Sociology
An introduction for nurses, midwives and health visitors

Caroline Cox, BSc(Soc), MSc(Econ), SRN
Director, Nursing Education Research Unit, Department of
Nursing Studies, Chelsea College, University of London

BUTTERWORTH
HEINEMANN

Butterworth-Heinemann Ltd
Linacre House, Jordan Hill, Oxford OX2 8DP

℞ A member of the Reed Elsevier plc group

OXFORD   LONDON   BOSTON
MUNICH   NEW DELHI   SINGAPORE   SYDNEY
TOKYO   TORONTO   WELLINGTON

First published 1983
Reprinted 1985, 1987, 1989, 1991, 1992, 1994, 1995

© Butterworth-Heinemann 1983

British Library Cataloguing in Publication Data
Cox, Caroline
  Sociology: an introduction for nurses, midwives
  and health visitors
  1. Sociology   2. Nursing – Social aspects
  I. Title
  301'.024616   HM51

ISBN 0 7506 0305 4

Library of Congress Cataloguing in Publication Data
Cox, Caroline
  Sociology: an introduction for nurses, midwives
  and health visitors
  ISBN 0 7506 0305 4
  Includes bibliographical references and index.
  1. Sociology   2. Medical care – Social aspects.
  Public health – social aspects. I. Title
  [DNLM: 1. Sociology – Nursing texts.   2. Nurse-patient
  relations.   WY87 C877c]

Printed in Great Britain at the University Press, Cambridge

Preface

If you are training to be a nurse, a midwife or a health visitor this book is written for you. It will not turn you into a sociologist, but it will introduce you to the world of sociology, in the hope that some of what it has to offer may be useful to you in your professional practice.

The book is written primarily for the newcomer to sociology. It gives an introduction to the subject, providing a brief overview of the different approaches within it. There are also short accounts of ways in which sociologists have studied some key aspects of society. They include those which are especially relevant to our understanding of the social context of health care, such as family life or social inequality.

The book may also be useful for those who, having already studied some sociology, would like to think further about its relevance to professional practice. The second part of the book, which discusses various aspects of the sociology of health care, will hopefully be of interest to you, as well as to the newcomer.

Having identified the book's objectives, it is also important to identify some of its limitations, especially its omissions. In any introductory textbook, the author has to be selective. Consequently, some entire topics have had to be omitted (for example, sociological accounts of political and economic systems); and in discussions of areas which have been included, much is missing. However, the references at the end of each chapter, together with suggestions for further reading, may go some way towards remedying these deficiencies by offering guidelines to readers who wish to pursue topics at greater depth.

Another aspect of the need for selectivity is the choice between 'old' and 'new'. Some regard it as a virtue to make a point of quoting the most recent work. I have not always chosen to do this, but have preferred at times to refer to longer established studies. Inevitably, my choices will occasionally offend people familiar with the range of options: I can only apologise for any sins of omission and commission.

One other problem needs to be mentioned, by way of clarification. It arises from the blurring of boundaries between sociology and other subjects. For example, there are no clear demarcation lines between some approaches in sociology and psychology. Therefore, especially in the more 'clinically' oriented chapters on patient care, reference is made to the work of practitioners in other fields, such as psychology and psychiatry. For this, I make no apology. Interdisciplinary boundaries are somewhat arbitrary, and if a study enhances our understanding of the social aspects of health care in general, or of the care of particular kinds of patients, it seems appropriate to include it.

Moving now from apologies to acknowledgements, I gladly acknowledge many debts of gratitude. I owe much to the nursing students at Chelsea College who shared with me their endeavours to relate sociology to nursing: I learned a great deal from their academic discoveries and from their sensitive appraisal of sociology in the light of their 'real life' experience of nursing. To Dr. John Marks and to many other colleagues who kindly devoted much time and patience to reading the manuscripts, I am deeply indebted: their critical comments, based on wide experience in both social and natural sciences, and in the philosophy of science, have greatly improved the book; the remaining shortcomings are mine. I am also grateful to Bob Pearson, of Butterworths, for his professional expertise and advice. His enthusiastic assistance with the text editing, illustration research and the writing of the summaries together with the seemingly innumerable tasks associated with producing a book, has been invaluable. Finally, my heartfelt thanks are due to Mrs. Jean Dowsett who has demonstrated that divine attribute of creating order out of chaos, by transforming mountains of hideous notes into neatly ordered pages, with a miraculous combination of efficiency, serenity and never-failing kindness. If the book achieves its purpose, the kindness and help of all of these people will have been justified.

The purpose of all our endeavours is the enhancement of the quality of care we provide for those for whom we are professionally responsible. And in so far as our professional responsibilities involve an appreciation of the social dimensions of health care, sociology has something to offer. This book could be a small part of that offering.

London   Caroline Cox

Contents

Part III
Using sociology: understanding society   39

3   Population structure and change   41

4   Family and kinship   51

Part V
Conclusion 195

Part I

Introducing sociology

A monastery on Mount Athos, northern Greece (Courtesy BBC Hulton Picture Library)

(. . . on Mount Athos there is an ossuary, where the bones of the monks are placed — see p. 1)

1 The relevance of sociology

The gods did not reveal, from the beginning,
All things to us; but in the course of time,
Through seeking we may learn, and know things better.
But as for certain truth, no man has known it ... .

Xenophanes (ca. 570–480 B.C.)

There is an old Chinese proverb: 'Give a man a fish and you feed him for one day; teach him how to fish and he can feed himself for a lifetime.' The purpose of this book is not to 'give' you sociology; rather it is to offer you some of the insights and information which sociology can provide so that you can continue to use and develop them in your professional practice as a nurse, a midwife or a health visitor (throughout the book, the terms 'nurse' and 'nursing' will be used in the generic sense to include the related professions of midwifery and health visiting, except where these are the specific subjects under discussion).

1.1 Why sociology?

You may well ask: 'Why do I need sociology?' In order to start to answer this question, I would like to invite you to come with me, in imagination, to the coastline of northern Greece. There we will find a rugged peninsula which juts out into the Aegean Sea, with majestic mountains, dense forests and precipitous cliffs. It is called Mount Athos and is also known as 'The Holy Mountain'. Most of us could not visit it in person, for it has become a sanctuary for monks and hermits who have come there, over the centuries, to seek a life of prayer. They live in conditions of utmost simplicity — some in monasteries, others in solitude in little huts, caves or even on ledges of rock on the cliff face. But they all share a common goal, which is dramatically symbolized when they die. For on Mount Athos there is an ossuary, where the bones of the monks are placed; but instead of the bodies being laid alongside each other, they are intermingled. For example, all the femurs or all the scapulae are kept together. Thus their fellowship in death demonstrates very vividly how they were all 'members one of another' in life.

And so are we all, for to be human is to be social. We cannot become fully human without social relationships and without the culture which is the heritage of any society — with its knowledge, language and ways of understanding the world. A moment's reflection will remind us that we are in a social situation from the moment of birth to the time of our death, and it is very likely that for each of us these two momentous events will take place in a hospital.

Social influences also help to shape us into the kinds of people we become and they affect the way we behave in our daily lives. Therefore, some understanding of these influences can help us to understand human behaviour better — both other people's behaviour and our own.

1.1.1   Sociology and nursing

The foregoing gives an indication of sociology's relevance to us as nurses, since we all know that nursing is essentially concerned with people and with human behaviour.

The Briggs Report (1972) described nursing as 'the major caring profession'. The word 'caring' implies a relationship, and relationship immediately implies a social situation. As professionals we wish to be as effective as we can in fulfilling our responsibilities in the social situations in which we practise our profession. We therefore need to have as much information as possible about the various factors affecting these situations, so that we can respond appropriately. These can be summarized in the form of an equation, which highlights different aspects of the human condition which we might need to take into account:

$$\text{Human behaviour} = f(\text{Individual characteristics} + \text{Social situation})$$

In this equation, f stands for the interrelationship between the characteristics of individuals and the social situation in which they are placed, which can each be subdivided further:

$$\text{Individual characteristics} \begin{cases} \text{Physical} \\ \text{Psychological} \end{cases}$$

$$\text{Social situation} \begin{cases} \text{Social structure} \\ \text{Culture} \end{cases}$$

It is fairly clear what is meant by physical and psychological characteristics of individuals, although they are not always easy to measure. However, it may be helpful to define the terms 'social structure' and 'culture' as they are used by sociologists.

Social structure refers to the building blocks of a society, like families, schools and hospitals — or larger units, such as the education system or the Health Service. Culture refers to a more intangible but no less important area of human experience — the world of man's knowledge, beliefs, ideas and values. This may sound rather vague, but if we recollect that martyrs choose to die for their beliefs and ideas, we shall not underestimate their importance. Culture is also important in a nursing context, because cultural influences can affect the ways in which people respond to pain and illness. Later we shall see that anthropological and sociological studies have shown how people from different ethnic and cultural backgrounds react in very varied ways to similar pathological conditions (see Chapter 9).

The equation therefore helps us to remember that, when we are caring for people, we need to bear all four 'levels' in mind: physical, psychological, social structural and cultural. Obviously, there may be times when one level has over-riding priority. If a patient is in acute physical pain — for example, with renal colic — his first and overwhelming need is for pain relief, because the pain is so intense that it virtually obliterates all other thoughts and concerns. At other times, patients may be so distraught with fear and anxiety that the priority will be to try to alleviate psychological distress. Some patients awaiting surgery or investigation are very fearful and anxious, and research has shown how the availability of nurses to discuss anxieties and to offer information and reassurance can be highly beneficial (see Chapter 9). However, these physical and psychological priorities do not occur in a social vacuum and it is in helping us to understand the social setting of our patients that sociology can make its contribution to nursing.

1.2 What is sociology?

The *Concise Oxford Dictionary* briefly defines sociology as 'the science of the development and nature and laws of human society', but it will be seen from this section that sociologists view sociology from completely different standpoints and that it is, in reality, a wider and more complicated subject than can be adequately conveyed by a short definition.

Sociology is a relatively young subject. It was given its name in the nineteenth century by a Frenchman, Auguste Comte (1798–1857) and for this reason he is sometimes regarded as its 'founding father' (*Figure 1.1*). Comte was very keen to establish sociology as a science and he somewhat arrogantly saw it as the 'queen of the sciences'. He also saw sociologists as people who should wield great influence in the affairs of men, on account of their scientific knowledge of human society. His grandiose view of himself and of sociology can be seen in the way he used to sign his letters: 'The Founder of Universal Religion, Great Priest of Humanity'!

Other writers who are often also called 'founding fathers' of sociology include Karl Marx (1818–1883), Max Weber (1864–1920) and Emile Durkheim (1858–1917). We will look at some of their works later because they are still very influential. They are important both in their own right and because they established various traditions or 'schools' within sociology which are still with us today.

1.2.1 The sociological terrain

Before we consider particular writers, it might be helpful to the newcomer to look at a sketch map of the sociological terrain (*Figure 1.2*). Precisely because socio-logy consists of a number of different traditions or schools, it can appear very confusing. But do not be alarmed — the confusion is in the subject, not just in your mind!

Figure 1.1   Auguste Comte, sometimes called the 'founding father' of sociology, 1798–1857 (Courtesy BBC Hulton Picture Library)

The purpose of a map is to provide an orientation and to show how different features in a landscape relate to each other. This map locates some of the main schools in sociology according to their relationship to two continua: from *microsociology* to *macrosociology*; and from those sociologists using primarily *objective* data to those concerned more with *subjective* experiences. At one end of the horizontal continuum there are sociologists whose starting point is *people*. These sociologists study the effects of social settings, such as a hospital ward, on the people

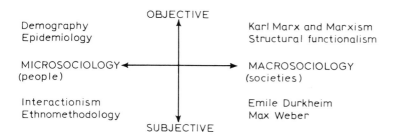

Figure 1.2   Sketch map of the sociological terrain (After Cox, 1979)

who experience them. They may also move on to consider wider aspects of the social setting such as the organization of the hospital or the Health Service. At the other end of the horizontal continuum, macrosociological studies begin by looking at whole *societies*, and the implications of particular ways of organizing a society for the people who live in it. For example, Marxists are highly critical of all capitalist societies: they emphasize the conflicts in such societies and they work towards bringing about a socialist revolution, in line with Marx's theories of history and social change (see Chapter 5).

The vertical continuum indicates how some sociologists work primarily with relative *objective*, quantitative or measurable data — such as infant mortality rates or the distribution of wealth and poverty. At the other end of this continuum are the more *subjective* sociologists who are particularly concerned with the less tangible world of ideas, beliefs and knowledge — the more qualitative aspects of human experience. Sociological perspectives here may be microsociological and concerned, for example, with social experiences which damage or enhance a person's self-esteem. In the macrosociological categories are sociologists who are interested in the influence of collectively held ideas such as religious beliefs and scientific knowledge. Here we find the sociology of science and the sociology of religion. Max Weber, for example, tried to show how religious beliefs have accounted for some of the major developments in human history (see Chapter 7).

These, then, are a number of the features we can identify when we look at our sketch map of sociology. We will now consider, briefly, each of the schools or perspectives identified on this map. Obviously, this introduction will be over-simplified, but its purpose will be achieved if you begin to understand something about the main characteristics of each type of sociology.

1.2.2 Microsociology

We will start at the microsociological end of the horizontal continuum.

Demography and epidemiology

These microsociological areas are not really sociological schools, but disci-plines in their own right. They are, however, included here because they give information on population change and on the social distribution of disease and death which is widely used in the sociology of health care. For example, as we shall see in Chapter 5, even in Britain today with its well-established 'welfare state', there are marked social class differences in the number of children who die in the first year of life — a worrying fact which poses a challenge for all concerned with infant and child health.

Interactionism

This rather daunting term, which is sometimes called *symbolic interactionism*, refers to a school in sociology which focuses on the effects of particular kinds of social relationships on the individuals who experience them. Important concepts used by interactionists include: (1) *self-image* (how we see ourselves); (2) *self-esteem* (how we evaluate or appraise our self-image); (3) *self-fulfilling prophecy* (the way in which other people's expectations may help to change us so that we become like their expectations).

For example, sociological studies of education have considered whether the act of 'labelling' a child as a success or failure has positive or negative repercussions. It has been suggested that negative repercussions may include a tendency for the child who is labelled a failure to go into a downward spiral of loss of self-confidence and further failure (see Chapter 6).

Interactionists have also undertaken a great deal of work in the sociology of health care, notably in thought-provoking accounts of the processes of depersonalization and loss of identity which may occur in institutions like psychiatric hospitals (see Chapter 10).

Ethnomethodology

This even more alarming term refers to work carried out by sociologists who adopt an intensive case-study approach. They attempt to portray in detail the experiences and behaviour of particular social groups so as to give the reader a sympathetic understanding of the way of life of these groups and of how they view the world. Detailed case studies, like good novels, can provide insights into the experiences of other people whose lives may be very different from our own. The research methods used by ethnomethodologists include participant or non-participant observation, to enable them to become intimately acquainted with the group under study. This inevitably leads to problems because the sociologist can rarely become a real member of the group, so his perceptions and accounts will always be coloured by his own personal interests and experiences. Also, his presence in the group may alter the way in which the group behaves. Nevertheless, careful and detailed case studies can help us to understand situations and experiences alien to us in a more intimate way than would be possible by other means.

1.2.3 Macrosociology

We now move from the microsociological to the macrosociological end of the continuum. Here we introduce some of the founding fathers of sociology — Karl

Marx, Max Weber and Emile Durkheim — and the sociological traditions which have stemmed from their work.

Beliefs of the founding fathers

For *Karl Marx* and his followers, the way in which economic production is socially organized is of fundamental importance. The crucial distinction is between those who are owners of the means of production (such as land or factories) and those who are not. Different types of social relationships are associated with this distinction between owners and non-owners, such as the relationships of superordination and subordination — or 'boss' and 'worker' in everyday language. These relationships are reflected in the concept of *class*, a central idea in Marxist theory, and in the conflicts between classes. Marxists believe and teach that *class conflict* is inevitable in societies which allow private ownership of the means of production and that the forces of history will lead ultimately to revolution and to the establishment of socialist societies which will be characterized by the public ownership of the means of production. Marxists claim that these socialist societies will not suffer from the conflicts endemic in their predecessors and that they will be free from undesirable features such as exploitation or alienation found in capitalist societies.

Max Weber took issue with Marx in several ways. For example, he argued that there is more to human history and to social change than the economic characteristics of societies — important though these are. He did not believe that man's destiny is shaped primarily or solely by economic forces. Instead, he thought that man could shape his own destiny by his beliefs and ideas. He also argued that Marx's theory of social class was inadequate, for it did not take account of other important social divisions such as social status and political power (see Chapter 5).

The latter part of the twentieth century is an opportune time to assess the theories of Marx and Weber, for one-third of the people in the world now live in societies with Marxist governments, which provide a valuable testing ground for studying how Marxism works in practice; and we can also look critically at our own society, and other western capitalist societies, to consider the extent to which Marx and Weber's ideas ring true here.

✝ *Emile Durkheim* is the last of the founding fathers whom we will be considering. He became the world's first professor of sociology in 1896, in Bordeaux. Like Comte, he was concerned to show that sociology is a science and in *The Rules of Sociological Method* (Durkheim, 1968 translation) he set out to demonstrate that sociology is not essentially different from the natural sciences. He believed, for example, that social phenomena can be measured and that even if it is not possible to conduct laboratory experiments with human beings, we can undertake comparative studies which serve a similar purpose. In other words, we can look at different societies and try to establish the causes and effects of different social phenomena.

His famous study on suicide (Durkheim, 1952 translation) vindicated his belief in scientific sociology. Here, he chose to study a human action which we might think would be the most personal and private of all — the taking of one's own life. Hitherto, explanations of suicide had been at the level of individual psychology. However, Durkheim wanted to prove the need for sociology by demonstrating that *social* influences are at work in promoting or inhibiting suicide, and he succeeded in showing that suicide rates do differ very significantly between social groups. He found, for example, that members of some religious groups are less prone to commit suicide than others, and that suicide rates are correlated with social factors such as loneliness and economic well-being. These variations do not always occur in ways which might have been expected, since sometimes suicide rates are high for societies whose people enjoy a high standard of living and are lower among those who are poorer. *Table 1.1* shows that some of these trends are still apparent. As Durkheim himself said many years ago: 'At each moment of history, therefore, each society has a definite aptitude for suicide.'

TABLE 1.1 Suicide death rates per 100 000 population

Country	Rate	Year
Australia	11.1	1977
Austria	24.8	1978
East Germany	36.2	1974
France	15.8	1976
Hungary	40.3	1977
Italy	5.6	1975
Japan	17.6	1978
New Zealand	9.3	1976
Poland	12.1	1976
Republic of Ireland	4.6	1977
Sweden	19.0	1978
U.K.:		
England/Wales	8.0	1977
Scotland	8.1	1977
N. Ireland	4.6	1977
U.S.A.	12.5	1976
West Germany	21.7	1976

(Source: World Health Statistical Report, W.H.O., Geneva, 1980.)

You might speculate on why these societies have these patterns of suicide. It is perhaps fairly easy to find a reason for the low rates in Eire and Italy, but why should Austria's rate be double that for Australia, and why should East Germany's rate be significantly higher than that for West Germany? If you would like some clues, you will find them in Durkheim's book, which can be obtained through your local library.

In the meantime, we can perhaps agree that Durkheim succeeded in making these points: (1) that even such an intimate and individual act as suicide may be subject to social influences; (2) that, therefore, not all human behaviour can be explained by psychology or physical science; (3) that there is thus a case for sociology as an academic discipline; and (4) that careful comparative sociological studies can have some similarities to the traditional methods used in the natural sciences.

Structural functionalism

Finally, we come to a contemporary sociological school which has some of its roots in Durkheim's work: structural functionalism. Functionalists are interested in the structure of societies and in ways in which changes in one part of a society may set up chain reactions leading to changes elsewhere. For example, some functionalist studies of families in modern societies have described how family life and relationships have been influenced by industrialization. Some of these changes affect the ways in which families provide for relatives in times of illness and other crises and are therefore of interest to professional practitioners concerned with the provision of health and welfare services (see Chapter 4).

The concept of role

The term 'role' has been widely used by functionalists, as well as by other sociologists such as the interactionists. The idea is not new, nor is it specific to sociology. Shakespeare immortalized it in his account of the different roles we play throughout our lives:

All the world's a stage,
And all the men and women merely players:
They have their exits and their entrances;
And one man in his time plays many parts,
His acts being seven ages ... .
(*As You Like It*, ii, 7, 139f.)

Sociologists often describe human beings as 'playing' parts — with one person fulfilling diverse roles, such as husband, father and greengrocer; or mother, nurse and secretary of the local tennis club. Some of these are family roles; others are occupational or recreational roles. The term 'role' refers to the ways in which society expects a person who occupies a given position to behave. Roles carry duties and obligations and they may also confer rights and privileges.

A number of variations on the theme of role have been developed. One variation is *role conflict*, which occurs when someone experiences conflicting demands within one role (for example, when a nurse does not have enough time to fulfil her clinical and administrative duties and to talk to patients) or conflicts between two or more roles (as with a mother who also has a job and finds it hard to reconcile this with the demands of motherhood). *Role strain* refers to stress which may be encountered in trying to fulfil *role obligations* (such as the anxiety experienced by student nurses who feel inadequately prepared for responsibilities which they may be asked to undertake on the wards).

We shall come across the concept of role again in a number of contexts. For example, in Chapter 8 we will discuss T. Parsons' account of the 'sick role' — which describes the behaviour which society expects of those who are ill — and his analysis of the role of the doctor.

1.3 Issues and problems in sociology

Two of the major issues are: (1) can, or should, sociology be a *science*? (2) Can, or should, sociology be, or attempt to be, *value-free*, i.e. impartial and objective in the sense of being free from bias?

1.3.1 Can, or should, sociology be a science?

The answer to this question naturally depends both on the nature of sociology and on what we mean by 'science'. The characteristics of science have been extensively discussed by many people. We will refer here to the work of one of the leading contemporary philosophers of science, Karl Popper. In his book *Conjectures and Refutations* (Popper, 1963), he describes science as essentially a continuous quest for knowledge. Reality — whether it is the reality of the physical universe or of human life — is so complex that we can never attain a full and final understanding of anything. Instead, we must always see our knowledge as provisional — perpetually up for testing and for possible revision in the light of new evidence. The title of his book illustrates this whole approach to science: all we know is seen as tentative conjecture, never as final truth. If this is so, any claims to knowledge should always be capable of being turned into hypotheses which can be put to the test. If they do not stand the test they are seen to be false, and new theories and hypotheses must be developed. When hypotheses do stand up to testing, we can have provisional confidence in them and can regard them as the best available knowledge. Thus, according to Popper, the whole scientific enterprise is built on the principle of *falsifiability*. You can see from the following brief summary that this is a very humble and tentative view of scientific knowledge:

> 'But just because it is our aim to establish theories as well as we can, we must test them as severely as we can; we must try to find fault with them; we must try to falsify them. Only if we cannot falsify them in spite of our best efforts can we say that they have stood up to severe tests.'

Popper also stresses the dangers of other views of the nature of knowledge, as when one person or group of people believe that they have grasped the ultimate 'truth' and are justified in imposing this on other people. In another book *The Open Society and its Enemies* (Popper, 1966) he applies his philosophy of science to the social sciences and to the ways in which societies are organized. He draws a distinction between two kinds of thinker and two kinds of society. First there are those thinkers — philosophers or sociologists — who believe that they have such a sure understanding of the ways in which societies work that they want to organize society according to their own blueprint. Alternatively, there are those who agree with Popper that reality is so immensely complex that it is impossible to understand it fully. These thinkers, therefore, believe that any attempt to change society should be relatively small scale, at least at first, so that the effects of change can be critically evaluated and carefully monitored. In other words they advocate 'piecemeal' reform rather than wholesale revolution.

Identified here, in these two fundamentally different approaches to social science and to social change, is one of the major ideological and political conflicts of the twentieth century. On the one hand, there are those who agree basically with Popper's position of adopting a cautious view of the nature of knowledge and especially of knowledge of social affairs; they also adopt a cautious approach to social change, preferring reform to irreversible revolution. This approach can be generally characterized as the *liberal* tradition and is a feature of what Popper calls an 'open society'. Such a society is 'open' because knowledge is open to challenge and to revision; social policies are open to criticism and to pressures for change; there is a relatively open circulation of ideas, information and criticism, and people are relatively free to dissent and to leave. Such societies have a free press; free elections with genuine choice between political leaders and the philosophies they represent; academic freedom in teaching and research; and freedom to form pressure groups to try to bring about change. They may also have many problems with which we are familiar, such as inequality and unemployment.

The alternative philosophy and policies are found in those people who, throughout history and in the present day, believe that they have achieved a grasp of the 'truth' and are so confident in the rightness of their cause that they feel justified in imposing this on other people. Examples include, in the past, some of the great religious tyrannies such as Roman Catholicism at the time of the Inquisition, or the dogmatism of Hitler's National Socialism and anti-Semitism. In the modern world, perhaps the most obvious alternatives to the open societies are Marxist societies. Basically, Marxists believe that Marxism provides such a satisfactory understanding of the nature of man and of society that they have a mission to bring into being the kind of society which Marx advocated. They believe that revolution, not reform, is needed, since they think that nothing short of a complete transformation of society, and particularly of the way in which the economy is organized, will achieve the desired results. In their eyes, anything less, in the nature of reform, may provide temporary alleviation of social problems, but is essentially a mere tinkering with surface structures.

If we attempt to evaluate the effects of such revolutionary change we need to compare the situation before and after socialist revolutions have occurred, taking into account the effects of other changes such as industrialization. We also need to compare societies which have undergone revolutions with those which have not. There is an inevitable problem in comparative studies, in that some data are not directly comparable or are even not available. However, some differences are readily apparent. Marxist societies are not generally 'open' to the same extent as their liberal counterparts. For example, there are many more restrictions on the circulation of information, on the freedom of the press, on the freedom of election to government, on academic freedom to teach and to research, and on freedom to dissent, to criticize and to emigrate. Such restrictions may be justified by Marxists as being in the common good. It is important to recognize that some of the differences between these two types of society reflect the age-old tension between freedom and equality. The liberal societies of the west are characterized by many more freedoms, which many cherish; however, socialist societies put more emphasis on social equality, which is felt by many to justify the infringements of freedom.

Therefore, these differences between western and Marxist societies, which are well known and are there for all to observe, are open to different interpretations. This issue of interpretation of social phenomena raises the second question which we asked.

1.3.2 Can, or should, sociology be value-free or impartial?

The answers to this question will inevitably be linked to the answers to the question of whether sociology is a science. We can identify two ways of categorizing the different kinds of sociology.

First, there are sociologists like Durkheim, who try to develop a sociology which is akin to the natural sciences. They work with data which they can measure and manipulate in ways which approximate as closely as possible to well-established scientific methods.

Secondly, there are sociologists who follow in the tradition of Max Weber. They believe that sociology should try to develop as a science, using the main scientific criteria in evaluating their work; however, they also believe that sociology must inevitably be a different kind of science. This is because sociology deals with human experience and not only do we need to observe and to measure, but we need also to *understand* the motivations and meanings behind the behaviour we observe. An example may make this clear. If a visitor from outer space were to go into a local bank in the high street he would observe people on two sides of a counter, separated by a glass screen, handing over pieces of metal and paper. He could not obtain from these observations, however detailed and accurate they were, any understanding of the whole system of banking which lies behind what he sees. Nor could he appreciate the feelings of anxiety experienced by the customer with an overdraft! Therefore, many sociologists argue that we need to develop a science of human behaviour and of human society which takes account of the *meanings* behind the behaviour we observe. In order to do this we need what Weber called *'verstehen'* — the power of intuitive understanding or empathy whereby we can identify with people's motivations and feelings. It is in this approach to sociology that we find those sociologists whom we call *subjectivists*, for they are concerned with people's subjective experiences as well as with their outward behaviour.

There are other ways in which sociology differs fundamentally from the natural sciences. For example, men are not molecules. The people who are the subjects of a study may respond to the sociologist or to his findings in ways which change the situation, so that nothing is held constant. Another difference lies in the fact that there may be different versions of the same 'truth'. No one doubts that the Vietnam War took place, but if one were to ask an American and a Russian for an account of that war, one could expect very different answers. Both might give accurate versions of aspects of the war, but the totality was so complex and the interpretations would be so varied that one could not expect either to give the complete 'truth' about what happened. Each account would inevitably be partial and so to some extent biased.

Although this example is extreme, similar problems arise with many subjects studied by sociologists. The subject matter of sociology is often controversial and commentators, whether sociologists or not, are unlikely to be impartial and unconcerned about the issues involved. There are, therefore, no clear answers to the questions we have asked — whether sociology is a science or whether it can be value-free. Sociologists who believe that their work should be as value-free as possible try to make their findings as impartial as they can. It is generally recognized that it is virtually impossible to be completely value-free, because we all feel deeply about controversial issues. However, we can try to minimize the effects of personal bias and prejudice by being scrupulously honest and open in the collection and presentation of data, and by making our data available for public scrutiny and alternative interpretation. We can also declare our own interests, so that other people can make allowances for our possible bias and can put forward alternative interpretations of our findings.

It is therefore appropriate that I should state my own position, so that you can take it into account when you read this book. Essentially, I support Popper's interpretation of the nature of science and his argument in favour of open societies. This is because I believe that reality is so complex that we should take a humble, tentative and self-critical approach to our understanding of it and to attempts to change it by social policies. I would, therefore, also favour bringing about social change by reforms (many of which are needed, I believe, as I am not complacent about many of the social problems confronting us) rather than by revolution — which presupposes that we can be sure that the new society will be so much better than its predecessor that a revolution, with all its costs, would be justified. As far as my allegiance to particular sociological schools is concerned, I believe that we need the insights provided by all of them. Each has limitations, but each can also make some contribution to our understanding of human behaviour. We can ask no more and should expect no less.

■ Summary

An introduction is given to the subject of sociology — what it is, why we need it and why it is relevant to health care workers. Some common terms are defined and an account of the early workers in the field and their philosophies is presented. A specific definition of sociology is avoided because the founding fathers themselves disagreed as to its precise nature. Certainly it is concerned with people and human behaviour, but it is open to debate whether it is a science like the natural sciences, as believed by August Comte and Emile Durkheim, or a different kind of science, as argued by Max Weber.

. The author's view is that we should pursue our quest for knowledge in a free and open way, constantly revising our beliefs in the light of new evidence. In this she supports Karl Popper's interpretation of the nature of science and his concept of an 'open society', and favours the use of reforms rather than revolution to solve our pressing social problems. She concludes that we should draw on the insights provided by all schools of sociological thought, in our attempts to understand society and the social context of health care.

16

■ Questions

1. 'Men are not molecules.' Do you think this means that sociology can never be a 'science'?
2. Why was Durkheim so interested in suicide? Do you think suicide is a subject which is relevant to sociology?
3. Write brief notes on any three of the following:
   (a) interactionism;
   (b) ethnomethodology;
   (c) 'role' and 'role conflict';
   (d) the 'open society';
   (e) 'value-freedom'.

References

Briggs Report (1972). 'Report of the Committee on Nursing', London, H.M.S.O.

Cox, C. (1979). 'Who cares? Nursing and sociology: the development of a symbiotic relationship', *Journal of Advanced Nursing*, vol. 4, pp. 237–252.

Durkheim, E. (1952 translation). *Suicide: A Study in Sociology*, London, Routledge & Kegan Paul (first published 1897).

Durkheim, E. (1968 translation). *The Rules of Sociological Method*, New York, Free Press (first published 1894).

Popper, K. (1963). *Conjectures and Refutations: The Growth of Scientific Knowledge*, London, Routledge & Kegan Paul.

Popper, K. (1966). *The Open Society and its Enemies* (2 vols.), London, Routledge & Kegan Paul.

Further reading

Cotgrove, S. (1978). *The Science of Society. An Introduction to Sociology*, London, George Allen & Unwin. A useful introductory textbook for the newcomer to sociology.

*MacRae, D. (1974). *Weber*, London, Fontana/Collins.

*Magee, B. (1973). *Popper*, London, Fontana/Collins.

*McLellan, D. (1975). *Marx*, Glasgow, Fontana/Collins.

* Three readable books from the Fontana Modern Masters series which provide succinct accounts of the works of these influential writers.

Part II

Introducing health care

Florence Nightingale at Scutari, by J. Barrett (Courtesy BBC Hulton Picture Library)

(. . . if we go back in time, we can see the achievements [in health care] of the twentieth century in a better perspective — see p. 19)

2 Health care from the classical era to the present day

We are so familiar with modern developments in health care that it is difficult for us not to take them for granted. But if we go back in time, we can see the achievements of the twentieth century in a better perspective — the perspective of history. This journey in time will also show us how other sciences have contributed to medical knowledge and give us some feeling for the interconnectedness of human endeavours in different fields.

2.1 Origins in Ancient Greece and Rome

The origins of western medicine are found in the classical era of Ancient Greece and Rome. Greek civilization was built on ideas of health which can be found in the famous Hippocratic writings. They are as timely now as they were over two thousand years ago:

> 'Life is short, science is long: opportunity is elusive, experiment dangerous, judgement is difficult. It is not enough for the physician to do what is necessary, but the patient and attendants must do their part as well, and circumstances must be favourable.'
> (Hippocrates, translated, Lloyd, 1978.)

The Greeks' view of health was embodied in their religious worship and can still be appreciated today by visiting the famous shrines such as those at Delphi, Delos and Olympia. These shrines emphasize the idea of man's complete well-being: spiritual, social and physical. They all contain temples symbolizing man's relationship to the gods; a theatre for acting out man's place in the universe and his relationship with his fellow men and women; and a sports stadium, where athletes offered their physical achievements as part of their worship. Hence the enormous importance of the Olympic Games, which were held at Olympia every four years for over 1000 years.

2.1.1 Hippocrates

It was in this kind of world that the first great physician, Hippocrates (460–375 B.C.), began to develop a *science* of medicine. Doctors and students came from far and wide to study with him at the island of Cos, and many of the ideas which were developed there have remained influential across the centuries. They include the importance of careful observation; the concept of internal harmony; and the need to study the influence of the environment on the individual. Hippocrates also laid the foundations of professional ethics in the famous Hippocratic Oath (*Figure 2.1*).

THE HIPPOCRATIC OATH

I SWEAR by Apollo the healer, by Aesculapius, by Health and all the powers of healing, and call to witness all the gods and goddesses that I may keep this Oath and Promise to the best of my ability and judgement.

I will pay the same respect to my master in the Science as to my parents and share my life with him and pay all my debts to him. I will regard his sons as my brothers and teach them the Science, if they desire to learn it, without fee or contract. I will hand on precepts, lectures and all other learning to my sons, to those of my master and to those pupils duly apprenticed and sworn, and to none other.

I will use my power to help the sick to the best of my ability and judgement; I will abstain from harming or wronging any man by it.

I will not give fatal draught to anyone if I am asked, nor will I suggest any such thing. Neither will I give a woman means to procure an abortion.

I will be chaste and religious in my life and in my practice. I will not cut, even for the stone, but I will leave such procedures to the practitioners of that craft.

Whenever I go into a house, I will go to help the sick and never with the intention of doing harm or injury. I will not abuse my position to indulge in sexual contacts with the bodies of women or of men, whether they be freemen or slaves.

Whatever I see or hear, professionally or privately, which ought not to be divulged, I will keep secret and tell no one.

If, therefore, I observe this Oath and do not violate it, may I prosper both in my life and in my profession, earning good repute among all men for all time. If I transgress and forswear this Oath, may my lot be otherwise.

Figure 2.1

2.1.2 Galen

Another significant figure in the history of ancient medicine is Galen (ca. A.D. 130–200), a Greek physician practising in Rome, who developed the science of anatomy by dissecting apes and pigs (the use of human bodies was prohibited). He located the cranial nerves and described the structure of the brain. He also suggested a theory of heartbeat, which was based on the contraction of muscles. He incorporated many of the ideas of Hippocrates concerning health and illness, and he remained the dominant medical authority until the Renaissance. During these intervening centuries, however, the Christian church was also very influential: religious orders looked after the sick and infirm in hospitals and monasteries; and the prevailing religious faith gave meaning to human problems of suffering and death, which were accepted as God's will. Throughout this time women, as well as men, were respected as healers and their contributions in caring for those in need were highly valued.

2.2 Developments in anatomy, physiology and public health in Renaissance Europe

Galen's work provided the basis of medical knowledge and health care for nearly fourteen centuries. During those long years, medical science in Europe made no significant progress. Europe had descended into the Dark Ages. Then the universities emerged, the Renaissance dawned and the natural sciences began to burgeon. Man began to feel master of the natural world and of his own destiny. The foundations of many religious beliefs were shaken and practices which had been forbidden by religion were now tolerated.

For example, in 1315 at the University of Bologna, an Italian, Mondino, began to teach anatomy by dissection of the human body. It was the first time this had been done for over 1500 years: as we have noted, even the mighty Galen had had to restrict himself to dissecting animals and so could not avoid errors in human anatomy. But it took a further 200 years for this pioneering work to reach maturity in Vesalius' epoch-making book *On the Structure of the Human Body*, in 1543. This was the first major work of modern medicine and paved the way for later breakthroughs.

We now enter a time which was relatively optimistic. Although life was still hard and was often cut short by famines or epidemics, for many people it was becoming more enjoyable and more worth living. So man became interested in prolonging life — an interest reflected in another famous work, the *Book on Long Life*, written in 1560 by Paracelsus Still following Hippocrates, Paracelsus stressed the importance of public health and of man's control over the physical and social environment. He put his teaching into practice by draining the swamps around

Venice and clearing the Venetian harbour of pollution — a great achievement! Paracelsus also looked after his own personal health by adopting a rigid low-calorie diet. And to good effect, for he lived to the ripe old age of 98!

The next key advance came in the field of physiology. Modern physiology has its origins in the work of William Harvey and his discovery of the circulation of the blood. His book *De Motu Cordis et Sanguinis in Animalibus* ('On the Motion of the Heart and Blood in Animals'), published in 1628, was as important for medicine as Newton's *Principia* was for the physical sciences. Harvey's ideas grew from his studies at Padua, where his teacher Fabricius was the first person to demonstrate the operation of the valves in veins, giving Harvey the first clues to his own theory. *Figure 2.2* shows a model of the anatomy theatre in Padua where Harvey stood and watched Fabricius' anatomical demonstrations, and *Figure 2.3* illustrates Harvey's original work, in which he demonstrated that the flow of blood in veins is towards the heart.

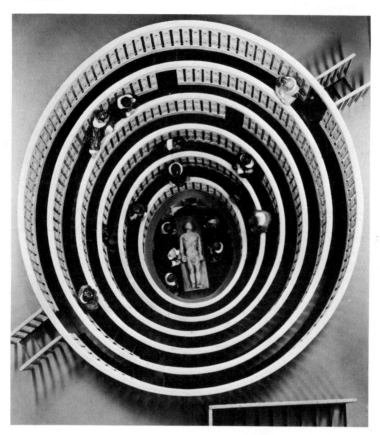

Figure 2.2   Model of the anatomy theatre at Padua built in 1594, where Harvey watched Fabricius' anatomical demonstrations (Courtesy The Wellcome Institute Library, London; from Stages in the Growth of Modern Medicine, 1st series, no. 3)

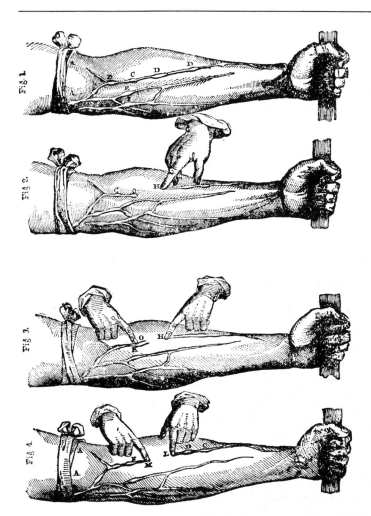

Figure 2.3 Diagram, from Harvey (1628), showing that the valves in veins only allow blood to flow towards the heart (Courtesy J. M. Dent, publishers, London)

So, by the seventeenth century, medical science had advanced in knowledge of anatomy, physiology and public health.

2.2.1 The experience of being a patient

Now let us turn briefly to the plight of the patient. What was it like at that time to be ill or injured? How were patients treated and what kind of health care was available?

Very little was available in the way of drugs or medicines. Surgery was a crude and desperate remedy, full of terror and danger for the unfortunate patient. It was thus usually reserved for the wounds of the battlefield and undertaken to avoid gangrene. Because of the conditions of the time, wounds often became infected and amputation was necessary to prevent the dreaded gangrene spreading. Operations were carried out with a butcher's skill and boiling oil was used as a means of cautery to stop bleeding. Some progress was made by a French surgeon, Ambroise Paré, in 1536, when he ran out of boiling oil; he used a simple dressing instead and found that the wound healed better! He also developed methods of ligature for tying off blood vessels to stop bleeding, and he made use of simple dressings and bandages. *Figure 2.4*, from a fresco in the Sorbonne, shows Paré doing an operation. There has been a battle and Paré is treating a wounded soldier. The dangers are emphasized by the presence of the bishop giving a blessing, and being ready to administer the last rites in the all-too-likely event of death.

Figure 2.4   Paré operating on a wounded soldier in the sixteenth century (Courtesy The Wellcome Institute Library, London; from Stages in the Growth of Modern Medicine, 1st series, no. 2; after a fresco in the Sorbonne)

At this time, hospitals were often relatively advanced and pleasant, symbolizing the Hippocratic ideal of treating the 'whole patient' in an appropriate, healing environment. *Figure 2.5* shows the hospital of Santa Cruz in Toledo in the sixteenth century. Another equally ancient hospital of the Knights Templar in Rhodes can be visited today and is just as clean, airy, restful and pleasant. So we can see that some of these early hospitals were in many ways more therapeutic and sanitary than

Figure 2.5   The hospital of Santa Cruz at Toledo in the sixteenth century (Courtesy The Wellcome Institute Library, London; from Stages in the Growth of Modern Medicine, 1st series, no. 5)

those which were to develop centuries later during the Industrial Revolution, some of which are still with us today. There are few wards in modern hospitals which look as good for nursing patients as the hospital in Santa Cruz.

2.3   Major developments in the eighteenth and nineteenth centuries

As we move on now through time, the number of significant developments in medical knowledge increased and only some of them can be mentioned here.

2.3.1   Advances in chemistry and physiology

In the eighteenth century the famous chemist, A. Lavoisier, made a great contribution to physiology when he separated 'air' into two gases and developed his theory of respiration. *Figure 2.6* is based on a drawing by Madame Lavoisier and shows her husband undertaking an experiment in his laboratory in Paris in 1789.

Figure 2.6 Lavoisier undertaking an experiment on respiration in his laboratory, in Paris, 1789 (Courtesy The Wellcome Institute Library, London; from Stages in the Growth of Modern Medicine, based on a drawing by Madame Lavoisier)

He is analysing gases which are being inhaled and exhaled, studying the relationship of respiration to exercise (note the treadle) and observing the effects on the subject's pulse rate.

Lavoisier's work came to an abrupt end during the French Revolution, when he was sent to the guillotine in 1794. However, he paved the way for progress in physiology, pharmacology, biochemistry and experimental medicine.

2.3.2 The rise of clinical medicine

Despite many such advances in knowledge, doctors still could not operate on patients' bodies to study what was happening internally. The risks of such surgery were far too great. However, a breakthrough occurred with the development of the stethoscope, which enabled doctors to listen to changes within the body — for example, to hear fluid in the lungs. The stethoscope was invented by a Frenchman, Laënnec, and its use was publicized in 1819. *Figure 2.7*, also based on a wall painting in the Sorbonne, shows Laënnec listening to chest sounds. He was particularly interested in tuberculosis, and unfortunately died of it at the age of 45.

Another important pioneer of modern medicine was Edward Jenner (1749–1823), who was born in a Gloucestershire village and became a country doctor. During the course of his work, Jenner noticed that cows sometimes developed

Figure 2.7   Laënnec using his newly invented stethoscope early in the nineteenth century (Courtesy The Wellcome Institute Library, London; from Stages in the Growth of Modern Medicine, 2nd series, no. 3, based on a mural in the Sorbonne)

ulcers on their udders and became unwell — farmers used to say that they were suffering from 'cowpox'. Milkmaids who milked these cows tended to develop inflammation on their wrists and hands, together with a fever; it was also noticed that those who had suffered once from cowpox never succumbed to the dreaded disease of smallpox. On the basis of such observations, Jenner undertook some experiments. In 1796 he took pus from a milkmaid's sore and transferred it to some scratches he had made on the arm of a healthy boy. The boy subsequently developed the signs and symptoms of cowpox. Jenner then proceeded with the experiment to a stage which was exceedingly dangerous: he introduced pus from the spots of a smallpox victim into further scratches on the boy's arm. Mercifully, the boy did not succumb to smallpox. The experiment was repeated with other patients, and so the process of vaccination was established.

2.4   Major developments in the nineteenth century

Further into the nineteenth century there are three other major advances we need to describe if we are to understand our own era; the rise of the germ theory of disease and the developments in surgery of anaesthesia and antisepsis.

2.4.1 The germ theory of disease

Bacteria had first been observed in the seventeenth century by a Dutch microscope maker, Anton van Leeuwenhoek. But it was not until the middle of the nineteenth century that Louis Pasteur linked bacteria with the theory of contagion and demonstrated that germs caused particular diseases such as anthrax, chicken pox and cholera.

Louis Pasteur was born in France in 1822 and graduated as a chemist at the age of 25. His research activities were very diverse, but he was particularly interested in microbes. Many contemporary scientists believed that these organisms emerged spontaneously and Pasteur set out to challenge this theory of 'spontaneous generation'. In order to do this, he set up an experiment with meat broth, showing that it would go 'bad' if exposed to microbes in the air, but would not do so if microbes were excluded. He took twenty boiled broths to the top of Mont Blanc, opened the containers in the pure mountain air and resealed them; twenty others were exposed to the polluted air of Paris. Only four of the flasks opened on Mont Blanc subsequently fermented, in contrast to all of those exposed to the Parisian air. He thus demonstrated the possible existence of microbes in the air and disproved the theory of spontaneous generation.

Pasteur also experimented with wine, having been asked by French wine manufacturers to study reasons for wine going sour. He recommended that the wine should be heated to 50–60°C, suspecting that the souring was caused by microbes and that this treatment would destroy them. The method was successful and is familiar to us now as the process of pasteurization, used to render milk safe for human consumption.

Applying his ideas on microbes to disease, Pasteur discovered that hens could be made immune to chicken cholera by the administration of a mild dose of cholera bacteria. Similarly, he gave a public demonstration of vaccination against anthrax in sheep, by injecting 24 sheep with a mild culture of anthrax and later injecting these same animals, plus another 24, with a fatal dose of anthrax microbes. Two days later the sheep which had been vaccinated were alive and well, while the others lay dead. Pasteur then, like Jenner, took the great risk of experimenting with a human being. He chose that most deadly disease, rabies, and injected into a nine-year-old boy, who had been bitten by a rabid dog, an extract made from the central nervous system of an animal suffering from rabies. Happily, the boy developed no symptoms and was restored to health.

Pasteur's work was of immense importance because it encouraged attempts both to prevent and to cure disease. Prevention could be achieved by public health measures — such as vaccination for smallpox, following Jenner's and Pasteur's work, or by sanitation and control of water supplies. As for cures, the isolation of pathogenic bacteria paved the way for the identification of substances which would destroy them, and thus for the revolution in therapeutics of this century.

2.4.2 New horizons in surgery: anaesthesia and antisepsis

Any surgeon faces three major problems: stopping bleeding, suppressing pain and preventing infection of wounds. The first problem, as we have seen, had been solved with the discovery of methods of ligature of blood vessels, but we have to wait until the latter part of the nineteenth century for solutions to the other two. Until this time, surgeons could do little to help patients to withstand the pain of surgery. Patients had to be held or tied down and surgeons had to work as quickly as possible. Some surgeons developed skills to the point where they could amputate a leg and tie off the arteries in less than 30 seconds. But such speed made refinement difficult; nor was sophisticated internal surgery possible.

Anaesthesia

Humphrey Davy, in 1797, suggested the use of nitrous oxide, or laughing gas, as an aid to surgeons. However, his ideas were not followed up for over 40 years until, on 16 October 1846, the first surgical operation was performed with a general anaesthetic. *Figure 2.8* is a model based on a contemporary drawing of this epoch-making event, which took place in Boston, U.S.A. The patient is having a tumour removed from his neck. Note that the surgeons and assistants are still wearing everyday clothes and there is no attempt to establish an aseptic environment.

Clearly, anaesthesia was an enormous blessing in the alleviation of suffering. It also allowed for great increases in the scope and practice of surgery. However, for a while it led to increased hazards, because of the large numbers of patients who

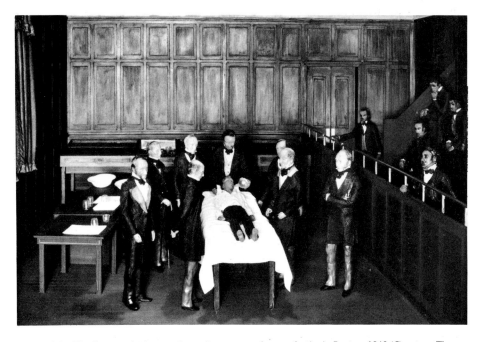

Figure 2.8   The first surgical operation using a general anaesthetic, in Boston, 1846 (Courtesy The Wellcome Institute Library, London; from *Stages in the Growth of Modern Medicine*, 2nd series, no. 4, based on contemporary paintings)

died from subsequent infection of wounds. Hence the great significance of that other breakthrough: antisepsis. Some feeling for what surgery was like in the era preceding antiseptic techniques can be obtained by visiting the operating room preserved from those days, which is situated in Southwark, near London Bridge.

Antisepsis

In 1867, the 'Lancet' reported a successful operation for a compound fracture of the leg, carried out by the surgeon Joseph Lister. What was significant was not the operation, but the manner in which it was done. Lister used a new technique which was to reduce dramatically the death rate for such a procedure, which up till then would have been higher than 50 per cent. Lister had been thinking about Pasteur's ideas on germs, and on 12 August 1865, when an 11-year-old boy was run over by a cart and had multiple injuries to both legs, he operated using carbolic acid as a disinfectant. The wound healed rapidly and cleanly. So began an era of antiseptic, later to become aseptic, techniques, which has enabled surgeons to undertake operations which previously would have been unthinkable (*Figure 2.9*).

Figure 2.9 Lister operating in 1877 using an antiseptic spray of carbolic acid. Note that there is no attempt to exclude germs and bacteria, but merely to kill those that were present Aseptic techinques came later (Courtesy The Wellcome Institute Library, London; from Stages in the Growth of Modern Medicine, 2nd series, no. 5)

2.5 Twentieth century developments in medical knowledge and health care

2.5.1 The control of infection*

We now have some idea of the state of medical knowledge and health care at the beginning of this century. But many of the benefits from the increase in knowledge only came in later decades. At the turn of the century, life was still 'nasty, brutish and short' for many people. For example, in 1900, a married couple who were planning to have a child had to reckon with an appreciable risk of the mother dying in childbirth. The maternal mortality rate was nearly 5 per 1000 live births, compared with 2 in 10 000 nowadays. Also, there was a probability of 1 child out of every 7 dying in the first year of life, compared with less than 1 in 50 now. Infectious diseases also took an enormous toll of life; for every person who dies from them now, 60 would have done so forty years ago — especially from whooping cough, measles, diphtheria and tuberculosis. Think of the contrast. Nowadays, in the western world, the possibility of a mother dying in childbirth, or of a child not surviving to adult life (except perhaps being killed in a road accident), hardly crosses parents' minds. And people do not expect to catch infectious diseases or, if they do, they expect to be cured.

The situation has changed very fast — so fast that many people have completely forgotten what things were like only forty years ago: the wards of fever hospitals; the sentence of lifelong invalidism that a diagnosis of pulmonary tuberculosis entailed; young children blue and exhausted from paroxysms of whooping cough; children dying from diphtheria; the virtually inevitable death from meningococcal meningitis. All these were commonplace phenomena of our own century, yet now they are things of the past in our society. How has this happened? The main causes have been revolutions in therapeutics and in preventive medicine, combined with improvements in the general standard of living.

2.5.2 Therapeutics and preventive medicine

Drugs

At the beginning of this century, physicians and surgeons had only a very limited array of effective drugs: nitrous oxide, ether and chloroform to help the surgeon; opium and morphine for pain relief; digitalis for heart failure; quinine for malaria; and aspirin, the first synthetic drug, which was introduced in 1899.

---

* Much of the material in this and succeeding sections is adapted from Norton (1969), reprinted by permission of Hodder and Stoughton Ltd, publishers, London.

The explosion in therapeutics since then has resulted in the vast array of drugs with which we are familiar. A glance at a pharmacopoeia will bring home dramatically how much progress has been made in just a few decades of human history.

The search for new drugs continues. For example, until fairly recently the American drug industry was bringing on to the market about 400 new drugs, or combinations of old drugs, every year. It is this context that we need to consider when discussing the pharmaceutical industry or debating the issues involved in tragedies such as those which occurred with the drug thalidomide.

One of the most dramatic results of this revolution in drug therapy is in the changing incidence of deaths from infectious diseases (see *Figure 2.10*). Remember, too, that this fall in the number of deaths in the first half of life needs to be seen in the context of a growing population.

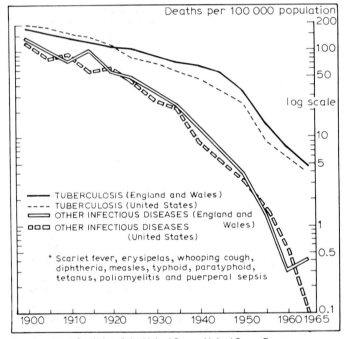

Sources: Vital Statistics of the United States, United States Dept. of Health, Education and Welfare, Registrar General's Statistical Reviews.

* Note: 1965 was an epidemic and 1960 an interepidemic year for measles in England and Wales and in 1965 measles caused two-thirds of its deaths from "other infectious diseases".

Figure 2.10   Death rates from tuberculosis and other infectious diseases in the U.S.A. and England and Wales, 1900–65 (From Norton, 1969, reprinted by permission of Hodder and Stoughton Ltd, publishers, London)

Social factors

It is important to point out that other factors were also at work (see McKeown, 1979). Social factors, such as a rise in the general standard of living and improvements in diet, housing, sanitation and work conditions, were all important contributors to the decline in death rates. However, drugs were also significant. *Table 2.1* shows that deaths from streptococcal infections (scarlet fever, erysipelas, puerperal sepsis) fell by 80 per cent following the introduction of sulphonamides in 1935; deaths from diphtheria fell dramatically after the immunization programme began in 1940; the largest drop in deaths from tuberculosis occurred in the decades 1945–65, after the discovery of streptomycin; and deaths from poliomyelitis fell significantly in the years following the mass vaccination campaign beginning in 1956.

TABLE 2.1 Deaths from certain infectious diseases (1925–65) in England and Wales

Disease	1925	1945	1965
Scarlet fever and erysipelas	1838	201	12
Whooping cough	6058	689	21
Diphtheria	2774	694	0
Measles	5337	728	115
Puerperal sepsis	1110	76	4
Meningococcal infection	354	527	112
Typhoid and paratyphoid	388	44	8
Tetanus	159	79	21
Tuberculosis — all forms	40 392	23 468	2282
Poliomyelitis	156	126	3
Population (in millions)	38.9	42.6	47.9

(Source: Registrar General's Statistical Review for various years.)

Therefore, the twin effects of rising standards of living and the discovery of so many effective drugs have revolutionized the patterns of disease and death in western societies. However, in medicine and health care, success often breeds new problems. We all have to die of something. Cures for some diseases mean that we may survive but, in due course, will inevitably suffer from something else instead. *Figure 2.11* shows how, with the fall in tuberculosis, there has been a dramatic rise in the incidence of lung cancer. Some of the most pressing problems now facing us are not infectious diseases, but malignant diseases, cardiovascular diseases, the diseases of old age and certain psychiatric problems.

We will be looking in later chapters at some of the implications of these changing patterns of disease and death and at the problems they pose for the provision of health care.

2.5.3   Diagnostic procedures

Remember that, until the last century, it was very difficult to have any idea of what was going on inside the body. This made accurate diagnosis very difficult. In the

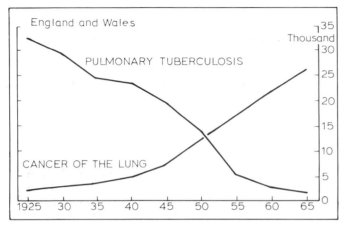

Source: Registrar General's Statistical Reviews Part I. Tables, medical.
Table 7 I.C.D. numbers 002 and 162, 163.

Figure 2.11   Deaths from pulmonary tuberculosis and lung cancer,
England and Wales, 1925–65 (From Norton, 1969, reprinted by permission
of Hodder and Stoughton, publishers, London)

twentieth century, a whole range of diagnostic procedures has developed. For
example, the x-rays discovered by Röntgen in 1896 were very soon being used to
diagnose fractures and internal lesions. And now we are so familiar with the reper-
toire of investigations undertaken in the pathological laboratories, such as
analysing cell tissues and body products, that we may take them for granted. However, it is not so long ago that doctors had to taste patient's urine to see if it was
sweet, thus indicating diabetes. Some experienced physicians who could judge
whether a patient was a diabetic by other clinical signs, used to teach students by
dipping one finger into the urine, and surreptitiously licking another!

2.5.4   Surgery

Surgery is probably the area which most often hits the headlines, as it is seen to be
'heroic' and dramatic. As we know, advances have been multitudinous, and all
were made possible by the nineteenth century breakthroughs in anaesthesia and
antisepsis. Surgical techniques are continuing to improve, as is illustrated by one
tragic example: it was recently reported that in Northern Ireland the terrorists
have changed their policy of shooting people in the knees to shooting them in the
ankles — apparently because surgeons have become so proficient at replacing
kneecaps that shooting in the knees was not seen to cause sufficient damage. As is
often the case, advances in technology may stem from situations of conflict and
'man's inhumanity to man'.

2.5.5   Radiotherapy

Another twentieth century development is radiotherapy, which is used when there is a need for the selective destruction of cells. Also, there have been recent developments in the use of laser beam therapy — for example, to destroy malignant cells, in the treatment of some conditions of the cervix, or to 'burn on' a retina which has become detached.

2.5.6   Psychiatry

In the field of psychiatry there have been twin developments — advances in physical treatments and in psychological methods. The latter lie more in the realm of behavioural science and we will be discussing some aspects of the care of the mentally ill in Chapter 10. In the area of physical treatments, there is first and foremost the revolution in the development of drugs, of which there are two kinds: those used for the treatment of the psychoses such as schizophrenia, and those for neuroses such as depression or acute anxiety states. In addition, there have been other developments such as the use of electroconvulsive therapy (ECT). All these advances represent as dramatic a revolution in the care of the mentally ill as has occurred in the care of patients with physical illness.

Overall, the revolution in psychiatric treatment has meant that official policy has been able to change to what is called an 'open door' policy. Many people who, in early days, would have had to remain incarcerated in psychiatric hospitals all their lives, can now live in the community for at least part of the time. Also, life within hospitals has changed greatly, with the virtual disappearance of the need for physical restraints, locked doors and padded cells. And all this has happened in living memory and largely since the World War II.

2.5.7   Contributions from the sciences

It is important to emphasize that many of the advances in medicine and health care have been a result of contributions from diverse sciences. If we list a few of these, we can more easily appreciate just how interdisciplinary medical knowledge has now become. As a matter of routine, modern health care draws on the following sciences:

Biochemistry: in the analysis of body fluids and the light this subject has shed on a myriad of diseases such as anaemia and diabetes.
Electrical engineering: in the development of machines such as those used for electrocardiographs and electroencephalographs.
Immunology: in preventive health care and transplant surgery.
Physics: with x-rays and radiography; laser beam therapy; the use of radioisotopes.

Physiology: in the understanding of respiration and developments in anaesthesia.
Polymer science: with the development of materials for use in orthopaedic and arterial surgery, such as artificial hip joints and heart valves.
Psychology: in psychoanalysis and behaviour therapy.
Statistics: in epidemiology and the development of mathematical research techniques.

2.6   Current issues in health care

Let us finish this historical overview by reminding ourselves of some of the dilemmas posed by advances in health care and the ethical issues they raise.

2.6.1   Changing patterns of disease and death

As we have already noted, achievements bring new problems in their wake, and we must all die of something. But now that so many of the diseases which used to kill people in infancy or childhood have been eradicated, many more people survive to middle and old age only to succumb later to other disabilities or diseases and thus to create new demands for health care.

Also, more effective ways of caring for people who suffer disabilities such as spina bifida, or who are injured in serious accidents, means that there are more people who are more or less chronically handicapped. Therefore, our population now contains more elderly people, who are prone to the diseases of old age, and more chronically sick or disabled people. Many of these people cannot be cured, but need care — and this raises numerous problems of how best to use scarce resources. High technology medicine is immensely expensive, as writers such as Ivan Illich point out (Illich, 1975), and we only have a limited budget available for health care. There is therefore a real conflict between different groups who urgently require money and staff for various worthwhile purposes. For example, who can balance the need for a renal dialysis unit, which can save a number of lives, against the care of the elderly or mentally ill in the community? These are tough, difficult questions of priorities, which in a free democratic society should be the concern of us all.

2.6.2   The quality of life and its termination

Given modern technology, it is now possible to keep people alive to an extent undreamed of before in human history. Whether by using, say, antibiotics, or heroic surgery, or life-support systems in intensive care units, we can now keep someone alive when 'nature's way out' would have been death. Agonizing questions confront perhaps the patient, often the relatives, and frequently the medical and nursing staff, about the quality of life which the patient may expect. Arthur Hugh Clough made the famous statement: 'Thou must not kill, but should not strive officiously to keep alive.' However, reality can be heartbreakingly complicated and uncertain. The enormous advances in health care have now put man increasingly in the almost god-like position of having the power of decision of life and death over his fellow men. In such decisions, there are no easy answers.

These are ultimate issues of great human significance. If we are to play a responsible role as citizens in our own society, as well as in our professional role as nurses, we need to think about them seriously and to work out our own moral position. For there can be nothing of greater importance than the life and the quality of life — and death — of our fellow human beings.

■ Summary

An overview of health care, from the classical era of Greece and Rome to the highly technological approach of the present day, is given. It is shown how the development of medicine into a complex science owes much to Hippocrates, who also laid the foundations of professional ethics, and to Galen, who developed the science of anatomy. During the Renaissance, dissection of the human body was undertaken by Mondino, which preceded the crucial anatomical work of Vesalius. In the sixteenth century Paracelsus stressed the importance of public health and the environment; and in the next century Harvey made the momentous discovery of the circulation of the blood.

Further significant advances were made in the eighteenth and nineteenth centuries, including the theory of respiration (Lavoisier), the invention of the stethoscope (Laënnec) and the discovery of vaccination (Jenner), while the nineteenth century saw the rise of the germ theory of disease (Pasteur), the development of anaesthesia (Davy) and the use of antiseptic techniques (Lister).

In the present century, the twin effects of the rising standards of living in western society and the discovery of effective drugs have revolutionized the pattern of infectious diseases and death rates. But now we are faced with increases in malignant and cardiovascular diseases, diseases of old age and psychiatric problems. Modern medical and health care and advanced technology enable us to extend the lives of very sick people, which poses ethical questions concerning the best use of scarce resources and the quality of life — and death — of our patients.

■ Questions

1. Why was Hippocrates so important? Do any of his ideas still have anything to offer us today?
2. What were the major contributions to medical knowledge of:
   (a) L. Pasteur;
   (b) A. Lavoisier;
   (c) E. Jenner;
   (d) J. Lister?
3. Give a brief account of some of the major developments in medical knowledge and practice in western societies over the past 100 years.
4. What are some of the implications for the provision of health care of the major medical advances of the twentieth century?

References

Harvey, W. (1628). *De Motu Cordis et Sanguinis in Animalibus* (On the Motion of the Heart and Blood in Animals); see translation by Franklin, K., *The Circulation of the Blood and Other Writings*, London, Dent, 1963 (Everyman edition).

Illich, I. (1975). *Medical Nemesis*, London, Calder & Boyars.

LLoyd, G. E. R. (Ed.) (1978). *Hippocratic Writings*, Harmondsworth, Pelican.

McKeown, T. (1979). *The Role of Medicine: Dream, Mirage or Nemesis?*, Oxford, Basil Blackwell.

Norton, A. (1969). *The New Dimensions of Medicine*, London, Hodder & Stoughton.

Further reading

McKeown, T. (1979). Cited in the References above. A book which discusses the relative contributions of social and medical factors in reducing morbidity and mortality rates. The author contends that modern medicine is excessively mechanistic and he offers an extended discussion on the concepts of health and disease.

Singer, C. (1957). *Anatomy and Physiology from the Greeks to Harvey*, New York, Dover. A well-illustrated and fascinating historical account.

Part III

Using sociology: Understanding society

View from top of Buckingham Palace showing immense crowds (Courtesy John Topham Picture Library)

(About 4000 million people now live on the earth — see p. 42)

3 Population structure and change

3.1 World population

The number of human beings on the earth has been increasing since the beginnings of the human race. Initially, for many thousands of years, the increase was slow because it was difficult for man to survive in harsh conditions, with only very primitive means of looking after himself. Death rates were very high, with disease, disaster, famine and warfare all taking their toll. It is estimated that the total human population was probably still only in the region of 5 million (about half the present population of London) by the year 7000 B.C..

Estimates of the growth of world population are inevitably very tentative and different sources suggest different figures, but they all show trends similar to that in *Table 3.1.*

TABLE 3.1   World population statistics

Year (A.D.)	Population (millions)
1	170
1000	265
1500	425
1650	545
1850	1200
1930	2000
1950	2500
1975	3900
2000	5750 (est.)

(Adapted from McEvedy and Jones, 1978)

The dramatic rate of world population increase is clearly shown in *Figure 3.1.* It took 1650 years for the population to increase from 170 million to 545 million, but since then it has grown increasingly rapidly, exceeding 1000 million by 1850. By 1950 it had more than doubled to reach 2500 million and will have more than doubled again by the turn of the century.

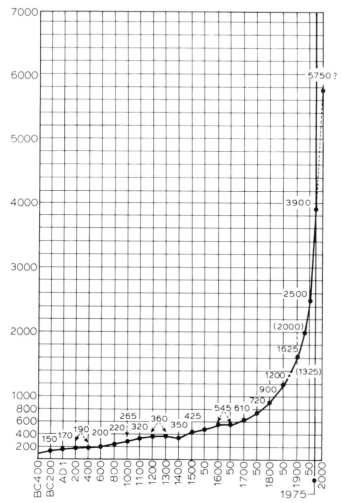

Figure 3.1 Graph showing the dramatic increase in world population (From McEvedy and Jones, 1978, reprinted by permission of Penguin Books Ltd; © Colin McEvedy and Richard Jones, 1978)

3.1.1 Thought-provoking statistics*

(1) About 4000 million people now live on the earth, which is about *5 per cent of all those who have ever lived*, in the two million years or so that men have inhabited the earth.

(2) The *present rate of doubling of the world population* is 35 years. If growth continues at this rate (it is actually exceeding it at present) the world population

---

* From Lewis (1981), by courtesy of Heinemann, publishers, London.

would exceed a million, million, million people in about 1000 years' time. This would mean that there would be about 1500 people per square metre of the earth's surface — including the sea!

(3) The *present annual increase in the world population* is approximately 80 million per year (greater than the combined populations of the U.K., Eire, Norway and Sweden). This amount is being added *every* year.

(4) The number of people killed in the Pakistan tidal wave in 1970 was 200 000. At the present rate of population growth, this figure would be made up in approximately one day.

3.1.2 Reasons for the increase in world population

A country's net population growth or decline depends on the difference between the birth rate (BR) and the death rate (DR) plus net migration (M). The growth rate (GR) for any given country can be expressed as

$$GR = BR - DR + M$$

On a world scale there is no migration, so the global population is calculated as

$$GR = BR - DR$$

As we saw in Chapter 2, death rates from many killer diseases have fallen dramatically during this century. Although the industrialized societies have experienced steeper declines in death rates than the developing countries, the worldwide use of powerful antibiotics such as penicillin and streptomycin, together with the important insecticide DDT, has meant that developing countries, too, are showing falling death rates. However, birth rates have not dropped proportionately and in many places life expectancy is increasing as standards of living rise with the spread of industrialization. The result is the growth in population which we have just been discussing.

It is therefore perhaps no accident that the first person to think seriously about the consequences of imbalance between birth and death rates was living in England at the time when the Industrial Revolution was just beginning to gain momentum. He was the Reverend Thomas Malthus (1766–1834).

3.2 Population theory of Malthus

The idea which is central to Malthus' work is that populations would tend to grow at a rate which cannot be matched by increases in the production of food and so the larger numbers of people would literally swallow up the food supplies. Malthus was a careful scientist and he tried to gather evidence for his theory by observation and by travel. He also tried to give his work mathematical precision by contrasting two types of progression or rates of growth. First, he argued that population tends to increase by *geometric progression*. For example, over 30 years a population of 1000 might double; it could double again over the next 30 years to 4000, and would then reach 8000 after only 90 years. This is the kind of progression which we have just seen is being followed by the world population in the twentieth century.

Secondly, the means of subsistence (chiefly food) tends to increase *at most* by *arithmetic progression*; that is, by particular amounts over a period of time. For example, the yield of 1000 lb. of wheat per acre *might* increase to 2000 lb. over 30 years, to 3000 lb. over the next 30, and reach 4000 lb. by 90 years, and so on. The resulting gap between the growth in the size of the population and food supplies is illustrated in *Figure 3.2*.

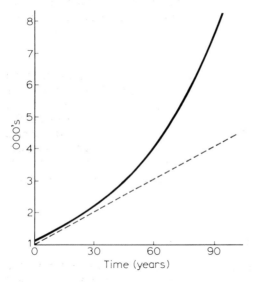

Figure 3.2   Diagrammatic representation of Malthus' simple theory of the relationship between population growth and food supply (solid line = population, in thousands; broken line = wheat, in 000's lb. per acre)

We can obtain some feeling for the significance of Malthus' ideas if we imagine breeding rabbits and having to rely on a limited plot of land for their food. However hard we tried to improve the output from that piece of land, it would not be very long before the rabbits multiplied to such a number that food supplies ran out.

Whether the minute details of Malthus' theory are accurate or not, the basic principle that food supplies *increase* less rapidly than populations, which *multiply*, implies a gloomy prospect for mankind: starvation.

3.2.1 Developments since Malthus

In 1798, Malthus published his famous *Essay on 'Population'*, in which he made his grim prophecy. However, since then a number of developments have taken place which have prevented his alarming predictions from becoming reality for the entire world population, although particular countries have experienced acute problems in feeding their growing populations. A population crisis on a global scale has been averted so far, for several reasons. For example:

(1) There have been breakthroughs in agricultural techniques which have increased food supplies beyond all expectation.
(2) Huge new areas of land have been opened up, as in the Americas, Australia and Russia.
(3) Revolutions have occurred in bulk packaging, storage and transport, so that food can be brought from the farthest corners of the earth to fill the shops in towns thousands of miles away. It is a stimulating exercise to stop for a moment in the middle of shopping in a supermarket and take note of how many foods on sale have come from very distant places.

Consequently, the fall in the death rate and the resulting rise in the population which followed from the Industrial Revolution have not as yet brought about the disaster prophesied by Malthus. Some of the saving factors have been products of the Industrial Revolution itself, such as the development of agricultural machinery and the railways. So, whatever undesirable results the Industrial Revolution brought in its wake, such as blackened cities, urban slums and industrial pollution, it is important to remember that it also brought unprecedented benefits to mankind and allowed our planet to sustain a population which could never otherwise have survived.

3.2.2 Remedies for the future?

But what of the future? As we have seen, the world's population is now increasing, as Malthus foretold, at a rapid geometric progression; if it continues at its present rate it will double again in 35 years. And some of the developments which saved us before, cannot do so again. It is difficult to see what new areas of the earth's surface can be drawn upon, and there is a limit to the extent to which more intensive farming techniques can continue to improve the output of crops or livestock. Consequently, unless we can discover other forms of food, or radically new and at present inconceivable ways of improving the output of existing kinds of food, the bleak future predicted by Malthus may yet come true, with the grim spectres of famine and misery.

An alternative remedy could, of course, be found in effective means of limiting the number of births. It is interesting to note that in many industrial societies there has often been a period in the early stages of industrialization when births have outnumbered deaths and the population has grown quickly. Later the birth rate often tends to drop and population growth decreases. This has been the case in Britain, as we shall see. Here, it happened spontaneously. However, in some other countries, deliberate attempts have sometimes been made to limit population growth. For example, in modern China, with its vast population, the government actively discourages parents from having more than one child. Should they decide to go against government policy and have a second baby, they are liable to suffer many disadvantages, such as poorer housing, family allowances and education. There are therefore real disincentives to having a family even of a size which we in Britain would regard as normal.

3.3 The population in England and Wales

The figures in *Table 3.2* show how the population of England and Wales has been steadily increasing over the past 1000 years, with some fluctuations in earlier centuries, reflecting ravages of epidemic disease such as the plague or the Black Death. We can see how the numbers started to 'take off' in the late eighteenth century — at the dawn of the Industrial Revolution — and why Thomas Malthus, writing at the time when this was just beginning to happen, was so prescient.

TABLE 3.2   Population statistics for England and Wales

Year	Population (millions)
1086	1.5
1348	3.7
1400	2.1
1540	3.2
1690	5.0
1750	6.5
1801	8.9
1851	17.9
1901	32.5
1951	43.8
1971	48.9

(From Lewis, 1981, by courtesy of Heinemann, publishers, London)

The really dramatic changes have occurred during the last 150 years. This is because a high birth rate was maintained *after* the death rate had begun to fall. This was very understandable, for it took time to realize what was happening. People expected to see many of their children die; consequently, it was customary to 'invest' in a large number of children, so that at least some would be likely to survive. As the report 'Prevention and Health: Everybody's Business' (D.H.S.S., 1976) reminds us:

'A century ago only six babies out of ten survived to adulthood, such were the ravages of disease, undernourishment, squalor and ignorance. The expectation of life at birth for a British boy born between 1871 and 1880 was 41 years, for his sister, 45.'

Nowadays, the expectation of life at birth for a boy is around 70 years, and for a girl, 76 years.

It was in the latter years of the nineteenth century and the early years of the twentieth century that life expectancy began to rise, and consequently many of the babies born at the turn of the century who would previously have died, did not do so. They are still with us today, as our 'senior citizens'. Gradually, parents began to appreciate this change and to start having smaller families. The birth rate began to drop, first with the middle classes and later through most of the rest of the population. There are, of course, some notable exceptions, such as Roman Catholics, who have religious objections to artificial forms of birth control. But by the 1930s the birth rate was dropping so far that many people were afraid that we would not be able to maintain ourselves as a population and that an actual decline would set in. As you can see, this has not happened. But what has happened is a change in the structure of our population.

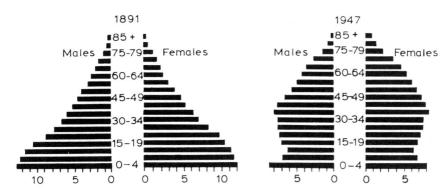

Figure 3.3   Population 'pyramids' for Britain, in 1891 and 1947 (From Young, 1971, by courtesy of Oxford University Press, publishers, London)

Figure 3.3 shows population 'pyramids' with the percentage of people in each age group. These pyramids show the changing age distribution over the years, with more infants and children in 1891 and more elderly people, especially women, in 1947. The shape of the pyramid for 1891 resembles that of a developing country today, with its high birth rate and a large proportion of the population aged 15 years or less. The 1947 pyramid is typical of many advanced industrialized societies. The birth rate has subsided and the falling death rate has allowed many more people to survive to old age. The smaller numbers of people in the 4–15 age group reflect the drop in the number of births during World War II.

Changes in the structure of a population have far-reaching repercussions, with many implications for health care (see Chapter 12). They also have implications for family life, as we shall see in the next chapter.

48

■ Summary

Statistical data are given which demonstrate the dramatic increase in world population over the past 2000 years, and it is stated that the present world population could double in 35 years if the present rate of growth is sustained. The growth rate is largely dependent on reductions in the death rate, which has greatly declined due to better health care and rising standards of living in industrialized societies. In the developing countries, immunization, antibiotics and insecticides have been some of the factors which have helped to reduce death rates, although they are often still unacceptably high .

In the nineteenth century Malthus argued that population increases by geometric progression but that food supplies increase at best by arithmetic progression; the resultant gap between the number of people and the available food supply would mean starvation. His grim prediction has been averted on a global scale, with some exceptions, by improved agricultural techniques, vast new areas of fertile land being exploited, and advances in bulk packaging, storage and transport. Now, however, we must discover other forms of food or ways of improving the output of existing food. Alternatively, effective methods of limiting the numbers of births worldwide must be adopted to reduce population growth. This has happened in Britain, where the structure of the population has changed from proportionately more infants and children at the end of the last century to more elderly people in recent years.

■ Questions

1. Who was Thomas Malthus? Why was his work so important? Do you think that Malthus' work can help us to understand the population problems of today?
2. Give a brief description of population changes in this country over the past century. What is their significance for the provision of health care?

References

Department of Health and Social Security (1976). 'Prevention and Health: Everybody's Business', London, H.M.S.O.

Lewis, J. L. (1981). Project Director, *Science in Society: Teacher's Guide*, London, Heinemann Educational Books and Association for Science Education.

Malthus, T. (1798). *Essay on 'Population'*, Penguin edition, with a Foreword by A. Flew, Harmondsworth, Penguin, 1970.

McEvedy, C. and Jones, R. (1978). *Atlas of World Population History*, Figure 3.1, p. 342, Harmondsworth, Penguin Reference Books.

Young, J. Z. (1971). *An Introduction to the Study of Man*, London, Oxford University Press.

Further reading

Laslett, P. (1971). *The World We Have Lost*, London, Methuen. A book which is comple-
mentary to Wrigley's text (below), with many fascinating anecdotes and information
about research methods in historical demography.

Wrigley, E. A. (1969). *Population and History*, London, Weidenfeld & Nicolson. An authoritative account of population changes from pre-industrialized societies to the present day.
Well illustrated.

East End of London family, 1912 (Courtesy BBC Hulton Picture Library)

(. . . social problems created by this rapid growth of towns included slum housing, overcrowding and bad sanitation — see p. 53)

4 Family and kinship

Almost all of us have direct experience of family life. It is the environment into which we were born and where we spent our most formative years. Therefore, family relationships are among the deepest and most enduring of all human relationships. Consequently, discussion about the family as a social institution often arouses intense emotions, because so much is at stake — positively, in terms of happiness and fulfilment; or negatively, as with grief from the death of those we love. Also, as we shall see in Chapter 10, the influence of the family can be so powerful that certain kinds of mental illness may be attributed to unhappy family relationships.

What is happening to the family in contemporary society? Some people preach a message of doom. They point to rising divorce and illegitimacy rates, and conclude that the family is in danger of extinction. It is true that these rates have been rising quite steeply, but the reasons are complex and many sociologists interpret events differently, even arguing that the family as a social institution is perhaps happier and stronger now than it has been in the past.

In order to understand trends, we need to compare the present with the past — to look back in time once again. We shall also consider a variety of sociological approaches, with different interpretations of events, including contributions from structural functionalists and from interactionists, and we shall discuss some of the implications of demographic change for family life.

4.1 The family in a changing society

It is difficult for us, having been brought up in an industrial society, to appreciate the magnitude of the change which has taken place over the past 200 years. All aspects of social life have been transformed by the twin processes of industrialization and urbanization.

4.1.1 Family life in pre-industrial society

Since we live in modern society, with all its stresses and strains, it is perhaps understandable for us to have a romantic view of life in rural pre-industrial societies, conjuring up visions of pastoral charm and tranquillity resembling a painting by Constable. But reality could be very harsh. We have seen in Chapter 2 how vulnerable mankind was to the killer diseases: the imminent possibility of death and suffering lurked around the corner for everyone all the time. And most people suffered from poverty and recurring famine.

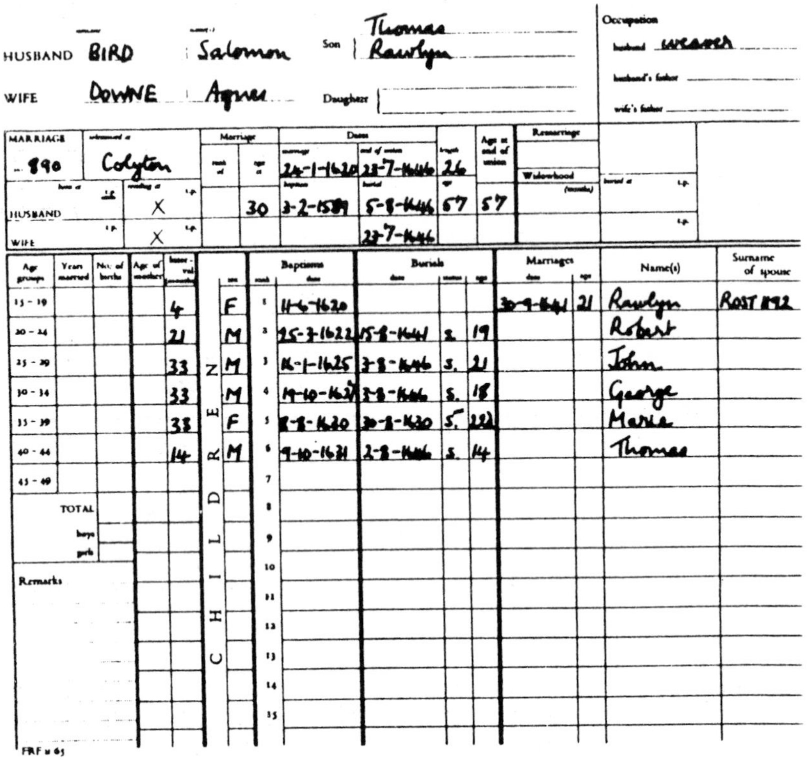

HUSBAND BIRD Salomon Son Thomas Rawlyn

WIFE DOWNE Agnes Daughter

Occupation: husband weaver; husband's father; wife's father

MARRIAGE 890 Colyton; Dates: 24-1-1620, 28-7-1646; length 26

HUSBAND X 30 3-2-1589 5-8-1646 57 57

WIFE X 28-7-1646

Age groups	Interval		Sex	Rank	Baptisms date	Burials date	status	age	Marriages date	age	Name(s)	Surname of spouse
15 - 19	4		F	1	11-6-1620				30-9-1641	21	Rawlyn	ROST #92
20 - 24	21		M	2	25-3-1622	15-8-1641	s.	19			Robert	
25 - 29	33	C	M	3	16-1-1625	3-8-1646	s.	21			John	
30 - 34	33	H	M	4	19-10-1627	3-8-1646	s.	18			George	
35 - 39	38	I	F	5	8-8-1630	30-8-1630	s.	22d			Maria	
40 - 44	14	L	M	6	9-10-1631	2-8-1646	s.	14			Thomas	
45 - 49		D		7								
TOTAL		R		8								
boys		E		9								
girls		N		10								
Remarks				11								
				12								
				13								
				14								
				15								

FRF u 65

Figure 4.1 Example of a family reconstitution chart, compiled from records in parish registers (From Wrigley, 1969, by courtesy of Weidenfeld and Nicolson, publishers, London)

Figure 4.1 illustrates how a particular family could be affected by the disaster of epidemic disease. This 'family reconstitution chart', derived from parish registers, shows how the entire family of Salomon Bird, a weaver, was wiped out in a few days: the mother died in July, followed by the father and three sons aged 21, 18 and 14, in August; two other children, one aged 19 and the other only three weeks old, had died in previous years. Such disasters must have been even more common when epidemics affected towns. For example, deaths from the plague in London reached astronomic proportions in 1625: 35 417 people died from it, compared with only 11, 17 and 16 in the previous three years.

4.1.2 Effects of industrialization and urbanization on family life

The Industrial Revolution depended on power-driven machinery. As water was the first source of power for large enterprises like mills, these were originally built in river valleys; and because they were dependent on the fall of water, they could not be too close together. However, with the development of the rotary steam engine, which was widely adopted after 1800, factories could be built close to each other in the towns, where coal supplies and labour were readily available.

Working class families

During the nineteenth century, people from the countryside poured into the nearest town and urbanization proceeded at a reckless pace. The figures in *Table 4.1* tell some of the story: the towns were growing more than twice as fast as the total population, which itself quadrupled during the century.

TABLE 4.1   Increasing urban population in England and Wales, 1801–1910

	1801	1851 *Population*	1910
England and Wales	10.5 m.	20.8 m.	40.8 m.
Birmingham	71 000	233 000	526 000
Manchester–Salford	95 000	401 000	714 000
Glasgow	84 000	329 000	784 000
London	1 117 000	2 689 000	7 256 000

The social problems created by this rapid growth of towns included slum housing, overcrowding and bad sanitation. Infectious diseases like tuberculosis took great toll of families crowded together, with poor food and excessive work; and other epidemic diseases spread rapidly through insanitary drainage systems and contaminated water supplies.

The problems of housing can still be seen in the remnants of the notorious 'back-to-back' houses in some cities: small, dreary and with inadequate sanitation, they provided cramped and unhealthy homes for vast numbers of the urban working classes (*Figure 4.2*). Also, in many cities, the environment was literally blackened by industrial processes such as those of the iron industry, which was growing very fast. All day long, smoke belched from blast furnaces, and towns in industrial regions became blacker and blacker. Charles Dickens, in *The Old Curiosity Shop*, gives an impression of the Black Country in the English Midlands, in about 1840:

'On every side, and as far as the eye could see into the heavy distance, tall chimneys crowding on each other, poured out their plague of smoke, obscured

Figure 4.2   Graphic portrayal of London slum dwellings (From the drawing 'Over London by Rail', by Gustav Doré, ca. 1870, by courtesy of the BBC Hulton Picture Library)

the light and made foul the melancholy air... . Dismantled houses here and there appeared, tottering to the earth propped up by the fragments of others that had fallen down, unroofed, windowless, blackened, desolate, but yet inhabited. Men, women and children, wan in their looks and ragged in their attire, tended the engines... begged upon the road, or scowled half-naked from doorless houses... . But night-time in this dreadful spot! Night, when the smoke was changed to fire, when every chimney spurted up its flame, and places that had been dark vaults all day, now shone red hot, with figures moving to and fro within their blazing jaws, and calling to one another with hoarse cries, — night when the noise of every strange machine was aggravated by the darkness; when the people near them looked wilder and more savage... .'

Such was the environment in which many working class families lived. The conditions in which they worked — men, women and children — were often comparably horrifying. In the cotton mills, some of the worst features of the new industrialism prevailed: long hours, insanitary conditions, child labour. Large numbers of children were handed over to employers from the age of 7, to work for over 12 hours a day, Saturdays included, under the control of overseers who often used the whip on them. Sometimes children could work for 14 or 15 hours a day for 6 days a week, with meal times being used to clean machinery. Attempts to control this situation included the Health and Morals of Apprentices Act of 1802 and the Factory Act of 1819, but conditions in factories remained deplorable. Consider this evidence given to the Committee on Factory Children's Labour in 1831–32:

'At what time in the morning, in the brisk time, did those girls go to the mills?'

'In the brisk time, for about 6 weeks, they have gone at 3 o'clock in the morning, and ended at 10, or nearly half-past, at night.'

'What intervals were allowed for rest or refreshment during those 19 hours of labour?'

'Breakfast — ¼ hr, and dinner — ½ hr, and drinking — ¼ hr.'

'Was any of that time taken up in cleaning the machinery?'

'They generally had to do what they call dry down; sometimes this took the whole of the time at breakfast or drinking, and they were to get their dinner or breakfast as best they could; if not, it was brought home.'

Figure 4.3   Room occupied by a military tailor and his family, at 10 Hollybush Place, Bethnal Green, London, ca. 1860 (Courtesy BBC Hulton Picture Library)

'Had you not great difficulty in awaking your children for this excessive labour?'

'Yes, in the early time we had to take them up asleep and shake them when we got them on the floor to dress them, before we could get them off to their work... .'

Such was the story of factory life for many workers; but for others who still worked in their own homes (called outworkers), conditions could be equally harsh (*Figure 4.3*).

Middle and upper class families

So far, we have considered some of the worst conditions — those experienced by the working classes. Obviously, there were many families who did not have to live in such deprivation: the wealthy aristocracy and the prosperous middle classes. The quality of family life for them was naturally very different, and they were less vulnerable to material hardship. However, there were many aspects of their social life which were also perceived as problems. For example, the authoritarian Victorian family could be a source of hardship of a different kind, especially for women. A Victorian husband's description of the marriage relationship as 'We twain are one flesh and I am he' reflects a whole system of ideas, beliefs, values and laws which discriminated severely against women. For example, the fact that on marriage a woman had to hand over all her property to her husband, meant that she lost her financial independence and with it her autonomy and her freedom. Also, the expectation that married couples would have large numbers of children had obvious implications for women. With a family size of six children being very common, and anything up to 10 or 12 children not unusual, women could expect to spend a high proportion of their married life either pregnant or nursing babies. It is not surprising that many reached their forties in a state of physical exhaustion, looking and feeling old women by the time they were fifty — if they survived that long.

Thus, as we look back in time, we see that the quality of family life often left a great deal to be desired. What is happening to it nowadays, in the latter years of the twentieth century?

4.2 The family's changing structure

The structural functionalist school of sociology (see Chapter 1) analyses the impact of changes in one part of society on other parts, such as the effects of industrialization on family life. Because an industrial society depends on technological advance, it needs a mobile, adaptable population. The harnessing of new forms of energy has revolutionized industry, transport, recreation and domestic life: the use of coal to drive steam engines for factories and railways; the availability of electric power (the first power stations were built in the 1890s); the widespread use of the world's oil resources (since World War II); and the application of nuclear power to generate electricity in the 1960s and 1970s. Each breakthrough has brought new patterns of employment, with many people moving home to take advantage of the new jobs, resulting in one of the main characteristics of industrial society: *geographical mobility.*

Some of the repercussions of geographical mobility become clear when we consider different kinds of family structure. Sociologists differentiate between an 'extended' and a 'nuclear' family. An extended family consists of a large group of kinfolk living together, or in sufficiently close proximity to constitute a family unit. Such a family might consist of parents and children together with grandparents, aunts, uncles and relatives by marriage. Extended families are found mainly in pre-industrial societies. They may be organized around particular patterns of inheritance. They are called 'patrilineal' if inheritance of property and/or name passes from father to son; 'matrilineal' if inheritance is from mother to daughter. If the family is patrilineal, a newly wedded couple will tend to live with or near the husband's family; if matrilineal, with the bride's family. Such domestic arrangements may not be without their problems.

For example, in traditional China, a new bride had to leave home to live with her husband's family, where she was often unhappy. Mothers-in-law could be notorious for the way in which they treated such newcomers, who were very vulnerable, particularly until they had established some status by giving birth to children of their own — preferably sons. It was therefore hardly surprising that there was a high suicide rate among young brides.

Sociologists use the term 'nuclear family' to denote the simplest of all family units: the basic 'nucleus' of parents and their children. When flying over a modern city, one can see the reality of the nuclear family vividly portrayed in literally 'concrete' terms: miles upon miles of small dwellings designed to house these small family units, with little or no space to accommodate other members of the extended family. This can cause problems, especially for the growing number of elderly people in our midst. For as the employment situation requires families to move to find jobs, elderly relatives may be left far away, perhaps lonely and prone to the infirmities of old age.

However, many sociological studies have suggested that geographical separation does not necessarily mean disintegration of family ties. The term 'modified extended family' describes families who keep closely in touch with each other, despite living at a distance.

4.2.1 The family in modern Britain

Britain is such a heterogeneous society that generalizations are inappropriate. Sociological studies have described different kinds of family life in various parts of the country. Some of these studies show how the nature of work done by the family's breadwinner may influence family relationships. For example, studies of coal miners (Dennis, Henriques and Slaughter, 1956) and of deep-sea fishermen (Tunstall, 1962) show that where men work in dangerous, demanding and physically exhausting conditions they often develop close relationships, because their lives depend on each other. They therefore tend to spend their leisure time in each other's company, often in the congenial atmosphere of the local pub. Tunstall's study of trawlermen suggests that, as a result, 'Some men quickly come to regard their wives mainly as providers of sexual and cooking services in return for a weekly wage'.

A somewhat similar picture emerges from one of the famous sociological studies of family life in London's East End in the 1950s (Young and Willmott, 1957). At that time, many Londoners living in the East End were housed in appalling conditions. I remember accompanying a district nurse on home visits to families in tenement blocks with filthy, cold outside stairways, where entire families were housed in single rooms. These rooms opened on to corridors where all the families from one landing had to depend for their water on one cracked, filthy sink at the end of the corridor, with only one cold tap; there was also only one equally filthy lavatory. Home in such conditions was not the most comfortable of places for relaxation after a day's work and men would often prefer to spend their free time in local pubs or clubs. Young and Willmott found, therefore, that the main backbone of family life was provided by the women: although families were not matrilineal in the sense of inheritance of name or property, the most significant relationships were those of the female kinship system. 'Mum' and 'Gran' were round the corner, if not next door, and were key sources of support and help in everyday life. This female-centred kinship system thus provided a valuable mutual aid society or 'mothers' union'.

Subsequently, policies of rehousing and urban renewal resulted in the demolition of tenements and other slum dwellings. Families were rehoused — some still in London, others in suburban estates or in the satellite towns mushrooming in the countryside around the city.

Rehousing has resulted in new styles of family life and family relationships. For example, studies of families living in new towns suggest that there is often more 'home centredness', with husbands investing more time and interest in home and family life. Also, as wives are more likely to be geographically separated from their mothers, the conjugal relationship may be closer, with more companionship between husband and wife. To use the sociological terminology, 'segregated conjugal roles' have been replaced by 'integrated roles' or 'joint roles'. This process is described by Young and Willmott (1973) as the development of a 'symmetrical' family, because it is characterized by more shared experience and greater equality between husband and wife. However, the elderly members of the family who have been separated from their children and grandchildren can feel lonely and they may regret the loss of the valuable role they might have played in helping to care for the younger generation. Also, the relatively isolated nuclear family may miss the practical and emotional support which the extended family can provide, for there is no real substitute for 'Gran' if, for example, 'Mum' has to go to hospital or if the children are ill.

4.2.2 Women and employment

Another important and related development is the growing number and proportion of women, particularly of married women, who work in paid employment: 42 per cent in 1971 compared with 22 per cent in 1951. There are several reasons for this trend — a trend which has important implications for family life and relationships. For example, more women are marrying and marrying younger: the percentage of women who marry has risen steadily from 85 per cent in 1900 to 95 per cent in the 1970s; and whereas in the 1950s only one in six were married by the age of 20, this proportion increased to about one-quarter in the early 1970s. Consequently, there is a far smaller pool of unmarried women available for employment at a time when there is a greater than ever demand for 'women-power'. Another significant trend has been the tendency for women to have smaller families (see Chapter 3 for discussion of the falling birth rate) and for them to have their children earlier in life than previously. As a result, the years devoted to child-bearing and child-rearing are virtually over for many women by the time they reach their early or mid-forties, leaving perhaps a quarter of a century still available for 'active service' in the labour market.

The current demand for women to take up jobs outside the home is probably unparalleled in human history. Technology and industrial change have generated an unprecedented number of 'white blouse' occupations — in secretarial posts, banking or computer programming, to name but a few. Also, the greater wealth resulting from industrialization has enabled society to develop the vast range of health, welfare and educational services we now take for granted. These require women to work in occupations which, while not entirely a female preserve, are seen as predominantly women's occupations, such as nursing, physiotherapy, schoolteaching and social work.

This increase in the number of married women working outside the home has diverse implications for family life. Two examples which have been considered by sociologists are the relationships between husband and wife and between mother and child.

4.2.3 Husband–wife relationships

Several studies have shown that, not surprisingly, women who combine domestic responsibilities with work outside the home may experience considerable stress (Klein, 1960). Some women go out to work for economic necessity, others to alleviate the tedium of routine housework (Oakley, 1974). Whatever the reason, they often have to cope with role conflict. As we saw in Chapter 1, this can be of two kinds:

(1) Inter-role conflict, when the demands of two roles clash; for example, when a crisis occurs at work with pressure to stay late, beyond the time when children are due home from school.

(2) Intra-role conflict, when there are incompatible demands within one role, as when the diverse expectations of a wife/mother role exceed the time and energy available.

There is also the additional danger that the working wife may find herself doing two jobs, fitting in all the domestic tasks before and after a day's work outside home. It is because of this that many married couples have tended to move from the traditional 'segregated role relationship' where the 'woman's place is in the kitchen', to sharing domestic tasks, with the husband helping with cooking, shopping and caring for the children. However, it is important not to generalize. There are many regional variations in the ways in which families regard the issue of women working outside the home, as Yudkin and Holme (1963) pointed out:

'It was significant that many of the husbands in Viola Klein's study (1960) who disapproved of their wives working, or even of the idea of them working, simply stated that women's place was in the home, a cliché offered with no attempt at rationalization and clearly culled from a prevailing social climate. The influence of the neighbourhood and its traditions can be equally strong. Families in Lancashire or the Potteries feel very differently from the families of miners in Wales about wives and mothers working. A mother in one part of the country may feel very guilty if she goes out to work: a mother in another area may feel equally guilty if she does not.'

Whatever the prevailing ideas about married women going out to work and sharing domestic chores with their husbands, it is generally felt that it is the wife who should carry the primary responsibility for the care of children and that it is her career which should be subordinated to the needs of family life. This has resulted in the familiar three-phase pattern of employment for married women: post-school work and/or education; marriage and child-rearing; re-entry into employment. While many — perhaps most — women are satisfied with this arrangement, it can cause tension, and the break in career is reflected in the marked under-representation of women in 'top jobs'. Nursing is no exception: although only about 15 per cent in the profession as a whole are men, nevertheless they occupy approximately 40 per cent of senior posts.

Another result of the increase in women working in paid employment is the relative financial independence which they can enjoy. This means that women do not now have to place such a high premium on marriage as a financial necessity, as their Victorian forebears did. A century ago, the number of 'respectable' occupations available to middle class women was very limited — the position of governess being the most generally acceptable. Consequently, marriage was necessary as a means of financial support and the 'prospects' of the bridegroom-to-be were a matter for serious consideration. The pressures on working class women were even worse, for the kinds of jobs available to them were either in domestic service or in factories such as those depicted earlier in this chapter; neither kind of employment gave much autonomy or remuneration. Nowadays, the actual or potential financial independence of women has resulted in a tendency towards greater equality of relationships between husbands and wives; and in the event of an unhappy marriage, the wife has more financial freedom to enable her to contemplate separation or divorce.

Thus, the consequences of changing patterns of employment and the increase in the employment of married women have been complex and diverse. They vary from family to family and range from certain negative aspects such as tension, stress and overwork to outcomes which are generally seen as positive: more sharing and co-operation in family life and greater personal freedom and fulfilment (Rapoport and Rapoport, 1976). What have been the implications for children?

4.2.4　Parent–child relationships

One of the most comprehensive studies of the effects on children of their mothers going out to work is by Yudkin and Holme (1963). These authors found that, contrary to many people's expectations, most children whose mothers went out to work showed no ill effects — given certain conditions about the age of the child when the mother went to work and the arrangements made for his or her care while she was out. In general, it was suggested that very young children (under the age of 3 years) need to see enough of their mothers to develop a very close relationship, to the extent that it is probably desirable for the mother not to go out to work. But over the age of three, provided the 'mother substitutes' are warm, caring people and that there is continuity of care, children may actually benefit if their mothers do go out to work. They appear more self-reliant and less anxious than their peers whose mothers stay at home.

Yudkin and Holme also stress the importance of family life as a whole, warning against underestimating the father's contribution. For example, they point to detrimental effects if the father works such excessive overtime that he fails to establish deep and happy relationships with his children.

Among the recommendations put forward in the book are many practical proposals such as the provision of more day nurseries; special allowances for mothers with children under three years of age, to enable them to stay at home; more facilities for part-time work for women, geared to school hours; more arrangements for the care of schoolchildren after school hours — for example, in public libraries, play centres and on school premises; more provision for children during holidays, in the form of holiday camps as in the U.S.A. or other organized holiday facilities; and especial provisions for mothers who are the sole supporters of their children.

We have seen that the structure and form of family life has been subject to many changes. In conclusion, let us briefly speculate on future trends.

4.3 The future of the family

Attempts to anticipate the future of the family as a social institution require the following considerations:

(1) An understanding of the family's *functions* for society and for individuals.
(2) An analysis of *social trends*, which might indicate that the family as we have known it may be changing.
(3) A study of *alternative* ways of organizing human relationships.

4.3.1 The functions of the family

Any society, if it is to survive, must ensure that the population reproduces itself adequately, and that children are brought up to contribute appropriately to the life of the community. It is therefore not surprising that all socieities have some regulations for the control of sexual relationships and family life. These are often given the backing of law and are reinforced by religious ritual.

For example, the centuries old *Book of Common Prayer* of the Anglican Church begins the Marriage Service by identifying the central functions of marriage: '...duly considering the causes for which matrimony was ordained: First, it was ordained for the procreation of children, to be brought up in the fear and nurture of the Lord; Secondly, it was ordained for a remedy against sin....; Thirdly, it was ordained for the mutual society, help and comfort that the one ought to have for the other, both in prosperity and adversity.' The modern *Alternative Service Book* of 1980 is a reflection of the times, in that the order is reversed, with the function of companionship between husband and wife coming first, but the other central functions are still present: reproduction and the appropriate upbringing of children.

Socialization

The process of bringing up children to play an acceptable role in society is described in sociological terms as socialization. It is through the process of socialization that a 'raw' human infant develops into a social person, initiated into the beliefs and ways of life of his social group and able to play his own part in society. Sociologists differentiate between 'primary' and 'secondary' socialization. The family is the main agent of *primary socialization*, for in the early days and months of a child's life, this is his 'world' — it is here that he encounters his first experience of physical and emotional needs and their satisfaction. And although socialization is a lifelong process, some of the most significant developments occur during the highly impressionable and formative period of early childhood. Hence the immense importance of the family and the quality of family relationships.

The process of primary socialization has been described by the social psychologist, G. H. Mead, as consisting of three stages (Mead, 1934). First, the young child must learn that he has an existence of his own, independent of his mother. He learns to distinguish 'I' from 'me' and to begin to see himself as an 'object' as well as experiencing himself as a 'subject'. This paves the way for the second stage — the 'play' stage — when a small child begins to play certain roles, such as 'Mummy' and 'Daddy'. The significance of this stage is that the child is temporarily stepping outside himself, and viewing the world, and himself, from the perspective of other people who are significant to him — his 'significant others'. In doing this, he is identifying with them, and beginning to adopt their views, their values and their standards of behaviour; and he is also 'internalizing' the norms and expectations of the wider society. In the third stage, called by Mead the 'game' stage, the child plays games — but the significance lies in the fact that these are games with abstract rules. Thus the child is now internalizing more universal concepts of 'right' and 'wrong' and learning to cope with general principles. In Mead's terminology, he is in the process of developing an 'internalized generalized other'.

Primary socialization is characterized by close emotional ties, in which the child identifies with his 'significant others' and, because he cares about them and for them, their influence is very strong and goes very deep. As he grows up and enters into a wider circle of social relationships, he will continue the process of socialization — learning how to behave in ways which are socially acceptable in a wide variety of milieux, such as school and work.

However, much *secondary socialization* is more concerned with learning appropriate knowledge, skills and attitudes, and less with emotional involvement. Nevertheless, there are obviously some adult situations, such as marriage and the establishment of a family of one's own, which involve deep personal relationships and adjustments. The process of socialization is thus a very important part of human experience and we shall come across it again in different contexts; for example in Chapter 8, where we meet the concept of 'professional socialization', and in Chapter 10, where we consider the significance of socialization in some discussions of mental illness.

4.3.2   Social trends: divorce

Given the key role of the family in traditionally fulfilling the social functions of regulation of reproduction, socialization of children and provision of adult companionship and support, how may we interpret statistics, such as those in *Table 4.2*,

TABLE 4.2   Petitions for divorce: England and Wales, 1911–1979

Year	Thousands
1911	1
1951	33
1966	47
1971	111
1973	116
1975	139
1977	168
1979	164

(Source: 'Social Trends', Central Statistical Office, 1981).

which show steep increases in rates of divorce? These crude statistics are often cited as cause for alarm and defined as social problems of growing magnitude. However, great care needs to be taken in the interpretation of such figures.

For example, any discussion of figures for divorce must take account of changes in law, in financial circumstances and in social norms. McGregor (1957) gives a historical account which shows how the rise in statistics may be explained to some extent by the *increased availability* of divorce as a solution to an unhappy marriage. Although there may have been many equally unhappy marriages in earlier years, recourse to divorce was precluded because the law presented many barriers. Not only was the cost prohibitive for most people, but divorce could only be granted on grounds which were often difficult to prove, such as 'cruelty', which made court proceedings very unpleasant.

Important changes in the law include the Herbert Act of 1937 which removed the 'double standard' (by giving equal rights to both men and women) and increased the grounds for divorce to include desertion; and the Legal Aid Act of 1949, which helped to reduce the financial barriers, which had previously often been prohibitive. More recently, 'irretrievable breakdown' of a marriage has been recognized as a legal ground for divorce, giving further opportunity for couples who feel that their marriage has been a mistake to apply for legal dissolution of the marriage contract. This represents a radical shift from earlier legal policy, which had insisted on the proof of matrimonial offence as grounds for divorce.

These changes in the law reflect changes in public attitudes. Divorce no longer carries the severe stigma or the social penalties of earlier years when, for example, divorce might have meant the end of a career. Also, divorce is now not limited exclusively to those who can afford the costs of divorce proceedings: the availability of legal aid means that more people can afford it.

Such changes must be taken into account in any interpretation of the steep rise in divorce rates. It is not necessarily the number of unhappy marriages which has increased, but the number of unhappily married people who seek a resolution to their problems in the divorce court. An additional point which is relevant to the issue of whether marriage and the family as social institutions are declining, is the fact that a high proportion of divorcees remarry. It thus seems that it is the quality of the relationship which is the issue, rather than a rejection of the concept of marriage as such — a trend which has been cynically described as 'a triumph of hope over experience'. Sociologically, this trend is described by the phrase 'serial monogamy', implying that, for some people in contemporary society, marriage patterns have shifted from lifelong commitment to one partner to a series of relationships. This may be partly explicable in terms of the increasing demands made on marriage in modern society.

As we have seen, the geographical mobility required of the family in industrial societies is associated with the separation of nuclear family units from the wider kinship network and the support which they can provide. Married couples have to rely much more on their own resources. Moreover, the change from segregated role relationships to integrated conjugal roles means that husband and wife are much more dependent on each other for practical help and for companionship.

While this can be very rewarding and satisfying, it can also generate strains and stresses. And with the greater emotional investment in family relationships, the costs of unhappiness can be correspondingly greater, not only for the married couple, but also for their children. Many people believe that children may suffer more by remaining in a home which is ridden with conflict, than by a relatively amicable agreement to part company. Other couples may stay together for the sake of the children, but separate once the children have left home; this pattern is reflected in the growing number of divorces occurring after 20 years of marriage.

The overall situation is summarized by Cotgrove (1978);

'Marriage is more popular than ever, but the more exacting demands made upon it can only be discharged by spouses more adequately matched than the chances of Cupid's bow necessarily ensure. Moreover, there are always likely to be some who simply cannot match up to the heavy demands that marriage makes upon them. Divorce statistics certainly indicate that for some this pattern may be shifting from lifelong to serial monogamy; from one partner for life to a series of partners.'

4.3.3 Alternatives to the family

So far in this chapter it has been assumed that the family as a social institution is here to stay. It may change, but its continued existence has not been questioned. However, there are some who challenge this assumption. For example, the psychiatrist R. D. Laing and his colleague A. Esterson (Laing and Esterson, 1964) have claimed that emotional tensions and conflicts in some families may drive people to insanity (see Chapter 10). Also, many sociologists, especially those with a 'radical' or Marxist persuasion, see the family as a major obstacle to social change and argue that more attention should be paid to the development of alternatives. One sociologist who writes in this vein, D. Morgan, makes the point in this way (Morgan, 1975):

'The foundations for a critical perspective on the family are, as I hope to have shown, already present: not only in theories derived from a Marxian tradition but also in the recognition of the human costs as well as gains in family living as stressed by Laing and some radical feminists, in the various challenges to the centrality of kinship as a topic in anthropology and in the ethnomethodological practice of regarding the "given" and the process whereby it is defined and successfully maintained as "given" as itself problematic and a topic for investigation. Such critiques, although very different, demonstrate the precarious basis upon which the family exists and in doing so bring the family and its change, its abolition or even its maintenance within the ambit of human choice and human praxis.'

Some societies have tried to put such alternatives into practice, and the following paragraphs describe three such attempts.

Soviet Union and simpler divorce

The Soviet Union in the 1920s tried to weaken the family unit, which was seen as a reactionary influence, by making divorce so easy that it could be achieved by postcard. The subsequent social instability, falling birth rate and problems in providing for the children who suffered from family breakdowns were so acute that the experiment was abandoned (Timasheff, 1946). The family as a social institution was reinstated and protected by new legislation.

Israel and the kibbutzim

Another country which has tried to alter radically the role of the family in society is modern Israel, with its kibbutzim. Some of these are now well established, having been in existence for over 40 years. In many kibbutzim, most property is communally owned and children are cared for on a communal basis. While still babies, they are removed from the continuous care of their parents and accommodated in 'baby houses'. The mother usually returns to work soon after childbirth. Children remain in communal care, being brought up with other children of the same age and visiting their parents for a few hours each day. The primary tasks of child-rearing and the associated process of socialization are largely transferred from the parents to the community.

Britain and the commune movement

In Britain, the most radical alternative to the traditional family structure can perhaps be seen in the development of the commune movement. One account of this movement, by Abrams and McCulloch (1976), discusses the diverse philosophies which have motivated people to try to establish this alternative way of life, and of the problems and satisfactions they have encountered. Many of these philosophies represent a critique of the nuclear family and what is often seen as its 'repressive' characteristics. This is reflected in the formally stated objective of the commune movement: 'to create a federal society of communities wherein everyone shall be free to do whatever he wishes provided only that he doesn't transgress the freedom of another.'

Abrams and McCulloch identify seven 'themes' which characterize the commune movement, including concern over problems of the family as an institution; problems for women in contemporary society; and problems arising from the loss of community. Many were intended to be 'revolutionary' in one form or another. The analysis shows that most of them have been short-lived. However, the experience of the Israeli kibbutzim suggests that, under certain conditions, alternatives to traditional family life may become established.

■ Summary

The crucial role played by the family in the survival of society is emphasized. Reproduction and socialization — crucial to the continuation of society — are seen as functions of the family. However, the family as a social institution has been profoundly affected by changes in the wider society, particularly by industrialization and urbanization. Interpretation of these changes and our reaction towards them will depend on our own beliefs, values and experiences. Alternatives to the family structure have been tried with varying degrees of success in the early years of the Soviet Union, in the kibbutzim of Israel and in the communes of Britain.

Because the family is such a significant social unit and the relationships it engenders are so deep, we are likely to feel strongly about it. It is therefore important, the author feels, to take account of the available evidence before drawing conclusions on a subject so complex and of such profound significance.

■ Questions

1. What do you understand by the terms 'industrialization' and 'urbanization'? What effects did these processes have on family life in this country?
2. Write brief notes on the following:
    (a) the extended family;
    (b) the nuclear family;
    (c) socialization;
    (d) role conflict.
3. Discuss some of the reasons for the increase in divorce since 1900.
4. 'The family in modern society is losing its functions.' Do you agree?

References

Abrams, P. and McCulloch, A. (1976) *Communes, Sociology and Society*, London, Cambridge University Press.

Cotgrove, S. (1978). *The Science of Society*, 4th edn, London, George Allen & Unwin.

Dennis, N., Henriques, F. and Slaughter, C. (1956). *Coal is Our Life*, London, Tavistock.

Klein, V. (1960). 'Working wives', *Occasional Papers*, no. 15, London, Institute of Personnel Management.

Laing, R. D. and Esterson, A. (1964). *Sanity, Madness and the Family*, London, Tavistock.

Mead, G. H. (1934). *Mind, Self and Society* for a useful summary see 'Self', in *Sociological Perspectives*, Thompson, K. and Tunstall, J. (Eds.), Harmondsworth, Open University Press/Penguin Education, 1977.

McGregor, O. (1957). *Divorce in England*, London, Heinemann.

Morgan, D. (1975). *Social Theory and the Family*, London, Routledge & Kegan Paul.

Oakley, A. (1974). *The Sociology of Housework*, London, Martin Robertson.

Rapoport, R. and Rapoport, R. (1976). *Dual Career Families Re-examined*, London, Martin Robertson.

Timasheff, N. (1946). 'The attempt to abolish the family in Russia', in *A Modern Introduction to the Family*, Bell, N. and Vogel, E. (Eds.), New York, Free Press, 1960.

Tunstall, J. (1962). *The Fishermen*, London, MacGibbon & Kee.

Wrigley, E. A. (1969). *Population and History*, London, Weidenfeld & Nicolson.

Young, M. and Willmott, P. (1957). *Family and Kinship in East London*, Harmondsworth, Penguin.

Young, M. and Willmott, P. (1973). *The Symmetrical Family*, London, Routledge & Kegan Paul.

Yudkin, S. and Holme, A. (1963). *Working Mothers and Their Children*, London, Michael Joseph.

Further reading

Bell, N. W. and Vogel, E. F. (Eds.) (1960). *A Modern Introduction to the Family*, New York, Free Press. An interesting textbook, with discussions of family life in different societies.

Fletcher, R. (1962). *The Family and Marriage*, Harmondsworth, Penguin. A short, readable book, which traces trends in family life, showing how it is adapting to changes in the wider society. Basically, an optimistic account which challenges those who proclaim that the family is on the decline.

Rosser, C. and Harris, C. (1965). *The Family and Social Change*, London, Routledge & Kegan Paul. A useful overview of previous sociological studies and a discussion of the continuity of the extended family in the area of study: South Wales.

N.B. It may be noticed that these recommendations do not refer to very recent books. This illustrates the point made in the Preface: sometimes, 'older' references are chosen, because they have much to offer which is of continuing value.

In front of a relief kitchen in India (Courtesy John Topham Picture Library)

('Social class' and 'social stratification' are not just abstract sociological concepts . . . they can encompass the diversities of wealth and poverty . . . — see p. 71)

5 Social class and social stratification

5.1 Concepts and theories

'Social class' and 'social stratification' are not just abstract sociological concepts. They are words which refer to deep human experiences and relationships. For example, they can encompass the diversities of wealth and poverty; of social snobbery and social deference; and of inequalities in access to, and benefit from, various educational, health and welfare services. They may therefore be reflected in the tragedy of avoidable infant mortality, or the suffering of an impoverished, undernourished, lonely old person dying of hypothermia.

All societies are divided into social groups, which often have unequal access to material resources such as wealth, or to symbolic resources such as prestige. Examples of highly stratified and very unequal societies include the feudal system of medieval Europe or the Hindu caste system. In those societies, social mobility — movement from one stratum to another — was traditionally very limited. Generally, a person's status in society was 'ascribed' at birth and he would remain in that social stratum throughout his life. For example, when the feudal system was at its height, it was almost impossible for someone who had been born a serf to rise above that status, or even to move away from the land belonging to his lord. Traditional Hindu society's rigid system of castes is reinforced or legitimated by religious beliefs, based on ideas of 'uncleanness' and 'untouchability'. These concepts preclude social intercourse between people of different castes and make it very difficult for anyone to 'pass' from one caste to another.

In both types of society, the rigid stratification system was loosened by the growth of cities which provided unprecedented opportunities for social mobility, with new kinds of employment which did not fit readily into traditional categories. Also, once a person had moved away from his own village, where his social position was common knowledge, he could begin a new social life and aspire to rise in the social hierarchy. Status which is attained by a person's own performance is called 'achieved status'.

In industrialized societies, the system of stratification has become more complex, with increased social mobility and achieved status becoming much more widespread. Because so much is at stake, it is not surprising that two of the early founding fathers of sociology, Karl Marx and Max Weber, devoted much of their attention to the concepts and the realities of social class and social stratification.

71

Figure 5.1 Karl Marx, the German socialist philosopher; photograph taken in 1866 (Courtesy BBC Hulton Picture Library)

5.1.1 Marx and social class

In Chapter 1, we noted that Karl Marx (*Figure 5.1*) believed that the most important division in society is economic: between those who own the means of production (land, factories, etc.) and those who do not. The owners are in such a strong position that they were seen by Marx as a 'ruling class' who control and manipulate not only the economy, but also other key social institutions such as government and the law. Conversely, the non-owners are very vulnerable; they have nothing to sell but their labour. Because society is divided into these two classes, the bourgeoisie (the 'haves') and the proletariat (the 'have-nots'), Marx believed that conflict and revolution would be inevitable. These might be delayed for a while, because the proletariat suffered from 'false consciousness', which prevented them from being fully aware of their disadvantaged and exploited position. However, in time, 'true consciousness' would emerge. Then, the proletariat would be transformed from a loose collection of people who happen to share the same fate — a 'class in itself' — to a more cohesive and motivated social force — a 'class for itself'. This class would then lead a revolution to destroy capitalist society, and would usher in a new era — the era of socialist society. In a socialist society, the old divisions would be eradicated, because private ownership of the means of production would be abolished. With public ownership, there would no longer be class conflict, and people could live and work together harmoniously, without exploitation or oppression by a ruling class.

Because Marx laid such emphasis on the economic characteristics of society, he can be called a 'materialist' or an 'economic determinist'. In other words, he believed that material factors — the way in which the economy is organized — determine the characteristics of other social institutions and the quality of human relationships. The economy is seen as the 'infrastructure' whereas the rest of social life, such as law, religion, culture and education, is seen as the 'superstructure', dependent on and shaped by the economic base. In Marx's own words, the social organization of the means of production is 'the real foundation, on which legal and political superstructures arise and to which definite forms of social consciousness correspond'.

5.1.2 Weber and social stratification

Max Weber also recognized the importance of economic factors in shaping social life, but he was not an economic determinist. Weber differed from Marx in various ways (see Chapter 1). First, he was not basically a materialist but an 'idealist', in that he believed that man was not shaped or determined primarily by material, economic forces, but could help to shape his own destiny in accordance with his ideas and beliefs. This was part of the significance of Weber's analysis of religion, in which he showed that religious beliefs could influence man's economic behaviour (see Chapter 7). This is in direct contrast to Marx's view which saw religion as the 'opium of the people'. By this he meant that it alleviated the sufferings of oppressed people by giving them hope. It served the interests of the ruling classes by keeping the working class subservient and relatively contented with their position in life — a divine legitimation of the ordering of society.

Secondly, Weber's analysis of 'class' differs from Marx's. He sees it more in market terms as 'the amount and kind of power, or lack of such, to dispose of goods or skills for the sake of income in a given economic order'. Thus, a capitalist society does not consist of just two classes; it is a more differentiated system, with numerous groups offering diverse goods and services and being remunerated according to the value placed on them by other people. This results in many gradations of standards of living and 'life chances'.

This analysis is related to a third difference from Marx: whereas Marx's analysis of class is essentially unidimensional, based on the economic criterion, Weber's theory of stratification is multidimensional, taking other criteria into account. For example, in addition to the relatively objective economic dimension, Weber also highlighted subjective differences in stratification in the form of social 'honour' or *status*, as well as the important dimension of access to *political power*. These are often related, but not always, and Weber recommended that any analysis of social stratification should consider these three dimensions separately. For example, it is not difficult to think of people who score high on one dimension but low on another: an impoverished aristocrat who enjoys social honour and perhaps even a seat in the House of Lords, but who no longer owns the property belonging to his forefathers; a clergyman or a nurse, who enjoy public esteem, with a respected career, but are not rewarded with a high income; or, in collective terms, the rising to parliamentary power of the Labour Party, which was not based on an 'infrastructure' of ownership of the means of production.

5.1.3 Theory and reality: developments since Marx and Weber

Any theory needs to be tested by applying it to the real world and assessing its effectiveness in prediction and explanation. In social science, we have a particularly difficult challenge, because the theory itself may change the reality. For example, Marxists believe in the truth of Marxist analysis and work to try to achieve a Marxist society on a global scale. Their success is measured by the fact that approximately one-third of the world's population now lives under Marxist governments of some kind. Weber's analysis has also improved our understanding of other aspects of social stratification. In the rest of this chapter we will therefore consider four related topics in more detail:

(1) Developments in Britain in the twentieth century: Marxist analysis; the embourgeoisement thesis and the social action theorists; social mobility; social elites.
(2) Developments in socialist societies.
(3) Social class, stratification and ideology.
(4) Social class and health.

5.2 Developments in Britain in the twentieth century

5.2.1 Marxist analysis of social class and class conflict

Although Marx was born in Germany, he spent most of his working life in England, and as we have seen he predicted the inevitability of a revolution. However, this has yet to come to pass in England and many other industrialized countries. Many explanations have been forthcoming as to why this is so. For example, some writers have pointed to the growth of joint stock companies, where the people who own the capital are not the same as those who manage the companies. There is thus some dispersion of power and of vested interests. In addition, there has been a proliferation of middle class occupations in professions both new and old, such as social work or architecture, and in white collar occupations like ·banking and computing. There has also been a rise in the general standard of living and an expansion of the welfare state. It is thus suggested that, for the time being, the gap between the ruling class and the proletariat has been narrowed and class conflict defused. However, Marxists argue that the essential contradictions of capitalist society still persist and that class conflict is endemic. Sooner or later the working class will rise in revolt and replace capitalism with socialism (Miliband, 1969).

5.2.2 The embourgeoisement thesis

An alternative analysis was put forward in the years following World War II. Impressed by the rising standard of living being enjoyed by many people, including many in working class occupations, a number of social theorists suggested that Britain was becoming a 'middle class society'. The title of an influential book, *The Worker in an Affluent Society* (Zweig, 1961), encapsulates the mood which had begun to emerge in the late 1950s. In essence, it was suggested that class differences were being eroded by the relatively large pay packets of many manual workers, who could consequently purchase material goods and enjoy activities which had previously been the prerogative of the middle and upper classes — such as cars, television sets and holidays abroad. It was also suggested that working class people were beginning to feel less socially inferior. As one manual worker remarked to Zweig: 'I am working class only in the works, but outside I am like everyone else.' This kind of evidence was used to support the idea that 'we are all middle class now' — an idea summed up in the word 'embourgeoisement'.

The social action theorists

The embourgeoisement thesis did not pass unchallenged. Among the sociologists who took issue with it were some who may be described as 'social action' theorists. Their approach is within the general sociological tradition which has stemmed from the work of Max Weber. They do not, like Marxists, give axiomatic priority to economic aspects of life, although they do not underestimate their importance. Also, they adopt a more 'subjectivist' approach, using Weber's concept of 'verstehen' (empathy) to try to develop an understanding of the ideas, beliefs, values and attitudes which influence people's views of social life and the ways in which they behave.

In order to test the embourgeoisement thesis, a number of these sociologists decided to assess the extent to which relatively affluent manual workers had, in effect, become 'middle class'. In order to apply as severe a test as possible, they selected a situation which might be thought most favourable to the development of embourgeoisement: the affluent workers in the car industry in Luton. This town was chosen because the car workers who lived there had severed their connections with traditional working class communities. They were typically living in new houses in recently developed estates and their weekly pay packets amounted to more than the salaries of some of their white collar counterparts. Thus, the researchers maintained, if embourgeoisement was occurring anywhere, it should be occurring in Luton; if it was not found there, it would be doubtful if it would be found anywhere else.

So began the now well-known studies by Lockwood, Goldthorpe and their colleagues, summarized in Goldthorpe et al. (1969). The researchers distinguished three areas of analysis: economic, relational and normative. They found that in economic terms, although it was true that the car factory workers took home relatively large pay packets, these were bought at a high price. The men often had to work overtime, in long shifts with awkward hours, in noisy, hot conditions, with boring repetitive work, bringing little in the way of job satisfaction. Also, their jobs were very insecure — they could be given just a few days' notice. Thus, in general, their conditions of employment compared very unfavourably with those of white collar workers.

In relational terms, it appeared that there was not much social mixing between the social classes either at work or in the local community. It seemed as though segregation persisted during leisure hours and that there was little or no social assimilation of the affluent working class into middle class circles.

Finally, in normative terms — attitudes, values and beliefs — there was little apparent tendency to change to more middle class patterns, as might be exemplified by, say, a shift towards voting Conservative. There were, however, some changes; for example, there was the tendency which has already been noted in the discussion on family life (Chapter 4) for these working class families to be more 'home centred' than those in traditional working class communities.

Overall, the embourgeoisement thesis was not endorsed by Lockwood and colleagues, and it was suggested that it is unlikely to become a reality while such fundamental differences remain between social classes in terms of job security, opportunities for promotion and preferred life-styles.

Social mobility and social elites

Another approach to social class and stratification is the study of social mobility. It was mentioned earlier that some societies have virtually no mobility between different social groups. However, industrial societies are relatively 'open', in that there are opportunities for movement from one class to another. There are different kinds of social mobility: upward and downward; within one lifetime (intragenerational) or between parent and child (intergenerational); short range or long range (across the manual/non-manual work boundary, or from 'rags to riches').

Comparative studies (Miller, 1960) of social mobility patterns in industrial societies show that they all have a sizable amount of social mobility, although there is considerable variation between them. Britain, for example, has a significant amount of short-range upward mobility (from manual to non-manual work), but not very much long-range upward mobility (from manual worker origin to elite status). There are numerous possible explanations for this. For example, one of the factors affecting mobility rates is the ratio of vacancies in positions in different strata to the numbers of people available to occupy them. Industrialization tends to create an expansion of elite positions ('top jobs') which are filled by upwardly mobile people who 'rise from the ranks'. But, in general, there are many obstacles which prevent a very high turnover of the kinds of people at the top. For example, in Chapter 6 we see how many working class children and young people may be disadvantaged in the education system and tend to underachieve compared with middle class children. Since many top jobs require educational qualifications, they may therefore be at a disadvantage.

Also, different elite groups often interlock, resulting in a tendency for them to be self-perpetuating — a phenomenon described by Wright Mills (1956). He described the existence in the U.S.A. of interlocking political, economic and military elites, suggesting that they not only shared interests which were reflected in crucial policy decisions, but also shared social relationships such as school friendships and other informal connections which could influence recruitment to elite positions. A more recent account by a British author (Rex, 1974), offers a similar analysis:

> 'What certainly is the case is that elite members do have a tendency towards corporate identity, that they do practise techniques of selection and exclusion against potential entrants and that they share a sense of exercising, not merely power as do Mills' three elites, but authority which rests upon cultural legitimations.'

An understanding of the existence and significance of elites in shaping policy and in influencing public opinion is important. We shall return to this theme when we discuss the provision of health care and the allocation of scarce resources between competing groups (see Chapter 8).

5.3 Developments in socialist societies

The discussion of social mobility and of social elites leads appropriately to a brief consideration of developments in socialist societies in which, using the Marxist definition, social 'class' has been eradicated. For, in so far as class is a product of unequal relationships stemming from ownership or non-ownership of the means of production, the abolition of private ownership means the abolition of the basis of class and class conflict. Also, socialist societies claim that they strive for equality: any differences should be justified on the principle, 'From each according to his ability, to each according to his need'.

5.3.1 Inequalities in socialist societies

It is well known, however, that social differentiation and privilege persist in socialist societies to an extent beyond that which could be justified by the above maxim. First, in economic terms, there are several analyses which demonstrate that although differentials in incomes are not so large as they are in capitalist societies, marked inequalities persist. Parkin (1971) suggests that, in the early post-revolutionary days, socialist societies achieved a considerable levelling out of incomes. However, as they tried to improve their industrial, technological and scientific base, they needed more incentives to encourage people to train for key positions, and this led to wider income differentials. Consequently, although socialist societies are still more equal in income distribution than western societies, inequalities are increasing.

Income is not the sole measure of equality, important though it is. Other forms of inequality have become characteristic of socialist societies. For example, M. Djilas, the former Vice-President of Yugoslavia, has highlighted the power, prestige and privileges which accrue to members of the Communist Party, particularly to those who become Party officials (Djilas, 1966). Instead of the class-less society envisaged by Marx, socialist societies have developed a new type of class structure and a new kind of ruling class — the new 'owners' of the means of production:

> 'In practice, the ownership privilege of the new class manifests itself as an exclusive right as a party monopoly, for the political bureaucracy to distribute the national income, to set wages, direct economic development and dispose of nationalised and other property. This is the way it appears to the ordinary man who considers the Communist functionary as being very rich and as a man who does not have to work... . The new class obtains its power, privileges, ideology and its customs from one specific form of ownership — collective ownership — which the class administers and distributes in the name of the nation and society.'

There are also other inequalities in many socialist societies. For example, in a society such as the Soviet Union, Communist Party members have access to special shops, otherwise reserved for tourists and other favoured groups; priority allocation for their children in schools of their choice; and privileged housing, sometimes in pleasant villas or 'dachas'. Conversely, negative effects of socialist stratification systems can be seen in the discrimination practised against those who do not find favour with the Party. In many cases, Christians and other religious believers are discriminated against in the competition for jobs and housing, while young people may find difficulty in obtaining a place at university if their religious commitment is known. Even more extreme kinds of inequality and discrimination are experienced by some religious groups or other 'dissidents', who may be sent to psychiatric hospital or to the notorious labour camps of the Gulag Archipelago for their 'anti-socialist' beliefs (Conquest, 1968).

It is important to stress that there are differences between the various socialist societies and that therefore great care must be taken to avoid unwarranted generalization. However, it does seem that equality has not been achieved to the extent that those who envisaged a classless Utopia might have hoped. It also seems that, in analysing the development of class and stratification in both western and socialist societies, we need to consider briefly the ideological dilemmas involved in attempts to put into practice the ideal of equality.

5.4   Social class, stratification and ideology

In Chapter 1 a number of themes were touched upon which are relevant here. They include the question of the extent to which sociology can be value-free. This is particularly relevant in discussions about a dilemma which confronts every society: the conflict between freedom and equality. In thinking about these important matters, it is helpful to read some proponents of different views; that is why the list of books at the end of the chapter includes examples of social action theorists, Marxists and critics of Marxism.

5.4.1   Social action theorists

The work of authors such as Lockwood and Goldthorpe exemplify the ideas of the social action theorists. They follow in the tradition of Max Weber. As we have seen, in their analysis of social stratification they take a multidimensional approach, looking at economic, social and political variables.

5.4.2   Marxist writers

Sociologists of Marxist persuasion, such as Miliband (1969) or Westergaard and Resler (1975), use Marxist theories and concepts to analyse the structure and organization of capitalist societies. They highlight, for example, interlocking relationships between big business and government which are claimed to constitute an effective 'ruling class'. In support of their position they quote evidence of considerable concentration of wealth in the hands of a small minority of the population and they illustrate the process of 'legitimation' by suggesting that social institutions such as the education system, the churches and the mass media all support the *status quo* and keep the subordinate working class in a state of acquiescence. They predict that this state of affairs will ultimately be changed as the working class becomes more aware of social injustice and begins to challenge and ultimately to destroy the capitalist system. They see their role as helping to raise levels of consciousness and thereby to help to bring about revolutionary social change.

5.4.3 Critics of Marxism

These workers take issue with Marxists in several ways. We may briefly identify two of them: analysing the realities of Marxism in practice; and arguing a case for capitalism in moral, social and economic terms.

Those who look at the realities of Marxism in contemporary societies often highlight the price that has been paid in loss of freedom and human rights. The secrecy surrounding official figures makes estimates inevitably tentative, but it is reasonably conjectured by Conquest (1978) that, from Stalin's reign of terror onwards, around 40 million Soviet citizens have perished at the hands of their fellow countrymen — executed in purges, killed during the forcible collectivization of the land, or destroyed by the harsh conditions of the labour camps.

On the second point, the defence of capitalism, several writers have argued that it is the most appropriate way of organizing society in order to protect freedom and to promote economic development. Although crude *'laissez-faire'* capitalism can be brutal — as we saw in the discussion of the working class family in the nineteenth century — contemporary advocates argue that its main ill-effects can be avoided by the provision of an effective 'safety net', and that its advantages outweigh its disadvantages.

The essential concept, according to one of the most ardent advocates, F. A. Hayek, is the market. Hayek (1978) argues that reality is so complex that no one person or group of people can possibly have sufficient grasp of it to draw up comprehensive blueprints for social or economic policy. Attempts to do so result in stifling freedom, initiative and enterprise, and in economic inefficiency. Such inefficiency, which is a well-recognized characteristic of the 'planned economies' of socialist societies, benefits no one in the long run. Therefore, the defenders of capitalism argue that, provided there is a satisfactory basic standard of living for all citizens (the term 'satisfactory' inevitably begging many questions), all stand to gain from the kind of market economy which will generate most wealth and use resources most efficiently. Thus, western societies which tend, as we have seen, to have rather more inequality than their socialist counterparts, are also characterized by higher standards of living and more freedom. It is because of the close association between freedom, individual responsibility and morality that Johnson (1979) has argued that there is essentially a moral basis for capitalism.

In conclusion, we must each decide, on the basis of our own values and on the evidence available to us, in which direction we wish our society to develop. There is an onus of responsibility on each of us to make some contribution to the future by working for the kind of society we believe to be best. Victor Hugo said: 'Mightier than an army is an idea whose time has come.' What are *our* ideas?

5.5 Social class and health

5.5.1 Operational definition of 'social class'

Before discussing some of the detailed information concerning the relationship between social class and health, it is necessary to define the way in which 'social class' is used in this context. So far, in this chapter, we have been discussing the contributions of some of the major theorists, using their definitions of class and stratification. But for more detailed investigations a working definition is needed, and the Registrar General's classification is the one generally used. This attempts to take account of both economic and social aspects of a person's occupation. It contains five categories, with the middle category being subdivided into 'manual' and 'non-manual'. *Table 5.1* illustrates this. In general, women are allocated to a social class on the basis of their husband's occupation unless they are single, in which case they are classified according to their own employment.

TABLE 5.1   The Registrar General's classification of social classes

Social class	Description	Example	Percentage of population
I	Professional; executives	Judges Doctors Accountants	5
II	'Semi-professionals'; managers	Teachers Nurses	20
III N	Skilled non-manual	Clerks	15
III M	Skilled manual	Taxi drivers Plumbers	33
IV	Semi-skilled manual	Farmworkers Assembly line workers	19
V	Unskilled manual	Building labourers	8

(Adapted from Patrick and Scrambler, 1982)

5.5.2 Social class, mortality and morbidity

There are significant and persisting differences in the patterns of disease and death between social classes in Britain. These differences begin at birth and continue throughout life. Sir John Brotherston reviewed the situation in the Galton Lecture in 1975 (Brotherston, 1976), and others who have discussed the figures and their implications include Blaxter (1976), Morris (1979) and the Black Report (Black, 1980).

These reviews show, for example, differences between the social classes in perinatal and infant mortality rates, in child health and in adult morbidity and mortality. *Tables 5.2* and *5.3*, and *Figure 5.2*, illustrate some of these differences.

TABLE 5.2 Perinatal mortality rates: social class (legitimate single births only) per 1000 live and still births — England and Wales, 1950 and 1973

Social class	1950	1973	Percentage decrease (1950–73)
I Professional	25.4	13.9	45
II Managerial	30.4	15.6	49
III Skilled:	33.6	19.2	43
non-manual		17.3	
manual		19.7	
IV Semi-skilled	36.9	21.8	41
V Unskilled	40.4	26.8	34
All social classes (including armed forces, students, etc.)	34.9*	18.9	46

(Source: 'Population Trends', vol. 4, 1976).
* Estimated.

TABLE 5.3 Mortality of men by social class, ages 15–65 — England and Wales, 1970–72

Social class	Standardized mortality ratios*
I	77
II	81
III (non-manual)	99
III (manual)	106
IV	114
V	137

(From Morris, 1979, by courtesy of *The Lancet*)
* Refers to all men in England and Wales = 100.

Perinatal mortality

Table 5.2 shows perinatal mortality increasing consistently and persistently from social class I to social class V. However, it also shows that there has been an overall improvement over the 20-year period, with the rate for social class V dropping to almost that for social class I two decades earlier.

Adult mortality

Table 5.3 shows a similar trend of a steady increase in the death rate from social class I to social class V for men aged 15–65.

Morbidity

When we consider disease rates rather than death rates it is important to remember that the one is not necessarily a reflection of the other. Most illnesses are not lethal, although many may severely impair quality of life, especially those diseases which are both chronic and handicapping.

Also, it must be borne in mind that official statistics do not necessarily reflect the actual amount of illness and disability in the population. For example, many people may not seek medical help for certain ailments and they consequently will not feature in medical records and the official statistics. It is known that much illness goes unreported for many reasons and that some of these reasons are linked to social class. For example, a working class mother with small children who is dependent on public transport may find it much harder to visit her local doctor than her middle class counterpart who has a car. She will therefore be less likely to receive treatment and to figure in the statistics. The difficulties are likely to be even greater if the doctor works with an appointment system requiring a tele-phone call before a visit to the surgery: the patient without a telephone, who is most likely to be a working class patient, is again relatively disadvantaged.

Consequently, statistics of morbidity may not be very accurate indicators of the actual amount of illness in a community. The existence of unreported and

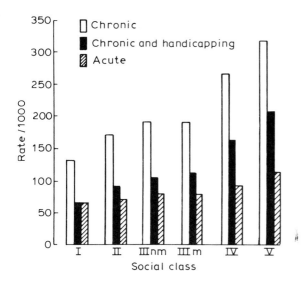

Figure 5.2   Rates of self-reported illness by social class, per 1000 people — men and women, all ages, Great Britain (From Blaxter, 1976, by courtesy of Academic Press)

untreated illness has been likened to an iceberg, with only the tip of the iceberg representing the conditions which are reported and treated. Thus, the data which are available are likely to be underestimates of the real amount of illness and impairment of health. But even as they stand, they show significant correlations with social class (*Figure 5.2*), and as Blaxter (1976) says::

> 'Even if examination is confined to the more stringent and objective condition of handicapping chronic illness, prevalence rates in Social Class V, at over 200 per 1000 people, are well over twice the rate of 75 reported in Class I.'

These inequalities in health have persisted despite the establishment of a 'welfare state' and of a National Health Service where treatment is free or heavily subsidized at the point of need. Some of the reasons are found in the differences in the standards of living; for example, in diet, housing and environment. Occupation may also be a contributory factor, and many working class occupations in particular bring health hazards. However, other contributory factors promoting inequalities in health may be (a) class differences in the uptake of health care and (b) class-related differences in the provision of health care.

5.5.3   The uptake of health care

This is a complex field. Many studies have demonstrated various aspects of the differential uptake of health care. One example relates to the use of facilities for children and draws on data from the National Child Development Study (Davie, et al., 1972). *Table 5.4* shows that among the children in the study at the age of seven, those with greater clinically defined needs for specialist services (needs which could have serious implications for their future) tended to use the relevant services less than others; also, more of them tended to be found among working class families.

TABLE 5.4   Need and service utilization

Percentage of 7-year-olds who:	Social class					
	I	II	III NM	III M	IV	V
Had poor dental health (10 or more DMF teeth)	6.5	8.8	10.0	9.7	11.4	9.6
Had ever attended dental clinic, dentist or orthodontist	83.3	79.9	80.9	76.2	72.5	67.6
Had not fully intelligible speech	5.5	8.4	9.5	14.9	18.3	22.1
Had ever attended for speech therapy	2.8	2.0	2.1	2.4	2.8	3.0
Had signs of past or present otitis media	6.8	5.8	7.7	7.4	6.8	9.6
Had ever attended a hearing or audiology clinic	8.6	7.0	7.9	7.7	7.6	7.1

(Adapted from Davie *et al.*, 1972)

5.5.4   The provision of health care

Class variations in the provision of health care may be found in literally 'concrete' terms (such as buildings); in staffing and in professional–patient relationships.

Hart (1971) has described the general situation as the 'inverse care law'. By this he means that the quality of care tends to be lower in those neighbourhoods which are already deprived, such as inner city areas, despite the fact that it is often these areas which have the greatest concentration of people with high rates of morbidity and mortality and who therefore could be deemed to need more health care.

There is also a tendency for deprived inner city areas to be served by general practitioners who operate from lock-up surgeries, with all the problems which this system creates for patients who need medical help 'after hours'. These problems are especially serious for patients who do not have a telephone, who have difficulty in communicating by telephone, or who live in areas where public telephones may have been put out of action by vandals.

Moreover, once a patient comes into contact with health care professionals, social class may influence the duration of a consultation and the quality of communication. Buchan and Richardson (1971), in their study in Aberdeen, found a social class gradient in the length of time that general practitioners spent with their patients (upper class patients had longer consultations than others); and Cartwright and O'Brien (1976) found that general practitioners tended to know more about their middle class than their working class patients.

In Chapter 9 we will return to the theme of the experience of being a patient. Here we will conclude with a reminder of the complexity of the relationship between social class, health and illness. Whereas the general standard of living has improved and there have been overall improvements in health (see *Table 5.2*), the persistent social class differences in health and in the uptake of health services present a continuing challenge to everyone involved in health care. It must also be recognized that many of the causes of class-related differences in mortality and morbidity stem from inequalities in the wider society — in general standards of living and associated life-styles. Sociology and epidemiology can enhance our understanding of some of these contributory factors. One of the most famous nineteenth century medical researchers, Rudolf Virchow (1821–1902), made the point cogently:

'Medical statistics will be our standard of measurement: we will weigh life for life and see where the dead lie thicker, among the workers or among the privileged.'

■ Summary

The sociological concepts of social class and social stratification are shown not to be abstract ideas but realities that confer immense advantages in terms of wealth, prestige, education and health care to some groups of people, with resultant disadvantages to others. There is discussion of the 'materialist' theories of Marxism and of the critics of his ideas such as Johnson, who argues that there is a moral basis for capitalism. Each of us is urged to decide which direction we wish society to travel and to take responsibility for making some contribution to the future of that society.

It is clearly demonstrated that there are significant and persistent differences in the patterns of disease and death between social classes in Britain, and that there are also class variations in the provision and uptake of health care. Despite overall improvements in the standard of living and health care of the disadvantaged groups, these and other inequalities present a continuing challenge to everyone involved in health care.

■ Questions

1. What do you understand by the following terms:
   (a) social mobility;
   (b) social status;
   (c) the 'embourgeoisement thesis';
   (d) the 'inverse care law'?
2. Compare and contrast Karl Marx's concept of social class with Max Weber's account of social stratification.
3. In what ways may social class be related to the provision and uptake of health care?
4. 'Now, more than ever, wealthier means healthier.' (Kennedy, The Reith Lecture, 1980.) Do you agree?

References

Black, D. (1980). 'Inequalities in Health' (the Black Report), Report of a Research Working Group, London, Department of Health and Social Security; reprinted in *Inequalities in Health*, Townsend, P. and Davidson, N. (Eds.), Harmondsworth, Penguin, 1982.

Blaxter, M. (1976). 'Social class and health inequalities', in *Equalities and Inequalities in Health*, Carter, C. and Peel, J. (Eds.), London, Academic Press.

Brotherston, J. (1976). 'Inequality: is it inevitable?', in *Equalities and Inequalities in Health*, Carter, C. and Peel, J. (Eds.), London, Academic Press.

Buchan, I. C. and Richardson, I. M. (1971). 'Time study of consultations in general practice', *Scottish Health Service Studies*, no. 27, Scottish Home and Health Department.

Carter, C. and Peel, J. (Eds.) (1976). *Equalities and Inequalities in Health*, London, Academic Press.

Cartwright, A. and O'Brien, M. (1976). 'Social class variations in the nature of general practice consultations', in *The Sociology of the National Health Service*, Stacey, M. (Ed.), Sociological Review Monograph no. 22, University of Keele, Staffordshire.

Conquest, R. (1968). *The Great Terror*, London, Macmillan.

Conquest, R. (1978). *Kolyma: The Arctic Death Camps*, London, Macmillan.

Davie, R. *et al.* (1972). *From Birth to Seven*, National Child Development Study, 2nd report, London, Longman/National Children's Bureau.

Djilas, M. (1966). *The New Class*, London, Allen & Unwin.

Goldthorpe, J., Lockwood, D., Bechoffer, F. and Platt, J. (1969). *The Affluent Worker in the Class Structure*, London, Cambridge University Press.

Hart, J. T. (1971). 'The inverse care law', *The Lancet*, vol. 1, pp. 1179–90; reprinted in *A Sociology of Medical Practice*, Cox, C. and Mead, A. (Eds.), London, Collier Macmillan, 1975.

Hayek, F. A. (1978). *Law, Legislation and Liberty*, London, Routledge & Kegan Paul.

Johnson, P. (1979). 'Is there a moral basis for capitalism? Dissenting thoughts in a collectivist age', *Encounter*, summer/autumn.

Miliband, R. (1969). *The State in Capitalist Society*, London, Weidenfeld & Nicolson.

Miller, S. M. (1960). 'Comparative social mobility', *Current Sociology*, vol. 9, no. 1.

Morris, J. (1979). 'Social inequalities undiminished', *The Lancet*, 13 Jan., no. 1, pp. 87–90.

Parkin, F. (1971). *Class, Inequality and Political Order*, London, MacGibbon & Kee.

Patrick, D. and Scrambler, G. (Eds.) (1982). *Sociology as Applied to Medicine*, Baillière-Tindall, London.

Rex, J. (1974). 'Capitalism, elites and the ruling class', in *Elites and Power in British Society*, Stanworth, P. and Giddens, A. (Eds.), London, Cambridge University Press.

Westergaard, J. and Resler, H. (1975). *Class in Capitalist Societies*, London, Heinemann.

Wright Mills, C. (1956). *The Power Elite*, London, Oxford University Press.

Zweig, F. (1961). *The Worker in an Affluent Society*, London, Heinemann.

Recommended reading

In this chapter I am not suggesting additional books for 'Further Reading' because it seems more appropriate to draw attention to some of those which have already been mentioned and to highlight their relevance:

1. For examples of Marxist accounts of social class in contemporary Britain, see either Miliband's *The State in Capitalist Society* and/or Westergaard and Resler's *Class in Capitalist Societies* (both cited in the References above).
2. For an account of the embourgeoisement thesis and the research which was designed to test it, see *The Affluent Worker in the Class Structure* by Goldthorpe *et al.* (cited in the References above).
3. For a readable and useful summary of the different approaches to social class and stratification, see the Open University's course: The Sociological Perspective, D283, Units 9–11, 'Stratification and Social Class'. These units may now be superseded, but should be available through libraries.
4. For a view of stratification from within a socialist society, see *The New Class* by M. Djilas (cited in the References above).
5. For an overview of persisting inequalities in health, see the book edited by Townsend and Davidson which presents the findings of the Black Report (cited in the References above, under Black, 1980).

Socrates, the Greek philosopher, 470–399 B.C. (Courtesy John Topham Picture Library)

(. . . said by some to be the first sociologist — see p. 89)

6 Education

In this chapter we will first try to clarify what we mean by 'education', then we will survey some of the key historical developments in education in western society. Finally we will discuss some contemporary issues in education and the contributions which a number of sociologists have made to our understanding of these issues.

6.1 What is education?

Many centuries ago Socrates, who is said by some to be the first sociologist, gave his version of what he meant by education: he compared it to his parents' occupations and considered that it was more like his mother's than his father's. His father was a sculptor, and so education in that vein would mean moulding and shaping other people to conform to his own ideals and expectations. However, his mother was a midwife, and Socrates preferred to think of his role as an educator being in some ways similar to her work — helping people to bring forth what was in them. This idea is embodied in one of the roots of the word itself — the Latin *e ducere* which means to 'lead forth' — and it has been an important characteristic of the liberal tradition of education in western societies. This tradition encourages people to think for themselves; to explore; to try to take account of all available relevant evidence before coming to conclusions; to be creative; and to achieve some form of self-fulfilment. Another root of the word education is the Latin *educare* which means to 'bring up children' — a meaning closely associated with the concept of socialization, to which we will return.

Education has other functions, too. At all ages and stages, whether in school, in university or in professional education, educators are also concerned with preserving and transmitting *knowledge* — including knowledge of our cultural heritage — with teaching *skills* and with encouraging certain *attitudes*. In institutions of higher education, especially universities, there is an additional responsibility to try to extend the boundaries of knowledge by *research*. Professions too have developed research as a basis for the knowledge which underpins their professional practice. Although nursing and midwifery have been somewhat slow to develop the research base for their own professional work, recent initiatives have begun to remedy this, and we have the formal recognition of the need to do so in the Briggs Report (1972) with its recommendation that 'Nursing should become a research-based profession'. So, to summarize: education is concerned with the teaching and learning of knowledge, skills and attitudes; with the process of generating new knowledge; and with helping people to achieve personal self-fulfilment.

6.2 A brief historical overview

6.2.1 Ancient Greece and Rome

The roots of our education system, like the roots of health care, can be traced back across the centuries to Ancient Greece and Rome. We know that education flowered in the centres of these early civilizations. Pupils received formal instruction from teachers in schools, while for some adults there were opportunities to study with such eminent scholars as Aristotle, Plato and Hippocrates. The Romans, with their famous organizational abilities, were the first people to have schools run by the government. They developed a network of schools throughout their empire, providing for three stages of education: primary schools for children aged about 6–12, for learning the 'three R's'; 'grammar' schools for boys of well-to-do families from about 12–16, where they could study Greek and Latin languages and literature; and schools of rhetoric, the art of public speaking, for young men who wanted careers in politics or other forms of public service.

Later, the Roman Empire was overrun by barbarian tribes who conquered Rome itself in A.D.410, and the period known as the Dark Ages began. Almost all centres of learning were destroyed and only the Christian church remained as the one bastion of any form of scholarship. For centuries, most people could do little more than concentrate on survival.

6.2.2 The Arab world

As Europe sank into darkness, other centres of civilization and scholarship emerged. For example, in the Arab world Baghdad developed as a fine city, famous for the study of mathematics and astronomy, and it was the Arabs who developed the system of numbers which we now use. Arab merchants had become acquainted with these numbers in their transactions with Hindus in India. The symbol for zero was added and the notation with which we are familiar was adopted. Its advantages for mathematical calculations can be readily appreciated if one imagines trying to do a sum the 'Roman' way, say multiplying or dividing

MDCXVI by MMDCXLVIII! In addition to developing new ideas and knowledge, the citizens of the Arab world also preserved the works of the ancient Greeks and Romans, safeguarding and translating the writings of great thinkers such as Plato and Aristotle.

6.2.3 The universities

So when Europe began to break out of the Dark Ages in the eleventh century, and as social conditions stabilized, there was a rich store of knowledge, old and new, ready to be learned and taught. Many new European centres of learning appeared, in the form of universities. Their early beginnings are so obscure that they have been described as a 'faint, murky cloud-wrapped dawn'. However, we do know that between 1100 and 1300, universities had been established in Paris, Bologna and many other cities.

In England, Oxford was the first town to have a university, which began with a group of scholars who were expelled from the University of Paris in 1167! They organized themselves into guilds of teachers, which established the residential colleges which have been a feature of the university ever since. By the early years of the thirteenth century, Oxford was a well-established university, with a chancellor, lecturing staff and faculties; the line of Chancellor has remained unbroken since 1221. England's other ancient university, Cambridge, was also a result of disorder and conflict: in 1209 some scholars retreated from troubles at Oxford and moved to Cambridge. By 1226 that university was also established, with benefactors and a chancellor. These two universities dominated the English scene for many centuries. However, three Scottish universities were established in the fifteenth century: St. Andrews, Glasgow and Aberdeen, with Edinburgh following in 1583.

6.2.4 Education Acts

Many schools were established during the centuries following the Dark Ages and some of them remain today. For example, the school attended by William Shakespeare can still be seen in Stratford-on-Avon. However, we have to wait until the nineteenth century for the extension of school education which eventually ensured that schooling would be available for every child and not just for a minority. The famous 1870 Education Act required local authorities to provide schools for all children, and was followed in 1880 by the first legislation which made schooling compulsory, albeit only up to the age of 10. During the next 100 years, successive Acts have increased the duration of compulsory education, but it was not until *after* World War II that *free secondary education for all* became available in Britain.

The 1944 Education Act, which required provision of this free secondary education for every child, resulted in the establishment of different types of school intended to suit the aptitudes and abilities of different children. This was called the 'tripartite system', because it consisted of three kinds of school: grammar, technical and secondary modern. The system, however, had not been in existence for very long before it came under numerous attacks, especially from social scientists and politicians.

6.2.5 Comprehensive schools

In 1965 the government changed the system of state secondary education by adopting a policy of comprehensivization. This required local authorities to prepare and to implement plans for abolishing grammar, technical and secondary modern schools, and replacing them by comprehensive schools. The extent of the changes which have followed is shown by the fact that, in 1965, less than 10 per cent of secondary schoolchildren were in comprehensive schools, whereas now, in the early 1980s, about 90 per cent are.

The issues involved in these developments in education are very complex and of profound importance. For example, they reflect the tensions between freedom and equality which exist in every society and the attempts to find a balance between them. They involve concern over educational standards and over ways in which children from all social backgrounds can be enabled to obtain maximum benefit from the educational system. Sociologists have contributed to these debates in a number of ways. The examples given here will illustrate some of them; others may be followed up in the Further Reading recommended at the end of the chapter.

6.3   Social class and educational achievement

The existence of a significant relationship between social class background and level of educational attainment has been a long-standing concern of social scientists and politicians. For example, in the days when the '11+' examination was taken by children at the conclusion of primary school, the tests were used as a means of selection for grammar and technical schools. Approximately 25 per cent went to grammar schools; the 75 per cent who did less well went to the secondary modern schools. It was found that a much higher proportion of middle class children were successful in the 11+ examination, and consequently went to grammar schools, than their working class counterparts (Douglas, 1964).

The policy of comprehensivization was designed, *inter alia*, to diminish the adverse effects of such early selection at the age of 11 and to keep open the avenues of educational opportunity for longer. Despite this, class differentials remain, with middle class children doing proportionately better in formal examinations, such as G.C.E. Ordinary and Advanced levels, and working class children generally performing relatively less well (Halsey, Heath and Ridge, 1980). These differences are also reflected in social class differences in entry to university, with middle class applicants faring statistically better.

Many factors have been put forward to explain these social class variations in educational attainment, two of which relate to the relationship between the home and the school and the relationship between learning and language.

6.3.1 Relationship between the home and the school

One of the classical studies in the sociology of education is *The Home and the School* (Douglas, 1964). This showed that the influence of the home environment on a child's attainment is multi-faceted. It includes tangible and material factors, such as a quiet room for homework and the availability of relevant books in the home, as well as more intangible factors such as parental interest and encouragement. Children from middle class families are likely to have an advantage because their homes will probably have more facilities conducive to study, and their parents are more likely to know how to take an informed interest in their educational progress. This does not imply that other parents are not concerned about their children's education, but that middle class parents are characteristically more likely to monitor effectively their children's scholastic progress and to be more confident in dealing with school staff. They are, therefore, more likely to raise problems and to discuss them with teachers. (The relative confidence of middle class people in dealing with institutions and their professional staff is a theme which will recur when we consider the use of health care facilities in Chapter 8.)

6.3.2 Relationship between learning and language

It has also been known for many years that children from lower working class homes tend to score significantly lower on tests of verbal ability. A number of researchers have tried to explore the reason for this. One of the most influential is a sociologist, B. Bernstein, who has analysed the language styles of different social classes, distinguishing two characteristic 'codes' of speech (Bernstein, 1961). He called one of them a 'restricted code', as it consists of simple sentence structures, with few adjectives and adverbs. This style of speech is often characteristic of working class communities and is appropriate for speaking about particular situations or highly specific topics. The other type of speech, called an 'elaborated code', is more complex, with longer sentences and more adjectives and adverbs. This allows for more distinctions to be made and facilitates discussion of a more analytical nature, particularly appropriate for 'universalistic' or abstract topics. This latter style is more characteristic of middle class speech, although middle class people may also use a restricted code.

The implications of the different speech styles for education are far-reaching, for as learning in school progresses beyond the 'three R's' to the discussion and analysis of more complex and abstract issues, an elaborated code is essential. Thus children from middle class homes who are familiar with this style of speech will have an advantage, while those who are less familiar with it may experience difficulties. Bernstein stresses that a restricted code is not necessarily linguistically or culturally inadequate — it can often be highly effective for very vivid and graphic communication. Anyone listening to the quick wit and ready repartee of Cockney patients in a hospital ward will appreciate its effectiveness! However, an elaborated code is inherently more appropriate for abstract analytical argument, and ability to use it opens the doors to bodies of knowledge in the sciences, arts and humanities. This is why it is important to teach the basic rules of grammar and syntax which facilitate the use of an elaborated code, to all children, particularly to those whose home background does not provide them with a ready familiarity with this linguistic style.

6.4 Educational policy: equality of opportunity and equality of outcome

Underlying the concern over differences in educational attainment between children from different social backgrounds is a related concern over the extent to which education may perpetuate existing social inequalities. Fierce arguments have raged over the extent to which the education system should be used as a means of 'social engineering', that is, to serve such social functions as making society more 'equal'. There are two kinds of equality which educational policy can try to achieve — equality of opportunity and equality of outcome.

6.4.1 Equality of opportunity

The 1944 Education Act, which made compulsory secondary education available for all children, free of charge, is one example of legislation designed to increase equality of opportunity. Similarly, the availability of higher and further education, with costs of tuition met by the state and with maintenance grants for those students whose parents have low incomes, represents an attempt to remove financial barriers to access to university and college. However, as we have seen, there have still been persistent social class differences in outcome, with middle class pupils tending to achieve more formal educational qualifications. We have already mentioned some of the reasons why this may be so; we now consider some others, relating to different kinds of school.

Independent and state schools

There are great differences between schools, exemplified by the small but thriving independent sector of education, containing the famous 'public' schools like Eton and Harrow, and other private schools. These include many of the former Direct Grant Schools which previously catered for sizable numbers of working class children who could not afford fees. This type of school was abolished by the Labour Government in the mid-1970s; the schools' governors then had to choose between becoming part of the local system of comprehensive schools or becoming independent and charging fees. Many chose the latter option and became independent.

It is well known that, on average, the independent schools obtain significantly higher grades in the public examinations of G.C.E. Ordinary and Advanced levels than schools in the state system (Kalton, 1966). Consequently, in so far as examination results act as passports to higher education, or to occupations requiring them as entrance qualifications, the continuing existence of an independent sector of education, with entry dependent on income, militates against equality of opportunity. This is one of the areas of conflict arising from the difficulty of reconciling equality and freedom.

Those politicians and social scientists who put relatively greater emphasis on equality are committed to abolishing independent schools. Those who put relatively more emphasis on freedom argue that these schools should be preserved — possibly in conjunction with some measures, such as the Assisted Places scheme, now in operation, which is designed to broaden access to them in order to increase equality of opportunity.

Differences within the state system

Differences also exist *within* the state system, where schools vary considerably in the levels of attainment reached by their pupils. Much of this variation is attributable to the kinds of factors we have identified, and comprehensive schools in catchment areas with a preponderance of middle class children are likely to have higher rates of examination success than those in socially deprived inner city areas. This may seem obvious, but research has also shown that schools do not merely reflect the social environment in which they are located. For example, Rutter *et al.* (1979) found considerable variety between schools which were located in the same deprived inner city areas. They suggest that teachers' attitudes and the ways in which they organize the school can significantly affect its ethos and important indices of school performance such as patterns of behaviour and truancy rates. So we can see that the situation is very complex and that attempts to enhance equality of opportunity are fraught with difficulties.

6.4.2 Equality of outcome

It is partly because of these difficulties that some people have been advocating equality of outcome as an aim of education. This may take the form, for example, of playing down those situations which lead to differentiation — like examinations with pass and failure grades. There are some people who oppose all examinations for this reason, and certain educationalists and politicians are arguing for a system of individual Pupil Profiles to replace examinations. The associated debates and arguments reflect many interrelated considerations which have to be taken into account. For example, other educationalists feel that a system of public examinations is necessary if there is to be any external and impartial monitoring of standards of teaching and learning. And many people working in universities and colleges, together with those who are responsible for selecting applicants to professional training or for jobs, require some indication of educational attainment and believe that standardized public examinations are the fairest and most reliable means of providing this.

The danger with personalized profiles and with teacher-assessed examinations is that the principle of 'externality' is lost and the teacher becomes the judge of his own teaching; also, personal bias may enter into assessment in ways which may be hard to avoid and could be unfair to particular children. So, as with equality of opportunity, attempts to achieve equality of outcome are fraught with problems. These are hard to resolve, because some of them are associated with the nature of the relationship between the education system and the wider society and particularly with society's occupational structure.

6.5   School and society

Schools do not exist in a social vacuum. We have already seen how some aspects of the wider social environment affect what goes on in schools, in our consideration of relationships between home and school. A structural functionalist approach to schools considers them in terms of their relationship to other parts of society; it also thinks of them as social systems and applies concepts of 'input', 'process' and 'output'. Homes and families clearly affect input, as they influence the children who come to school and their response to the education they receive there. But schools are also influenced in their output, by needing to prepare their pupils to play their part in the society which they will enter when they leave, particularly in the jobs to which they will go. These range, in any society, from jobs which society holds in high esteem, to those which are less esteemed, but may be equally necessary.

In our society, specific educational qualifications are generally required for highly esteemed jobs, such as those in the Registrar General's categories I and II (see Chapter 5). Those which are just as necessary but which do not require formal qualifications are designated as 'Unskilled manual work' in the Registrar General's classification. The education system must therefore prepare young people for many very different roles.

6.5.1   American and English systems compared

An American sociologist, R. Turner, has described the different ways in which two societies do this (Turner, 1960): the U.S.A., which he calls a 'contest' system, and England, which he describes as a 'sponsorship' system. In the U.S.A. opportunities for educational attainment are kept open for as long as possible, for as many children as possible, with little in the way of selecting or sifting children into different kinds of school. Even at the stage of leaving school there are many opportunities for continuing education, with 42 per cent of young people going to college of some kind. However, because expectations are consequently raised, elaborate mechanisms are required for 'cooling out' students who cannot make the grade (for not everyone can be a lawyer or a professor of nuclear physics!). They then have to adjust their sights accordingly, possibly feeling disappointed and disillusioned.

By contrast, Turner suggests that in England, especially under the former system of grammar and secondary modern schools, we tended to select and to sift people earlier, so that children and teenagers had time to adjust to the kind of job and its associated life-style in which they would be likely to find themselves. Thus the 11+ examination encouraged those who passed it and who went to grammar school to set their occupational sights relatively high and often to think in terms of going to university and entering the professions. The successful applicants to technical schools would be more likely to anticipate careers in applied science and technology, while the secondary modern schools would tend to give their pupils a curriculum with less academic content and a more directly vocational orientation. The system was called a 'sponsorship' system by Turner, because he saw it as making a very early decision about the type of schooling which children would receive, and the type of career they would be likely to choose, with the children who were successful in the 11+ examination being 'sponsored' or 'groomed' for the elite positions in society.

6.5.2 Selection in education

It was this feature of the tripartite system — making decisions and selecting pupils so early — that was regarded as one of its major defects. It was seen as detrimental for 'late developers'; it was also seen as favouring the middle class children at the expense of working class children, for it was the former who tended to perform proportionately better in the crucial examination. Therefore, it was felt by many people, in terms of both social justice and of efficiency of selection, that a system of selection and segregation at the age of 11 was undesirable. The comprehensive system of secondary schooling was intended as a remedy: selection would be abolished, children would be educated together in secondary schools serving local neighbourhoods, and educational opportunities would be kept open for all children for as long as possible.

This development has been described by another sociologist, J. Ford, as a 'gigantic experiment with the life chances of millions of children' (Ford, 1969). She suggests that the system has not succeeded in its objectives, for social class differences in achievement persist within comprehensive schools. These may be reinforced by streaming, with disproportionate numbers of middle class children in higher streams and working class children in lower streams. Also, as children tend to make friends with others in their own forms, the schools may perpetuate not only academic differences, but also social divisions, which may be more apparent because all the pupils are under one roof.

Evaluation of these developments raises once again the fundamental philosophical and political issue of the conflict between freedom, justice and equality. In essence, we as a society chose a single system of state education — the system of comprehensivization — in an attempt to increase social equality. In doing so, we abolished a more diverse system of schooling and so reduced freedom of choice, at least for those who had been in a position to choose. Similar dilemmas of choice between the values of freedom and equality are encountered in the provision of health care. The necessity of having to make such choices shows us that education and health are essentially and inevitably political issues — they raise profound questions of political philosophy and consequently they often raise feelings and lead to heated debates on questions for which there are no easy answers.

6.6   Educational selection within schools

We have considered briefly some of the relationships between schools and the wider society. We will now refer to some sociological studies of the processes occurring within schools. The examples chosen are concerned with another controversial issue related to the question of selection, but this time it refers to selection within schools rather than selection between them.

6.6.1   Streaming

The issue under consideration is 'streaming' — placing children in forms according to their perceived ability. Some sociologists have criticized this practice. They argue that selection has detrimental effects on those placed in lower streams. Their approach draws heavily on concepts and insights from the interactionist school of sociology, in particular the concepts of self-esteem, labelling and self-fulfilling prophecy. 'Self-esteem' refers to the way in which we see ourselves as a reflection of other people's views of us; we touched on these ideas in Chapter 1. It is suggested that those who are 'labelled' academic failures and relegated to lower streams may suffer damage to their self-esteem, morale and self-confidence. Moreover, teachers' expectations of them will be lower, with the possibility that a 'self-fulfilling' prophecy will result: the children believe they are seen as failures, teachers expect less of them, and they consequently perform less well.

6.6.2   Mixed ability teaching

It was partly because of this sort of critique that arguments for mixed ability teaching gained credence. It was proposed that this would avoid the detrimental results of selection; that children who learn quickly could still work at their own pace; that they would act as a stimulus to those who learn more slowly and would help them with their work. It was thus predicted that all would benefit. However, the reality of mixed ability teaching in some schools has not worked out so happily and has led to criticism. In some cases, quick learners have been held back, becoming bored, frustrated and under-achieving, while slower learners may feel demoralized when they see other children finding work so much easier, and become inhibited from asking questions.

Such disadvantageous results of mixed ability teaching have been identified in a report by Her Majesty's Inspectorate (1980) on schools in the Inner London area. For example, they say:

'There are however many classes and schools where expectations are too low and where, despite the efforts of the Authority's Inspectorate, teachers assume that mixed ability classes should be taught at a pace which is right for the pupil of slightly below average ability. The schools frequently blame their pupils' backgrounds for the poor results: this is largely unjustifiable. The fault lies in low teacher expectation, perhaps arising from unfamiliarity with the capabilities of abler children, and from lack of pace, interest and variety in the work of the class.'

6.7 Philosophical and political dilemmas

The examples of developments in education discussed in the foregoing paragraphs highlight the complexity of social life. Even if problems are identified and solutions are recommended and implemented, new problems arise in their wake. Education is a social institution of the greatest importance for us all. It has a profound influence on children who are exposed to its influence during the formative years of childhood and adolescence. Educational policies have repercussions spreading far and wide throughout society and, as we have seen, educational decisions involve some of the toughest philosophical and political dilemmas confronting every society. One of the toughest of these dilemmas is the conflict between freedom and equality. We therefore need to think clearly and to be fully aware of the philosophical and political commitments which underpin every policy and every argument.

The suggestions for Further Reading at the end of this chapter are intended to provide a 'broad spectrum' coverage, so that you can consider in greater detail the cases presented by the advocates of different viewpoints and make up your own mind on these important matters in the light of the arguments and evidence they put forward. If you do find the time and opportunity to do this, you will be following in the tradition of education in western liberal societies which we defined at the beginning of the chapter — acquainting yourself with the knowledge and ideas which are available and drawing your own conclusions.

100

■ Summary

An outline of the history of education is sketched: the 'grammar' schools of the Romans; the Christians and especially the Arabs who kept the light of education shining during the Dark Ages; the founding of universities in Europe and England; the institution of schools for all children in England following the Education Act of 1870; free secondary education for all under the Act of 1944; and finally the emergence of the modern comprehensive school system. We see that once again there is a class variation — this time in the performance of children at school. Sociologists have much to say about this phenomenon, and the views of Douglas concerning the influence of home life and of Bernstein regarding the relationship between learning and language are discussed.

Once more we are faced with ethical questions such as the difficulty of reconciling equality of educational opportunity with the freedom to choose independent education, for those in the fortunate position of choice. The areas of education and health, where similar tensions between freedom and equality exist, are thus seen to be inherently political issues which raise profound philosophical questions.

■ Questions

1. In what ways may social class affect educational achievement?
2. What do you understand by the following terms:
   (a) equality of educational opportunity;
   (b) 'elaborated' and 'restricted' codes of speech;
   (c) 'contest' and 'sponsorship' systems of education?
3. What do you think are the advantages and disadvantages of the policy of comprehensivization of secondary education?

References

Bernstein, B. (1961). 'Social structure, language and learning', *Educational Research*, June.
Briggs Report (1972). 'Report of the Committee on Nursing', London, H.M.S.O.
Douglas, J. W. B. (1964). *The Home and the School*, London, McGibbon & Kee.
Ford, J. (1969). *Social Class and the Comprehensive School*, London, Routledge & Kegan Paul.
Halsey, A. E., Heath, A. and Ridge, J. (1980). *Origins and Destinations: Family, Class and Education in Modern Britain*, Oxford, Clarendon Press.
Her Majesty's Inspectorate (1980). 'Educational Provision by the Inner London Education Authority', report by H. M. Inspectors, Department of Education and Science, November.
Kalton, G. (1966). *The Public Schools: A Factual Survey*, London, Longmans.

Rutter, M., Maughan, B., Mortimore, P. and Ouston, J. (1979). *Fifteen Thousand Hours*, London, Open Books.

Turner, R. (1960). 'Sponsored and contest mobility and the school system', *American Sociological Review*, vol. 25.

Further reading

Bowles, S. and Gintis, H. (1976). *Schooling in Capitalist America*, London, Routledge & Kegan Paul. A Marxist critique of education in contemporary western societies.

Carter, C. (1980). *Higher Education for the Future*, Oxford, Blackwell. A stimulating review of the present system of higher education in Britain, with suggestions for some radical changes.

Dawson, P. (1981). *Making a Comprehensive Work: The Road from Bomb Alley*, Oxford, Blackwell. A lively and thought-provoking book by a headmaster of a London comprehensive school which had an unenviable reputation for violence, and his account of how he set out to 'transform it into a safe place for pupil and teacher and an effective environment for learning'. The book also discusses a wide range of issues such as streaming and systems of support for problem children.

Flew, A. (1976). *Sociology, Equality and Education*, London, Macmillan. A philosopher's discussion of contemporary issues in education, written in a robust style from a standpoint that criticizes recent trends which have placed a higher premium on equality than on freedom.

Halsey, A. E., Heath, A. and Ridge, J. (1980). *Origins and Destinations: Family, Class and Education in Modern Britain*, Oxford, Clarendon Press. A research-based discussion of some of the relationships between — as the title suggests — family, education and social class. The book analyses changes in the education system and considers their implications for social justice.

Marks, J., Cox, C. and Pomian-Srzednicki, M. (1983). 'Standards in English Schools', National Council for Educational Standards, Arnellan House, Slough Lane, London N.W.9. A research report on a survey of the examination results of 350 000 children in 2000 schools, demonstrating wide variation of attainment between schools of similar types; also that the system of selective schools (the combination of grammar and secondary modern schools) attains better results than the system of comprehensive schools.

Pope John-Paul II's visit to Britain, 1982 (Courtesy John Topham Picture Library)

(What is crucial is that we never undervalue the importance of religion for many of our patients ... — see p. 108)

7 Religion and secularization

> 'If thy soul is a stranger to thee, the whole world becomes unhomely.'
>
> *(A 15th century Sufi man of prayer.)*

Religion may be a matter of great concern to you, or you may feel quite indifferent about it. Whichever is the case, it is important not to underestimate its sociological significance. It is no coincidence that the great founding fathers of sociology — Marx, Weber and Durkheim — all devoted much time to it; and more recently there has been and still is lively debate among contemporary sociologists about what is happening to religion in modern societies.

One point needs to be made at the outset. Sociology can describe religious behaviour and institutions, but it can never prove or disprove the ultimate truth or falsity of religious beliefs or the authenticity of religious experience.

In this chapter we will first look briefly at some of the ideas of two of the founding fathers; we will then consider the process of 'secularization' and the extent to which it is occurring in modern societies — both capitalist and socialist; and we will conclude by mentioning some of the implications of religious beliefs and practices for those who work in health care.

But before we take our discussion any further, it is appropriate to define what we mean by 'religion' in sociological terms. Durkheim (1969 translation) defined it thus: 'A unified system of beliefs and practices relative to sacred things.' This is a useful definition, as it emphasizes the universal significance of the 'sacred' as the central element of religious faith. For it is this transcendental dimension which differentiates religious belief systems from others — such as political ideologies like liberalism, socialism or Marxism. Durkheim's definition is also useful because it makes a distinction between beliefs and practices which, as we shall see, is helpful in discussing recent developments.

7.1 Marx and Weber's views of religion

7.1.1 Marx and the 'opium of the people'

A basic tenet of Marxist doctrine is that religion is a symptom of man's distress. This distress is caused by an unjust and repressive society, and one of the functions of religion is to help those who are oppressed to cope with their suffering. This view is expressed in the famous statement (quoted in Beeson, 1974):

> 'Religion is the sigh of the oppressed creature, the heart of a heartless world, just as it is the spirit of a spiritless situation. It is the opium of the people. The abolition of religion as the illusory happiness of the people is required for their real happiness.'

Marx and Engels (1955 translation) claimed:

> '...we have seen repeatedly that in existing bourgeois society men are dominated by the economic conditions created by themselves, by the means of production which they themselves have produced, as if by an alien force. The actual basis of the reflective activity which gives rise to religion therefore continues to exist, and with it the religious reflection itself.... It is still true that man proposes and God (that is, the alien domination of the capitalist mode of production) disposes.'

Marx and Engels (1955 translation) developed their argument to the point where they claimed that if only society would take possession of the means of production, 'then will the *last* alien force which is still reflected in religion vanish; and with it will also vanish the religious reflection itself, for the simple reason that then there will be nothing left to reflect'. It will therefore be interesting to examine the extent to which this prophecy has been fulfilled in those socialist societies where the private ownership of the means of production has been abolished (see below for some discussion of this).

7.1.2   Weber and the 'Protestant ethic'

Max Weber devoted a vast amount of time to the study of religion. One of his most famous books is called *The Protestant Ethic and the Spirit of Capitalism* (Weber, 1930 translation). In this book, and in other studies of religion, he took issue with some of Marx's ideas. For example, he challenged Marx's emphasis on economic forces as the major determinants of human history. Instead, Weber contended that man's ideas and beliefs, including religious beliefs, could influence his destiny.

In order to demonstrate his case, Weber undertook comparative studies which showed how capitalism had only originated in those societies where Protestantism prevailed. He pointed out that other great civilizations — such as China or India — had been equally ready, in economic and material conditions, to 'take off' into capitalism. But they had not done so. Why not? Because in each of these cultures the 'economic ethic' of the dominant religion was not conducive to the emergence of the 'spirit of capitalism'. So what was special in the Protestant way of life? Its characteristics included a great emphasis on hard work and stern warnings against the evils of extravagant living. Thus money which was earned could not be spent on frivolities; all that could be done was to reinvest it. Constant reinvestment resulted in the development of large private enterprises and the accumulation of capital, hence the economic conditions favouring the development of a capitalist economy.

However, there was another factor at work — one which at first sight appears paradoxical. It was this: for some Protestants, most notably the Calvinists, material success was not valued just for its own sake, but for its religious connotations. This was because they believed in the doctrine of predestination, which taught that only a limited number of people would be granted salvation, and that this elect group had already been chosen by God. We might surmise that this belief would lead to a fatalistic attitude, as everyone's destiny had already been decided. However, the Calvinists responded by looking for signs of divine favour which might indicate that they were among the chosen few. Material success was seen as such a sign, and striven for accordingly. This naturally reinforced the attitudes and behaviour conducive to the investment of capital and the growth of successful businesses.

Thus, Weber argued that there was a fundamental compatibility between theological belief and economic behaviour, which explained why capitalism emerged in Protestant Europe and not in other parts of the world. Discussion continues on the specific relationship between Protestantism and the rise of capitalism, and on the more general relationship between religion and social change. A useful overview can be found in the Open University (1972) course, cited in the References.

7.2 Religion in contemporary society

7.2.1 Religion in western societies

One of the great debates in the sociology of religion centres on the concept of secularization. By 'secularization', sociologists mean a decline in the social signifi-cance of religious beliefs, practices and organizations.

The background to the secularization debate

It has been suggested that secularization is likely to occur in modern societies for various reasons. For example, it has been argued that the rise of science may undermine religious faith. This is because the great successes of science and technology may encourage man to feel that he can achieve mastery over the physical world — in previous eras he could only try to influence it by magical and religious rituals. Also, a scientific way of thinking may encourage a 'rationalist' world view which has no room for the transcendental and the metaphysical. Finally, it has been suggested that the 'opiate' functions of religion may become less necessary as man's standard of living improves and/or as he suffers less from social injustice and oppression — say, with the demise of capitalism and the advent of socialism.

The 'evidence' for secularization

The arguments for or against secularization are often based on certain kinds of statistics, such as the numbers of babies brought to church for baptism or the proportion of young people coming for confirmation. Analysis of such figures for Britain shows some decline for both the Church of England and for the Nonconformist churches. For example, the number of infant baptisms in the Church of England fell from 623 per 1000 live births in 1885 to 531 in 1962, while the number of 15-year-olds who had been confirmed dropped from 371 per thousand in 1885 to 315 in 1960.

However, figures such as these are open to very different interpretations. One approach is taken by Wilson (1966), who regards these data as 'some sort of index of secularization'. If this is a valid measure, then it can be argued that organized religion has indeed been losing ground steadily over the past 100 years or so. There are, however, some exceptions: for example, the Roman Catholic Church has been increasing its membership (partly as a result of a net immigration from predominantly Roman Catholic countries such as Eire and Poland); and similar increases are found in other religious communities such as the Sikhs and the Muslims, with the influx of new settlers from places like India and Pakistan.

Despite these variations in the evidence concerning numbers, Wilson argues that religious beliefs, practices and organizations have lost influence — not only in Britain, but also in other western countries — during this century.

Different interpretations of the 'evidence'

There are other viewpoints. For example, another sociologist, David Martin, comes to a different conclusion (Martin, 1967). He suggests that what we need to explain is not the decline in participation in religious activities, but its persistence. In Victorian times there were strong social pressures to conform, and these often included the expectation that one should attend church. However, with the subsequent relaxation of these pressures, people are less likely to go to church just for the sake of appearances. Consequently, if they do go, their attendance is more likely to be voluntary and to reflect some genuine interest or conviction. Martin therefore suggests that one can interpret the statistics used by Wilson as indicating fairly high levels of religious participation, rather than the reverse.

Another point has also been made which casts doubt on the thesis that society is becoming more secular: it has been suggested that religious belief may be felt by many people to be a 'private' concern and that it is possible to retain one's faith without participating regularly in the activities of an established church. Some support for this view may be found in an international survey undertaken by Gallup Poll in 1968, which discovered that a very high percentage of people in European countries said that they believed in God — ranging from 60 per cent in Sweden and 73 per cent in France and Norway, to 77 per cent in Britain, 79 per cent in the Netherlands, 83 per cent in Finland and 85 per cent in Austria. Certainly, not all these people are to be found in church every Sunday, and it has been suggested that one reason for discrepancies between relatively low figures for church attendance and the higher figures for an alleged belief in God, may be some disillusionment with institutional religion, rather than a complete rejection of religious faith.

Obviously, this is a very complex issue, and we should not jump to simple conclusions. It is important to remember the different aspects of religion — beliefs and practices — which were highlighted in Durkheim's definition. We must therefore be wary of trying to infer too much from statistics which can only offer crude indicators of very limited facets of religious experience. For in so far as religion has provided man with ways of interpreting the ultimate issues of life and death, giving them meaning and purpose, it is unlikely to be 'explained' or 'explained away' very easily. This is perhaps why religion in socialist societies has not, so far, confirmed Marx's prediction that it would 'wither away' and 'vanish'.

7.2.2 Religion in socialist societies

It is impossible to generalize about religion and secularization in countries as diverse as the Soviet Union, East Germany, Poland, Albania or China. Their histories and cultures are so diverse and their present situations vary from the virtual annihilation of the church in Albania to its continuing strong influence in Poland. The interested reader can find some useful accounts of religious conditions in the U.S.S.R. and Eastern Europe in T. Beeson's book *Discretion and Valour* (Beeson, 1974) and in the publications of Keston College (see under Bordeaux, 1971, in the Further Reading).

All that can be said here is that, although generalizations are impossible, one thing is clear: in many socialist societies, religion has not withered away and shows no likelihood of doing so in the foreseeable future. For example, the work of Lane (1974; 1978) shows that some of the Christian churches in the Soviet Union are attracting new members; moreover, many of these are young people brought up in an education system which teaches a secular ideology, and in a state which invests large sums of money in atheist propaganda. Also, in the U.S.S.R. there has been sustained persecution of some of the churches and of individual believers. The extent of the suffering has been well documented: churches have been forcibly closed and many individuals have been imprisoned, sent to labour camps or treated as psychiatric patients for their religious beliefs (see, for example, the publications of Keston College). In Poland, it has even been argued that a process of 'desecularization' is occurring. Pomian-Srzednicki (1982) concludes his study thus:

> 'An examination of the concept of secularization in Polish material has revealed three main points: the concept is used by the political authorities as an instrument of anti-religious policy and repression; the available evidence does not unambiguously confirm a thesis of secularization for Polish society; there is very strong evidence for a thesis of desecularization in Poland. The final point is connected with certain features of Marxism–Leninism in power which appear to have strong desecularizing influences — in particular the failure to solve the problems it sets out to solve like the elimination of injustice and the provision of plenty.'

7.3 Religion and total patient care

In our professional roles we are probably closer than anyone else to patients when they are confronting the ultimate issues of life and death. The concept of 'total patient care' requires us to take account of all aspects of our patients' condition, including their spiritual needs and religious beliefs. Thus, if we share their faith, it may be appropriate to discuss their predicament in the light of that faith: it is our privilege and our duty to be available, although not, of course, to impose. If they have religious beliefs which they cannot share with us, it is our responsibility to ensure that they have the opportunity to discuss them with an appropriate person. What is crucial is that we never undervalue the importance of religion for many of our patients and their relatives. Although some may not care, for others it may be their most important and urgent concern, especially in times of crisis and impending death: for them, religion is that which is of ultimate significance — the very 'ground of their being'.

Perhaps this short chapter on religion can serve as a reminder of its significance, and of our responsibility in this most sensitive aspect of patient care.

■ Summary

Religion is of great sociological significance, and this is borne out by the time devoted to its study by the founding fathers of sociology. The views of Marx who saw religion as a symptom of man's distress and of Weber who contended that religious beliefs could influence man's destiny are contrasted. This is followed by a discussion of the debate concerning the rise of secularization and the decline in the social significance of religion. Science, rationalist thought and rising living standards, together with greater social justice, are said by some sociologists to have undermined religious faith. However, it is seen that there are different interpretations of facts and figures regarding religion in contemporary societies, and other sociologists maintain that there is an increase in religious belief, but not necessarily in institutionalized religion, and that religion in some secular socialist countries shows no signs of diminishing.

Professionally, the concept of total patient care requires us to take account of all aspects of our patients' condition, which includes their spiritual needs and religious beliefs. Indeed, for some patients and their relatives religion is the most important part of their life, and we must respect this whatever our personal beliefs may be.

■ Questions

1. Do you think that Britain is now a 'secular society'?
2. In what ways have Karl Marx and Max Weber illuminated our understanding of religion?
3. Compare and contrast recent changes in religion as a social institution in one capitalist and one socialist society.

References

Beeson, T. (1974). *Discretion and Valour: Religious Conditions in Russia and Eastern Europe*, Glasgow, Fontana/Collins.

Durkheim, E. (1969 translation). 'The social foundations of religion', in *Sociology of Religion*, Robertson, R. (Ed.), Harmondsworth, Penguin.

Lane, C. (1974). 'Some explanations for the persistence of religion in Soviet society', *Sociology*, May, vol. 8, no. 2.

Lane, C. (1978). *Christian Religion in the Soviet Union*, London, George Allen & Unwin.

Martin, D. (1967). *A Sociology of English Religion*, London, Heinemann.

Marx, K. and Engels, F. (1955 translation). *On Religion*, Moscow, Foreign Language Publishing House.

Open University (1972). The Sociological Perspective, Course D283; Block IV: 'Beliefs and Religion', Bletchley, Open University Press.

Pomian-Srzednicki, M. (1982). *Religious Change in Contemporary Poland: Secularization and Politics*, London, Routledge & Kegan Paul.

Weber, M. (1930). *The Protestant Ethic and the Spirit of Capitalism* (translated by T. Parsons), London, George Allen & Unwin.

Wilson, B. (1966). *Religion in Secular Society*, London, Watts.

Further reading

Bordeaux, M. (1971). *Faith on Trial in Russia*, London, Hodder & Stoughton. An authoritative account of aspects of the experiences of some religious believers in the U.S.S.R. The author is Director of Keston College (Centre for the Study of Religion and Communism, Keston, Kent), which publishes much well-researched information on religion in socialist societies.

Hector, W. and Whitfield, S. (1982). *Nursing Care for the Dying Patient and the Family*, London, Heinemann Medical Books. Chapter 1 has a particularly useful account of the views of different religions on death.

Hill, M. (1973). *A Sociology of Religion*, London, Heinemann. A useful review of the field covering, *inter alia*: some of the basic concepts; Weber's thesis on Protestantism and capitalism; the debates on secularization.

Martin, D. (1978). *The Dilemmas of Contemporary Religion*, London, Oxford University Press. A stimulating book by one of the leading sociologists in the field.

Sociology applied to health care

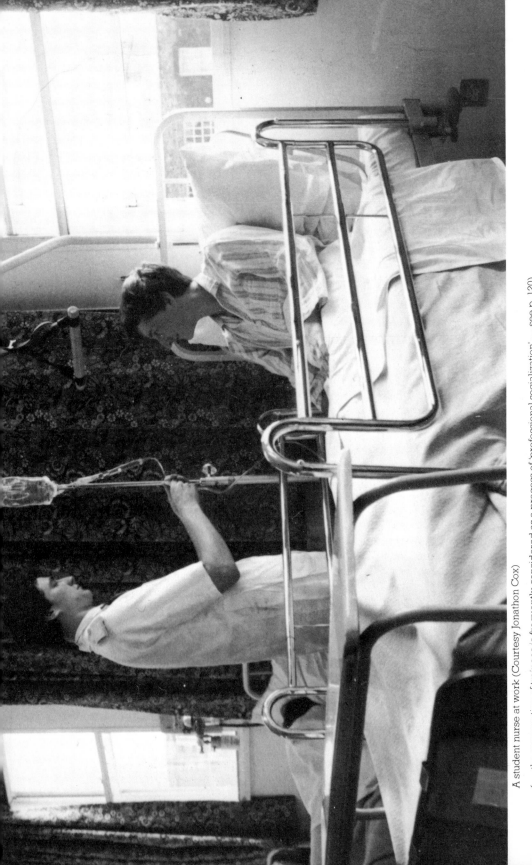

A student nurse at work (Courtesy Jonathon Cox)

(... the preparation of trainees is frequently considered as a process of 'professional socialization' — see p. 120)

8 The provision of health care

'Man has created new worlds — of language, of music, of poetry, of science; and the most important of these is the world of the moral demands, for equality, for freedom, and for helping the weak.'

(K. Popper, *The Open Society and Its Enemies*, 1966.)

In the next six chapters, which comprise Part IV of this book, we turn from our introduction to sociology to consider some of the ways in which sociology has been applied to the study of health care. Although not all the writers mentioned are sociologists — for example, some of them are psychologists, medical practitioners or historians — their work considers the influence of social factors on health care and therefore has sociological relevance.

The theme for the International Council of Nurses Congress in Los Angeles in 1981 was 'Health Care for All — a Challenge for Nursing'. Contributions from many countries indicated just how big a challenge this is. And, as we have seen in Chapter 5, there are still inequalities in health and in the use of health care facilities in Britain today, despite over two decades of welfare state provision and the National Health Service.

In this chapter we first briefly consider some aspects of the relationship between health needs and health care, drawing on the provocative and often controversial ideas of Ivan Illich. Then we refer to the work of three sociologists who write from different viewpoints. First, we consider Talcott Parsons' concept of the 'sick role' and his account of ways in which the roles of doctor and patient complement each other. Secondly, we note E. Freidson's account which highlights some of the potential problems and conflicts in doctor–patient relationships. Thirdly, we draw attention to a Marxist perspective on the provision of health care. Finally, we consider some ways in which sociologists have analysed the concept of a 'profession'. We look briefly at some of the criteria of professionalism, at the concept of 'professional dominance' and the process of 'professional socialization'.

8.1 Relationship between health care and health need

8.1.1 The contribution of Illich

The shortfall in the provision of health care, relative to health needs, has been a topic of interest for many writers concerned with both industrialized societies and with the developing countries of the Third World. One of the most controversial and stimulating contributions is found in the work of Ivan Illich. He uses the concept of 'iatrogenesis' to describe illnesses which are actually caused by medical practice and describes ways in which the activities of doctors may have harmful results (Illich, 1975). For example, he claims:

> 'It has been established that one out of every five patients admitted to a typical research hospital acquires an iatrogenic disease, sometimes trivial, usually requiring special treatment, and in one case in thirty leading to death. Half of these episodes resulted from complications of drug therapy; amazingly, one in ten came from diagnostic procedures. Despite good intentions and claims to public service, with a similar record of performance a military officer would be relieved of his command, and a restaurant or amusement centre would be closed by the police.'

Another theme in Illich's work is the misallocation of scarce resources. He points to the widespread tendency for investment in high cost, high technology, high prestige medicine and a consequent underspending on primary and preventive health care. Many people argue that this is a problem in Britain, with the 'Cinderella' services such as care of the elderly and the mentally handicapped suffering as a result of current priorities. Certainly there are issues here which need careful discussion and consideration. Moreover, anyone familiar with health care in the developing countries will recognize this problem, in a very acute form, in many of them.

For example, during a visit to Turkey I was shown hospitals with magnificent facilities bought at great expense from western countries (such as scanning machines and operating theatres, exceeding those of many British hospitals in their modernity). There was also no shortage of medical students, but the number of nurses and midwives was woefully inadequate. The consequences were disturbing. In one hospital there was only one nurse to care for a ward with 90 post-operative patients; and, in a country where the infant mortality rate was running at 150 per thousand, and where one-half of the population is aged only 15 years or less, there was an acute shortage of well-qualified community health care workers.

Clearly, higher levels of investment in preventive and primary health care, and a better ratio of nursing to medical staff, could do more to save lives and to increase life expectancy than current patterns of investment in high cost technologically oriented medical practice.

Illich's work is seen by many people as useful in highlighting problems of misallocation of scarce health care resources, but there is a deeper issue underlying his work. He was writing from a predominantly theological perspective and he is ultimately concerned with the belief that pain and suffering are important aspects of human life and that medical practice is effectively removing them. He suggests that people have forgotten how to look after themselves and how to cope with these ultimate experiences. Therefore, he urges a return to more self-reliance and a greater readiness to withstand the temptations offered by inappropriate medical alleviation of the afflictions inherent in our mortal condition.

Not surprisingly, Illich's book has been subjected to severe criticism, and he has been accused of underestimating the benefits of modern medicine. However, some of his recommendations may be worth considering. They include measures to increase individual responsibility for health and the development of low and middle level technology in health care.

Sociologists have also analysed the ways in which societies organize the provision of health care. Examples of two different approaches are offered here: first, the work of T. Parsons — who was one of the first sociologists to address himself explicitly to health and illness and whose work spans both macrosociological and microsociological approaches; secondly, a contribution from a Marxist perspective, by V. Navarro.

8.1.2   The contribution of Parsons

One aspect of Parsons' work (Parsons, 1951) comes from a structural functionalist perspective. He stresses the importance of health for the smooth running of society. In this context he develops the concept of the 'sick role', which involves certain rights and obligations. If fulfilled, these should restore the sick person to health as quickly as possible. The basic ideas are as follows:

(1)   The condition of being sick is essentially undesirable, both for the individual and for society. Its unpleasantness for the sick person is self-evident; its undesirability for society lies in the fact that it prevents the sick person from fulfilling his or her social obligations effectively. If people cannot work, or parents cannot look after their children, some important jobs are not being done, and disruptions will result. Consequently, there is an obligation on those who become ill to try to return to health as soon as possible.
(2)   The concept of the 'sick role' carries with it both rights as well as obligations. Therefore, if a sick person fulfils the prescribed obligations he is entitled to certain rights. These rights and obligations are summarized in *Table 8.1.*

TABLE 8.1   The rights and obligations of the 'sick role'

Obligations	Rights
Patient must wish to recover as quickly as possible	Patient is relieved of normal responsibilities and tasks
Patient must seek professional advice and follow prescribed treatment	Patient is accorded sympathy and support

Parsons recognizes that not all illnesses are sufficiently severe to require people to accept all the rights and obligations of the sick role. Trivial conditions may only need self-treatment, and do not necessitate taking time off work. However, Parsons' analysis describes ways in which society generally expects an ill person to behave, and it accounts for the general lack of sympathy accorded to malingerers or to those who fail to follow medical advice.

The doctor–patient relationship

In Parsons' analysis, the roles of doctor and patient are seen as reciprocal: the patient is required to trust the doctor and to follow his instructions; in return, the doctor makes his professional knowledge and skill available to the patient. This places doctors in a very powerful and influential position. Parsons suggests that they, too, are therefore bound by certain obligations which must be fulfilled if they are to enjoy their privileges. These are summarized in *Table 8.2.*

TABLE 8.2 The doctor's role: privileges and obligations

Obligations	Privileges
Must be guided by the interests of the patient rather than by self-interest	Considerable professional autonomy
Must apply a high degree of skill and knowledge	Occupies a position of authority *vis-à-vis the* patient
Must be objective, emotionally detached and guided by the rules of professional practice	Has the right to intimate examination of patients and to information concerning their personal lives

It will be seen that the potential problems inherent in the medical role — such as the need for intimate physical and personal contact — are reduced by the obligations to ensure that the relationship is guided by professional ethics and standards of behaviour (there are echoes here of the Hippocratic Oath which we encountered in Chapter 2). When this reciprocity is maintained, the doctor can fulfil his responsibilities to the benefit of the patient and of society, by restoring the patient to as healthy a state as possible.

Parsons' work was significant as it was one of the first sociological accounts of the social role of the medical profession. There have been subsequent criticisms and modifications. For example, whereas Parsons sees a basic harmony and reciprocity in the doctor–patient relationship, other sociologists such as Freidson (1962) point to various dilemmas and possible conflicts. He, for example, argues that doctors and patients embark upon their relationship with such differences in their knowledge and experience that they experience a 'clash of perspectives':

'It is my thesis that the separate worlds of experience and reference of the layman and the professional worker are always in potential conflict with each other . . . . The practitioner, looking from his professional vantage point, preserves his detachment by seeing the patient as a case to which he applies the general rules and categories learned during his protracted professional training. The client, being personally involved in what happens, feels obliged to try to judge and control what is happening to him. Since he does not have the same perspective as the practitioner, he must judge what is being done to him from other than a professional point of view.'

There are implications for nurses in Freidson's interpretation of dilemmas in the doctor–patient relationship. For example, it indicates the need for nurses to be available in an interpretative capacity if there is a 'clash' between the doctor's and patient's perspectives; also, Freidson's account may apply to any profession — nursing included — and can therefore sensitize us to possible communication problems in our own relationships with patients.

As already mentioned, the approach used by Parsons is essentially structural functionalist. He considers the role of the doctor in the light of the functions it serves in maintaining order and stability in society. However, there are other approaches which focus on conflict rather than stability. One of these is the Marxist viewpoint, exemplified in the work of V. Navarro.

8.1.3   The Marxist approach of Navarro

In Chapter 1 we saw that Marxists are predominantly concerned with economic factors in social organization and social change. Navarro (1975) is interested in the role of private capital in the provision of health care. He argues that in capitalist societies health care has become a commodity to be bought and sold, and that decisions on priorities will be guided by criteria of profitability. For example, if health legislation is likely to affect the productivity of an organization in profit terms, it is likely to be opposed or ignored. He also points to some of the effects on doctor–patient relationships when the profit motive is allowed to obtrude, suggesting that the doctor's decisions may be more influenced by monetary concerns than by the patient's well-being. These concerns are compatible with some of those voiced by Illich (1975). For example, Illich alleges that surgeons may undertake unnecessary operations in countries such as the U.S.A., where surgery brings financial rewards.

Navarro's work draws attention to the role of the state in the provision of health care. The interrelationships between the state and health care are very complex and vary from country to country. Whereas Marxist studies tend to focus attention on capitalist societies, it has also been suggested that there may be some similarities between capitalist and socialist societies. To achieve an adequate understanding of the complex relationship between the state and systems of health care, it is necessary to look at several different societies in order to discern parallels and differences which may transcend particular labels such as 'capitalist' and 'socialist'. Patrick and Scrambler (1982) indicate these complexities:

'Both capitalist and socialist societies have adopted a variety of strategies in relation to medicine . . . . Governments may wish to "buy off" political discontent by setting up a system of health care financing which makes health care more readily available, such as Medicare in the U.S.A., the Welfare State in the U.K. or the co-operative medical service in China. On the other hand, they might discover that attempts to cut back on such systems at a time of financial crisis generate social disruption. Governments might be eager to use the service of medicine in the control of deviants (U.S.A., U.K.), political dissidents (U.S.S.R.) or population growth (China), but might also wish to devote medical resources to other priorities.'

So far, in this chapter, we have been at the macrosociological level of analysis — looking at ways in which social systems operate, from structural functionalist and

Marxist perspectives. We now move towards the more microsociological end of the continuum in order to consider certain groups of people who work within these social systems — the professionals.

8.2   Sociological studies of the professions

Sociologists have been interested in the professions for several decades. Fifty years ago, Carr-Saunders and Wilson (1933) wrote a classical book which set the scene for much subsequent discussion. More recently, Freidson (1970a) has written specifically about the medical profession.

Most sociologists agree that for an occupation to be classified as a 'profession' it must meet certain criteria:

(1)   It must possess a *body of specialized knowledge.*
(2)   This knowledge must be *imparted to new members in institutions controlled by members of that profession.*
(3)   There should be a *'monopoly' of professional practice.* This means that in order to practise in the profession, a person must become qualified by passing recognized examinations, and have his or her name formally placed on a register of licensed practitioners.
(4)   Professionals are *accountable to members of the same profession,* because if the professional practice rests on a specialized body of knowledge, only fellow professionals can judge the overall quality of practice.
(5)   There is an *ethical code* which underlies professional practice. This consists of the kinds of principles described by Parsons (1951) in his description of the obligations inherent in the doctor's role (see above). In essence, they stipulate that the professional person must be committed to the principle of service, so that he puts the patient's or client's interests before his own.

There has been a great deal of discussion about whether nursing fulfils the criteria of professionalism. Readers can use their own judgement to assess the situation. Some writers argue that, in their view, occupations such as nursing and social work do not as yet possess all of the attributes of a true profession, and consequently they designate them 'semi-professions' (Goode, 1960).

8.2.1   Professional dominance

One may feel that discussion of whether a particular occupation such as nursing is a 'profession' is just an academic exercise. It may be. However, there are important social consequences which stem from the degree of power and influence which a particular professional group can command. Freidson (1970b), for example, has discussed the concept of 'professional dominance' with reference to the medical profession's dominant role *vis-à-vis* 'paramedical' occupations such as nursing:

'University training gave physicians and surgeons a stronger political position for persuading the state to subordinate to them such competitors as apothecaries, grocers, and barbers, not to speak of allowing them to prosecute the irregular practitioners. This could be so even when it was doubtful that the actual knowledge and skill of the university-trained practitioner in those days equipped him to practice any more effectively than his self-taught or apprenticed competitor.

'With the development of the university and the guild in European cities, then, rose a rudimentary organization of full-time health workers, organized at least in part under the supervision of physicians and surgeons . . . . Not until the twentieth century in Europe and North America did anything resembling a stable and extensive division of labor dominated by physicians emerge. In the nonindustrial countries of the world today, such a division of labor does not yet exist to any great degree.

'By the twentieth century the medical profession was at last able to establish a secure mandate to provide the central health service . . . . It is in this context that the development of the contemporary paramedical division of labor can be understood as something much more complex than merely rationally functional or technical differentiation. Because of the importance of social, political, and economic factors, there is great variation in the origin and present position of occupations related to health. Some historic specialties like dentistry survived fairly independently of the paramedical division of labor. Others, like pharmacy and more particularly optometry, were not fully integrated into the paramedical division of labor, being at least partially independent of it. Still others, like the bone-setter and, in the United States, the midwife, were taken over by the physician himself, laymen and amateurs being driven out of practice. Others, the most prominent of which is nursing, maintained an ancient function while being brought firmly under medical control . . . .'

Effects on the practice of midwifery

A current issue which might serve to illustrate this point is the present state of midwifery in Britain. Recent developments in obstetrics have resulted in changes in the practice of midwifery which are seen by many midwives as an erosion of their role and of their professional autonomy. For example, current obstetric thinking, which sees no birth as 'normal, except in retrospect', has profound implications for midwifery. For according to the World Health Organization's definition of the midwife, she is trained to care for the mother and baby during a normal pregnancy, delivery and puerperium. But if there is no such thing as 'normality' (until 'after the event'), there is no role or responsibility for the midwife. And research has shown that the organization of maternity care may reflect this thinking, in ways which are detrimental to pregnant women.

For example, Robinson, Golden and Bradley (1981) found that in nearly 60 per cent of cases where mothers visited hospital antenatal clinics for routine checkups, abdominal examinations were performed by midwives and then repeated by medical staff. This is clearly an unsatisfactory situation. First and foremost, the women are worried because they think something may be wrong; it also wastes their time having to wait to see the doctor. Secondly, it is an insult to the midwives because it implies that their clinical judgement is inadequate, despite the fact that they have been trained and qualified to assess pregnancy and to detect abnormalities. Thirdly, it is not the most appropriate use of the medical staff's time — instead of having to see so many women with whom they can often spend no more than a few minutes, it would surely be preferable if they reserved more time for those who have obstetric problems and who therefore need their specialist attention.

This example illustrates one way in which a dominant profession may be able to use its power to influence policy in ways which may be detrimental both to clients and to colleagues in less powerful positions.

8.3   Preparation for professional practice

Whether nursing is seen as a fully-fledged profession or not, it certainly fulfils a number of the generally recognized criteria for professional status, and the preparation of trainees is frequently considered as a process of 'professional socialization'.

8.3.1   Professional socialization

In Chapter 1 we mentioned the concept of socialization and in Chapter 4 we discussed its importance in the upbringing of children. Now we will consider its application in studies of the ways in which newcomers are initiated into medicine and nursing. These studies show how professional training serves two functions. First, it imparts a body of knowledge and expertise; second, and more subtly, it fosters 'appropriate' beliefs, values and behaviours.

Some of the classical studies of the socialization of medical students were undertaken in the U.S.A., but they are relevant elsewhere. One famous study, by Becker *et al.* (1961), described in detail how medical students felt about being placed in a distinctly subordinate position during their training and forced to go through what seemed like a 'trial by ordeal' before being allowed to enter the profession.

8.3.2   The uncertainty element in medicine

Another study, by Fox (1957), aptly called 'Training for uncertainty', describes how medical training places students in stressful situations because of the inevitable uncertainty in medical practice. The stress and anxiety are heightened by the students' painful awareness of this uncertainty, which contrasts uncomfortably with the public's confidence in their professional knowledge. In Fox's own words:

'Two basic types of uncertainty may be recognized. The first results from incomplete or imperfect mastery of available knowledge. No one can have at his command all skills and all knowledge of the lore of medicine. The second depends upon limitations in current medical knowledge. There are innumerable questions to which no physician, however well trained, can as yet provide answers. A third source of uncertainty derives from the first two. This consists of difficulty in distinguishing between personal ignorance or ineptitude and the limitations of present medical knowledge. It is inevitable that every doctor must constantly cope with these forms of uncertainty and that grave consequences may result if he is not able to do so. It is for this reason that training for uncertainty in a medical curriculum and in early professional experiences is an important part of becoming a physician.'

Fox then describes various ways in which students react to this uncertainty and learn how to live with it. For example, at certain stages in their training they prematurely adopt attitudes of 'certainty' and confidence, partly based on ignorance; later, they may acknowledge more uncertainty, but find it threatening and even 'blame the patient'. In their training they are, however, encouraged to voice and to share their uncertainty so that they can come to terms with this fact of medical life.

8.3.3   Stress and the student nurse

There are many similarities between the stress experienced by medical students and the experiences of student nurses as described by Davis (1966). Davis describes the stages through which student nurses pass as they progress through training. He emphasizes particularly their changing views of their own identities:

(1) *Initial innocence* — when students arrive with high ideals and eager desires to help their suffering patients. However, this stage gives way to frustrations as reality proves to be very different from their expectations.
(2) *Labelled recognition of incongruity.* The realization by students that nursing is not exactly in accordance with their preconceptions; this is a time of stress when they are afraid of being asked to take on more responsibility than they feel ready for.
(3) *'Psyching out'.* The adoption of various tactics and strategies to cope with the tensions involved in their training, including ways of 'putting on a front' for their teachers.
(4) *Role simulation.* A very self-conscious acting of the role of the professional nurse.
(5) *Provisional internalization* followed by *stable internalization.* Progressively successful and consistent stages of development of a fully professional identity, during which the values and the behaviours of the qualified professional nurse are not merely 'put on' by students — they actually identify with them and make them their own.

This study describes the ups and downs — the vicissitudes and satisfactions — of nurse training for a group of American students. British students often find it helpful to consider the extent to which it applies to their own situation, and take comfort from the fact that they are not alone in experiencing some of these painful processes.

In this chapter we have seen that the professional role entails various obligations. We have also seen that the process of training for this role may not be easy and that it involves stress of various kinds. One of the most distressing aspects of medical and nursing education and practice may be the element of uncertainty inherent in the knowledge base underpinning the professional's work. It is therefore perhaps important to remember in this context the words of J.B. Conant: 'There are areas of experience where we know that uncertainty is the certainty.'

As we can be certain that uncertainty will be a problem in a student nurse's training, students should be given maximum support, guidance and supervision — for their own sake and for the sake of the patients in their care. However, research has shown that very often students may be left to cope with their uncertainties with little supervision or support (Lewin and Leach, 1982). The need to remedy this situation is a theme which will recur in the next chapter, when we will be considering nurse–patient communication.

■ Summary

Despite the welfare state and the National Health Service there is still a shortfall in the provision of health care relative to health needs. The overview given of this topic of interest includes macrosociological accounts of the organization of health care and discussion of the health professions. The discussion refers to the controversial ideas of Illich, highlighting problems of misallocation of resources, the structural functionalist viewpoint of Parsons and the Marxist approach of Navarro concerning the role of private capital in the provision of health care. The ways in which sociologists have analysed the concept of 'profession' are also considered, as are the criteria for defining professionalism.

The element of uncertainty in medical practice and knowledge could be distressing to the student nurse. The author believes that, to counter this, trainees should be given maximum support, guidance and supervision for their own sake and for the sake of their patients.

■ Questions

1. Discuss any two of the following concepts:
   (a) the 'sick role';
   (b) 'professional dominance';
   (c) 'iatrogenesis'.

2. In what ways do sociological studies of professional socialization illuminate your understanding of nursing education?
3. Do you think that nursing is a profession? If so, give your reasons; if not, do you think it should strive to become one, and why?

References

Becker, H., Geer, B., Hughes Everett, C. and Strauss, A. (1961). *Boys in White: Student Culture in Medical School,* Chicago, University of Chicago Press.

Carr-Saunders, A. and Wilson, P. (1933). *The Professions,* Oxford, Clarendon Press.

Cox, C. and Mead, A. (Eds.) (1975). *A Sociology of Medical Practice,* London, Collier Macmillan.

Davis, F. (1966). 'Professional socialization as subjective experience: the process of doctrinal conversation among student nurses', in *A Sociology of Medical Practice,* Cox, C. and Mead, A. (Eds.), London, Collier Macmillan, 1975.

Fox, R. (1957). 'Training for uncertainty', in *The Student Physician,* Merton, R. *et al.* (Eds.), Cambridge, Mass., Harvard University Press; reprinted in *A Sociology of Medical Practice,* Cox, C. and Mead, A. (Eds.), London, Collier Macmillan, 1975.

Freidson, E. (1962). 'Dilemmas in the doctor–patient relationship', in *Human Behaviour and Social Processes,* Rose, A.. (Ed.), London, Routledge & Kegan Paul; reprinted in *A Sociology of Medical Practice,* Cox, C. and Mead, A. (Eds.), London, Collier Macmillan, 1975.

Freidson, E. (1970a). *The Profession of Medicine,* New York, Dodd Mead.

Freidson, E. (1970b). *Professional Dominance,* New York, Atherton.

Goode, W. (1960). 'Encroachment, charlatanism and the emerging profession', *American Sociological Review,* vol. 25 (Dec.), pp. 902–914.

Illich, I. (1975). *Medical Nemesis: The Expropriation of Health,* London, Calder & Boyars.

Lewin, D. and Leach, J. (1982). 'Factors influencing the quality of wards as learning environments for student nurses', *International Journal of Nursing Studies,* vol. 19, no. 3, pp. 125–137.

Navarro, V. (1975). 'Social class, political power and the state and their implications in medicine', *Social Science and Medicine,* vol. 9, pp. 351–363.

Parsons, T. (1951). *The Social System,* Illinois, Glencoe, Free Press; London, Routledge & Kegan Paul; see especially Chapter 10, 'Social structure and dynamic process: the case of modern medical practice'.

Patrick, D. and Scrambler, G. (1982). *Sociology as Applied to Medicine,* London, Baillière-Tindall.

Popper, K. (1966). *The Open Society and its Enemies,* vol. 1, London, Routledge & Kegan Paul.

Robinson, S., Golden, J. and Bradley, S. (1981). 'Antenatal Care, Preliminary Report on the Project on the Role and Responsibilities of the Midwife: Part I', *Midwives Chronicle,* January, vol. 94, no. 1116.

Further reading

Patrick, D. and Scrambler, G. (1982). *Sociology as Applied to Medicine,* London, Baillière-Tindall. Written by sociology teachers in London medical schools, this book offers concise and well-referenced accounts of many aspects of health care, including chapters on inequality and social class; medicine and social control; the health professions and evaluation of health care.

Patients may be confronted by a bewildering array of signs on arrival at hospital (Courtesy Jonathon Cox)

(. . . 'the experience of being a patient', even for non-serious illnesses, can arouse deep-seated fears and anxieties — see p. 125)

9 The experience of being a patient

'As sickness is the usual forerunner of death, it should therefore lead you seriously to consider, and reflect on your behaviour in life, and carefully to examine yourselves how far you are prepared for that great change.'

(*Directions and Prayers for the Use of the Patient*, Guy's Hospital, London)

Although the solemn words above date from the last century, they are timeless in their message. Most illnesses jolt us into remembering that we are mortal — that health is not something we can take for granted, and that death is inevitable, sooner or later. This is especially true for patients being admitted to hospital, who are likely to be worried about their condition and alarmed at the sight of seriously ill patients around them. Thus 'the experience of being a patient', even for non-serious illnesses, can arouse deep-seated fears and anxieties.

9.1 Interpersonal relationships between patients and professionals

This anxiety-laden situation can also make the patient very vulnerable in personal relationships, particularly with those people who are described somewhat inelegantly in sociological jargon as 'significant others' (see Chapter 4). This is why some sociologists and psychologists have turned their attention to the inter-personal relationships between patients and the professionals who care for them such as doctors and nurses. These studies are usually microsociological and frequently adopt an interactionist or ethnomethodological perspective (see Chapter 1).

9.1.1 Patients' evaluation of communication

Several studies have described patients' views on the care they receive in hospital or in the community. McGhee (1961), for example, visited patients about two weeks after they had been discharged from hospital and found that 65 per cent of them were dissatisfied with communication during their hospital stay, compared with less than 40 per cent who were unhappy about other aspects of their hospitalization such as medical or nursing care, food or noise. Cartwright (1964) found a similar proportion of her sample of patients in general wards would have liked to have been told more about their condition and treatment. And, more recently, Wilson-Barnett (1977) found that 40 per cent of all comments on this subject made by patients in her sample from general medical wards indicated their desire for more information. This desire is also felt by patients in the community who visit their general practitioners. Kincey *et al.* (1975) found that, although most patients said that they felt that their doctor had told them enough about certain aspects of their condition and treatment, only 56 per cent felt that they had been fully informed about diagnosis, aetiology, treatment and prognosis.

9.1.2 Factors associated with inadequate communication

Communication is a two-way process. Some of the problems in communication may be found in the attitudes and behaviour of professional personnel, others in the characteristics of patients. Research has identified some of the factors which affect the amount of communication with medical or nursing staff.

For example, Cartwright and O'Brien (1976) looked at relationships between patients' social class and consultations with general practitioners. They found that, on average, middle class patients spent longer with the doctor, asking more questions and discussing more problems. This was the case even when they had mentioned fewer symptoms than their working class counterparts during an interview before the consultation. This discrepancy may be accounted for by the attitudes and behaviour of both patients and doctors. For example, patients may be very diffident and refrain from asking questions. Diffidence may be related to social class, since middle class patients possibly feel more at ease with middle class doctors. Also, doctors tend to assume that patients do not want information unless they request it; so they may not volunteer it. Thus, those who do not ask, do not receive.

Doctors may also increase patients' reluctance to ask questions by their behaviour during a consultation: Cartwright and O'Brien's study also showed that doctors tended to like consultations in which conversation did not exceed five minutes and where patients only asked one question. Patients, especially those who are diffident, are likely to pick up the doctor's cues and to refrain from intruding further on his time.

A second example concerns nursing staff in hospital and shows how patients may be discouraged by nurses from asking for help or from talking about their fears and anxieties. Maguire (1978) interviewed patients with breast cancer and observed the extent to which nurses sat down and talked to patients who were showing obvious signs of distress. Instead of encouraging patients to talk about their worries, nurses tended to offer platitudes such as 'don't worry'. Maguire points out that many of the patients were terrified of their cancer spreading and of imminent death, although some of them had a favourable prognosis and could have been relieved of their fear by a factual discussion of their condition. Even for those whose future was more uncertain, it is reasonable to suppose that a sympathetic ear and an opportunity to talk about their worries might have been more appropriate than the combination of platitude and sedative which they were given.

The final example offers a salutary reminder that although patients may not always give obvious 'cries for help' or indications that they want more information, this does not mean that they do not need support. Wilson-Barnett (1981) emphasizes this point:

'My own research demonstrated that it is by no means always patients who *show* or *express* their distress who require the most psychological care (Wilson-Barnett and Carrigy, 1978). When patients were interviewed, we found that it was the quietest, least expressive patients who often reported most anxiety and depression throughout their stay in medical wards. However, these patients often received least attention from nurses although they were most at risk and most in need of support. For example, those who had been admitted for diagnostic tests or who had early stages of cancer were most likely to be very worried about their condition and to experience feelings of guilt. This could relate either to a lack of obvious debility, or to their worry that if the doctors could not make a diagnosis they may be considered as hypochondriacal . . . . There is no doubt that particular groups of patients in general wards (such as the very anxious, the undiagnosed, the severely ill or the unsociable) require really open communication with staff so that their needs can be recognised and satisfied.'

9.1.3   Reasons for inadequate communication

There are many reasons why staff may find it difficult to offer the 'open' communication advocated by Wilson-Barnett, and why patients may find it hard to express themselves or to receive and to understand information. Some of these reasons may be related to pressures on staff; others, to pressures on patients.

9.2   Pressures on staff

A Dutch sociologist, E. Cassee, discusses some of these problems (Cassee, 1975). He argues that the way hospital staff behave towards patients has an important part to play in the healing process and that successful 'therapeutic behaviour' is helped by open two-way communication. In other words, the staff must keep the patient informed about his illness and treatment, and encourage him to express his fears and anxieties. Cassee's research was designed, *inter alia,* to answer the question, 'Does therapeutic behaviour form part of the work of a registered nurse in the Netherlands?'. He found that only one aspect of the therapeutic role had been built into the work of the nurses in his study: providing information about nursing procedures. Much less emphasis was put on other aspects of communication, such as providing information about patients' conditions, or encouraging them to express their anxieties and fears. Patients were given the opportunity to talk about their anxieties in less than 50 per cent of cases, and only 15 per cent of the nurses stated that patients in their nursing units were usually asked for their opinions. Cassee suggests that this is very understandable:

'The reactions of those attending a training course for staff nurses gave us a clue with regard to a possible explanation of the findings . . . "Many nurses avoid this form of contact with the patient, since they do not know how to handle his reaction." The interesting thing here is that their motivation for withholding information is *not* "it is better for the patient because he cannot cope with it", but "it is better for the nurse because she does not know how to handle it". From an emotional point of view, therapeutic behaviour is risky for both nurses and doctors, because it requires a more intimate and personal approach to the patient. Such an approach can trigger off feelings which are difficult to control.'

Cassee suggests that nurses consequently tend to avoid making themselves vulnerable by retreating into defence mechanisms such as those described by Menzies (1960). These include strategies such as extreme task division, which allows the nurse to compartmentalize care and to avoid having to relate to the totality of the patient and his illness; or the 'depersonalization' of patients reflected in the ways in which nurses often talk about them — 'the "coronary" in bed 16'. In order to reduce the stress and anxiety which lead nurses to take refuge in these defence mechanisms, Cassee suggests that they need support and the opportunity to discuss their own anxieties and perplexities:

'Emotional openness between the members of the ward appeared to be especially important. Improvement of the quality of care should therefore start with the improvement of mutual communication between staff.'

9.3   Pressures on patients

While staff may often fail to give adequate information or allow sufficient opportunity for patients to discuss their problems, it may also be true that patients do not always 'hear' or remember what is said. For example, Ley and Spelman (1967) found that within a few minutes of their consultation, patients tend to forget between one-third and one-half of the information given by a doctor. This may happen for a variety of reasons. For example:

(1) Doctors use technical language which their patients do not understand.
(2) Patients do not have sufficient 'background' medical knowledge to appreciate the significance of what they have been told.
(3) Patients are anxious — and anxiety can inhibit memory.
(4) The information is given so quickly that they cannot take it in.

9.3.1   Ensuring adequate understanding

The importance of ensuring adequate understanding is illustrated very graphically in a study undertaken in Glasgow by Boyle (1970). He found that often doctors

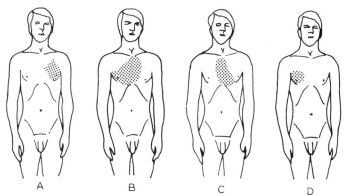

Distribution of positions of the heart. A, 47 patients (41.2%), 2 doctors (5.7%). B, 17 patients (14.9%), no doctors. C, 48 patients (42.1%), 33 doctors (94.3%). D, 2 patients (1.8%), no doctors.

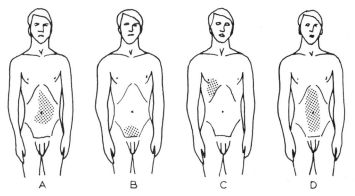

Distribution of positions of the bladder. A, 27 patients (24.1%), no doctors. B, 67 patients (59.8%), 35 doctors (100%). C, 9 patients (8.0%), no doctors. D, 9 patients (8.0%), no doctors.

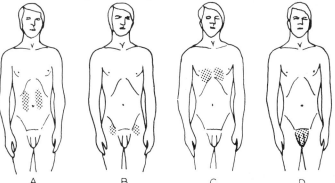

Distribution of positions of the kidneys. A, 52 patients (46.0%), 35 doctors (100%). B, 55 patients (48.7%), no doctors. C, 2 patients (1.8%), no doctors. D, 4 patients (3.5%), no doctors.

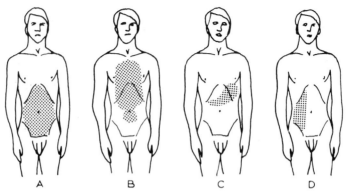

Distribution of positions of the stomach. A, 67 patients (58.8%), no doctors. B, 22 patients (19.3%), no doctors. C, 23 patients (20.2%), 35 doctors (100%). D, 2 patients (1.8%), no doctors.

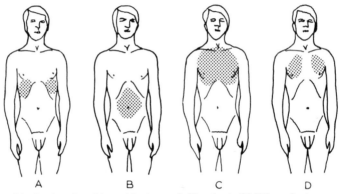

Distribution of positions of the lungs. A, 36 patients (33.3%), no doctors. B, 2 patients (1.9%), no doctors. C, 55 patients (50.9%), 35 doctors (100%). D, 15 patients (13.9%), no doctors.

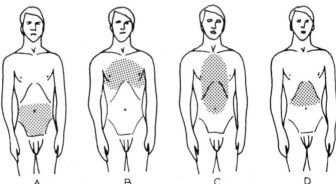

Distribution of positions of the intestines. A, 83 patients (76.9%), 35 doctors (100%). B, 1 patient (0.9%), no doctors. C, 13 patients (12.0%), no doctors. D, 11 patients (10.2%), no doctors.

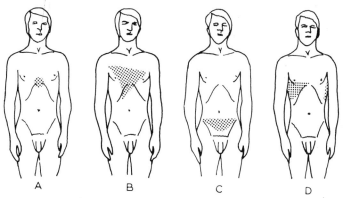

Distribution of positions of the liver. A, no patients, no doctors. B, 6 patients (6.1%), no doctors. C, 45 patients (45.5%), no doctors. D, 48 patients (48.5%), 35 doctors (100%).

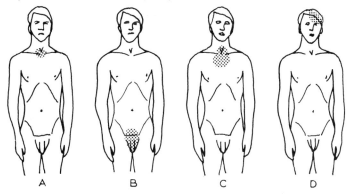

Distribution of positions of the thyroid gland. A, 72 patients (69.9%), 35 doctors (100%). B, 3 patients (2.9%), no doctors. C, 25 patients (24.3%), no doctors. D, 3 patients (2.9%), no doctors.

Figure 9.1   Patients' and doctors' perceptions of the location of organs in the body (From Boyle, 1970, by courtesy of the Editor of the *British Medical Journal*)

and patients were not 'talking the same language'. For example, terms used by doctors (such as 'palpitations' or 'bronchitis') meant very different things for doctors and patients. Also, many patients, understandably, had very little knowledge of human anatomy, so their ideas of the location of various organs in the body often differed significantly from those of the doctors. *Figure 9.1* illustrates the degree of discrepancy, particularly with regard to organs such as the thyroid gland, the kidneys and the liver. Such discrepancies, especially if they are not recognized, may obviously lead to risks of misunderstanding in giving and taking medical histories and in discussion of diagnosis, treatment and prognosis.

Imagine, for example, the unnecessary worries of a patient waiting to be admitted for an operation on his thyroid gland if he had the same ideas about the location of this gland as the patients in Boyle's B or D groups!

9.4 The importance of communication

There are many reasons why communication is important. For example, a number of researchers have demonstrated that anxiety and worry can increase pain and discomfort. Among these, both Hayward (1975) and Boore (1979) have worked with patients undergoing surgery and shown that they benefit from the opportunity to discuss their operations in advance. In this research, samples of patients were given information about their operation and about what to expect post-operatively. They were then compared with patients who had not been given this pre-operative 'counselling' session. Both research studies demonstrated beneficial results for the patients who had had the opportunity to discuss their operations beforehand. Hayward's patients appeared to feel less pain and needed less analgesia than the control group. Boore's patients had lower measures on physiological indicators of stress, such as urinary hydroxycorticosteroid levels, and fewer post-operative complications, such as wound infections, than those in the control group.

In summary, as J. Wilson-Barnett emphasizes:

'Throughout our communication with patients we must give time to develop our skills as observers, assessors, listeners and informers and then examine our effectiveness through the benefits to patients. This is not just a vague idea based on intangible evidence. Research has shown that improved nurse–patient communication does have measurable clinical and psychological benefits to patients.'

9.5 Subjective views of patients

9.5.1 Experiences of sociologists as patients

The studies mentioned so far in this chapter have involved researchers describing other people's knowledge or experiences. However some sociologists have given first-hand accounts of themselves 'on the receiving end'. They are valuable in that they enhance our understanding of what it really feels like to be a patient. These studies make no claim to being 'scientific' in the sense of being representative of all patient encounters with doctors or nurses, but they are still 'valid' in that they describe something which actually happened. The book by Davis and Horobin (1977) is an example of this approach in which sociologists record and analyse their own experiences with health care professionals.

9.5.2   Influence of culture on responses to pain and illness

Many studies have shown how people from different cultures vary in their behaviour when they are taken ill. For example, a study by Zborowski (1952) compared three groups of patients — Jewish, Italian and 'Old American'. Although all these patients were suffering from the same condition, they behaved very differently. The 'Old American' patients tended to be very stoical, reserved and kept the traditional 'British stiff upper lip', while the Jewish and Italian patients were noisy, uninhibited and very demanding. However, behind their noisy behaviour, the Jewish and Italian patients were worried about different problems: the Jews were primarily concerned about the meaning of their illness for their families and their jobs; the Italians were most anxious about the immediate relief of pain.

Studies such as these do not imply that some patients' behaviour is right or wrong; rather, they help us to understand what is most worrying patients, so that we can respond more sensitively to their spoken — and unspoken — anxieties.

9.5.3   Experiences of other patients

In addition, researchers sometimes involve themselves closely in the observation and discussion of encounters between patients and professionals, as in the work described in Wadsworth and Robinson (1976). One chapter in this book, 'People's accounts of medical encounters', by B. Webb and G. Stimson, gives vivid descriptions of patients' experiences and analyses ways in which they are recounted. The researchers found, for example, that patients and doctors rarely exhibit anger or conflict during a consultation; they tend to be 'emotionally flat' and fears are not usually brought out into the open. However, it was also observed that this lack of drama in the direct encounter was 'in marked contrast to the dramatic and emotional content of patients' accounts of their surgery encounters when talking to family and friends (or interviewers)'.

Webb and Stimson also suggest that when patients recount their experiences of consultations, they try to redress the inherent inequality between themselves and the doctor. They might 'get their own back' by mimicking the doctor or by calling him nicknames:

'A doctor is meant to give time to his patients: we heard of a doctor who had earned a reputation among his patients for conducting consultations at great speed and was known as "two-minute Todd" . . . . A doctor is meant to take care in examination and diagnosis: one woman described her doctor's "kerbside manner" saying when he visited at home he would stand at the door rather than examine her children.'

Stacey and Homans (1978) assess the value of such studies in this way:

'There is a richness of understanding of both the interactive process and the patients' point of view which cannot be achieved by survey methods alone. The insights which emerge from the conversations among patients are important. Some hold it against such works that one does not know how representative they are. This is to mistake the purpose. If such relationships can occur at all or anywhere, they are part of what constitutes the totality of the doctor–patient relationship. It is necessary to discover the character of such relationships before one can measure the prevalence of particular types.'

Yes, indeed. And one of sociology's contributions to health care may be the provision of more information about relationships between patients and doctors or other health care professionals. So we now turn our attention to some of the ways in which sociologists have described the care of particular kinds of patients: the mentally ill, the chronic sick, the elderly and the dying. In this respect we might consider the words of Florence Nightingale: 'How little the real sufferings of illness are known and understood. How little does anyone in good health fancy him or even herself into the life of a sick person.'

■ Summary

The experience of being a patient can arouse deep-seated fears and anxieties, making the patient vulnerable in relationships with 'significant others'; this is why sociologists and psychologists study the interpersonal relationship between patients and health care workers. Of crucial importance is adequate two-way communication between these groups of people, and this chapter describes pressures on both patients and staff that could prevent such communication — such as the attitudes of professionals; social class and the diffidence of patients; the tendency of nurses to discourage patients from talking about their fears; and the possibility that patients do not always hear or remember what is being said at consultation. Mention is made of the interesting, but inevitably subjective, accounts given by sociologists who themselves have been patients and of the influence of culture on patients' responses to pain and illness.

The author concludes this account of the microsociological studies of interpersonal relationships by suggesting that one of sociology's contributions to health care may be the provision of more information concerning relationships between patients and health care professionals.

■ Questions

1. In what ways may the study of sociology help us to have a better understanding of the experience of being a patient?
2. Why do you think that there seem to be problems in communication between patients and their nurses or doctors? Suggest some ways in which we might improve such communication.

References

Boore, J. (1979). *Prescription for Recovery,* London, Royal College of Nursing.

Boyle, C. (1970). 'Difference between patients' and doctors' interpretations of some common medical terms', in *British Medical Journal,* 2 May; reprinted in *A Sociology of Medical Practice,* Cox, C. and Mead, A. (Eds.), London, Collier Macmillan, 1975.

Cartwright, A. (1964). *Human Relationships in Hospital Care,* London, Routledge & Kegan Paul.

Cartwright, A. and O'Brien, M. (1976). 'Social class variations in health care and in general practitioner consultations', in *Sociology of the National Health Service,* Sociological Review Monograph No. 22, Stacey, M. (Ed.), University of Keele.

Cassee, E. (1975). 'Therapeutic behaviour, hospital culture and communication', in *A Sociology of Medical Practice,* Cox, C. and Mead, A. (Eds.), London, Collier Macmillan.

Davis, A. and Horobin, G. (1977). *Medical Encounters. The Experience of Illness and Treatment,* London, Croom Helm.

Hayward, J. (1975). *Information — A Prescription Against Pain,* London, Royal College of Nursing.

Kincey et al. (1975). 'Patients' satisfaction and reported acceptance of advice in general practice', *Journal of the Royal College of Practitioners,* vol. 25, pp. 558–562.

Ley, P. and Spelman, M. (1967). *Communicating with the Patient,* Staples Press, London.

Maguire, P. (1978). 'The psychological effects of cancer and their treatments', in *Oncology for Nurses,* vol. 2, Tiffany, R. (Ed.), London, Allen & Unwin.

McGhee, A. (1961). *The Patients' Attitude to Nursing Care,* Edinburgh, Livingstone.

Menzies, I. (1960). 'A case study on the functioning of social systems as a defence against anxiety', Report of the Nursing Service in a General Hospital, *Human Relations,* November, pp. 13–32.

Stacey, M. and Homans, H. (1978). 'The sociology of health and illness: its present state, future prospects and potential for health research', *Sociology,* vol. 12, 2 May, 281–307.

Wadsworth, M. and Robinson, D. (Eds.) (1976). *Studies in Everyday Medical Life,* London, Martin Robertson.

Wilson-Barnett, J. (1977). 'Patients' emotional reactions to hospitalisation', *Ph.D. thesis,* University of London.

Wilson-Barnett, J. (1981). 'Communicating with patients in general wards', in *Communication in Nursing Care,* Bridge, W. and Macleod Clark, J. (Eds.), London, H.M.&.M. Publishers.

Wilson-Barnett, J. and Carrigy, A. (1978). 'Factors affecting patients' responses to hospitalisation', *Journal of Advanced Nursing,* vol. 3, pp. 221–228.

Zborowski, M. (1952). 'Cultural components in responses to pain', *Journal of Social Issues,* vol. 8, pp. 16–30.

Further reading

Wilson-Barnett, J. (1979). *Stress in Hospital. Patients' Psychological Reactions to Illness and Health Care,* Edinburgh, Churchill Livingstone. A useful overview of much of the literature written by psychologists and sociologists on the importance of good communication between providers and recipients of health care, with particular reference to the relationship between information, stress and anxiety.

'Care' of a mentally ill person in the nineteenth century, reproduced from an etching by G. Cruikshank from the original drawing exhibited to the House of Commons Select Committee on Madhouses, 1815 (Courtesy BBC Hulton Picture Library)

(. . . if a person is coerced into such an institution, the experience may not be desired and may even be harmful — see p. 146)

10 Sociological aspects of the care of the mentally ill

This chapter is concerned with *sociological* aspects of mental illness. It will not therefore deal with other important approaches such as the psychodynamic tradition, with its emphasis on 'inner world' phenomena and the role of the unconscious, or the behaviourists, whose work is based on theories of conditioned learning. Instead we will concentrate on the discussion of: (a) contemporary challenges to the basic idea of mental illness; (b) social factors in the causation of mental illness; (c) mental illness as social experience; (d) current controversies — the 'over-use' and the 'abuse' of psychiatry.

10.1   Challenges to the concept of mental illness

The title of this chapter begs a question which is at the heart of much debate among sociologists: is there something which can be called 'mental illness'? You may think it strange that this question should be asked, especially if you have worked in a psychiatric hospital with patients who are clearly distressed and whose suffering is very real. However, when influential writers challenge the very idea of mental illness and consequently the basis of all psychiatric practice, we need to start by considering this challenge.

In this section we will begin with two medical critics — the psychiatrists T. Szasz and R.D. Laing — and then consider briefly the ideas of certain sociologists, who are usually called 'labelling theorists', as exemplified by the work of T. Scheff. Finally, since these critics represent some of the influential figures in the 'anti-psychiatry' movement, we will look at the anti-psychiatry approach.

10.1.1   Szasz: the 'myth' of mental illness

The American psychiatrist T. Szasz has vigorously challenged the concept of 'mental illness' (Szasz, 1961). He refuses to accept the idea that situations which are currently defined as mental illness, and treated as such, are actually 'illnesses'. Although he agrees that there may be illnesses associated with physical pathology

— such as cerebral tumours — which may affect behaviour, Szasz argues that other experiences and behaviours commonly called 'mental illness' should be seen not as 'illness' but as 'problems of living'. He carries his analysis to the dramatic conclusion: 'There is no such thing as mental illness'.

Szasz then proceeds to criticize the practice of psychiatry, condemning psychiatrists as oppressors — 'professional hirelings', 'jailers' and 'torturers' — and psychiatric hospitals as 'prisons' and symbols of oppression. It is clear that Szasz is very worried and angry about the plight of many psychiatric patients and, as we shall see, there are indeed many causes for concern. However, he has been criticized for ignoring the genuine suffering which is inherent in the conditions called 'mental illness' and for underestimating the compassion and sincerity of those who care for them.

Roth (1976), for example, takes issue with him on these points, claiming that he underplays the fact that for patients: 'their troubles are desperate, their sufferings are extreme; that, indeed, they feel, and are, very ill; that the psychiatrists who care for them are not guilty conspirators but earnest and compassionate men and women, trying to do what they can to help the sufferer in each individual case.'

10.1.2 Laing: the family and psychological stress

Another psychiatrist who challenges current ideas of mental illness is R.D. Laing. One of his main contributions centres on the notion of the family as a cause of schizophrenia. He and his colleague, A. Esterson, argue that certain families place their children in conditions of great psychological stress; for example, in situations where parents make contradictory demands so that the child cannot please them both (Laing and Esterson, 1964). These writers suggest that since it is impossible for the child to make a 'rational' response he will respond in a way which appears irrational, but that this is, in effect, quite rational given his impossible situation. They describe a number of families of schizophrenic patients and suggest that the family can be seen as a 'pathogenic institution'. Thus, for Laing, schizophrenia is not an illness, but a person's way of coping with intolerable social and emotional pressures. Also, like Szasz, Laing regards psychiatric practice as coercive and repressive and sees psychiatrists as people who use diagnosis and treatment to control behaviour which other people define as a nuisance. Even worse, they may collude with the very family which might have caused the problem in the first place.

Laing's work has, not surprisingly, been challenged. For example, he has been criticized by another psychiatrist, J. Wing, for not providing sufficient evidence and for being unwilling to set up appropriate studies using controls and comparisons to test his theories (Wing, 1978).

10.1.3 Labelling theorists

We now turn from medical challenges to the idea of mental illness to those made by sociologists who are called 'labelling theorists'. These sociologists are essentially dissatisfied with the 'clinical' approach of contemporary psychiatry which focuses on patients' individual characteristics in explaining and treating mental ill-ness. Instead, the labelling theorists emphasize the social processes whereby certain behaviour comes to be defined as 'mental illness' and certain people come to be labelled as 'mentally ill'. Labelling theorists do not claim that there is no such thing as mental illness or that mental illness is really a rational way of coping with an intolerable situation; instead, they claim that it is merely society's way of defin-ing particular types of behaviour.

Mental illness as 'residual deviance'

During the 1960s these ideas were developed in an extreme form by T. Scheff, who went so far as to suggest that labelling is the single most important cause of mental illness (Scheff, 1966). Scheff's argument was that certain kinds of behaviour do not fit into the general pattern of social expectations — they upset the taken-for-grantedness of everyday life. Some of these odd, bizarre or 'deviant' behaviours, which do not fit into other categories for which society has already provided a label (such as 'criminal'), form what Scheff calls 'residual deviance'. According to him, most psychiatric symptoms can be seen as instances of residual deviance, which have become part of society's cultural stereotype of mental illness. For people whose behaviour is categorized in this way, the consequences may be very grave: a process may be set in train which can be likened to the old saying 'Give a dog a bad name'.

The effects of labelling

The situation is regarded as very serious by Scheff and other labelling theorists because they believe that the very act of labelling a person has profound effects.

First, society will tend thereafter to see that person in terms of the label — he will henceforth always be seen as someone who is 'mental' or 'mad'. The labelling theorists thus emphasize the long-term negative effects of being stigmatized as a psychiatric patient.

Secondly, the results of labelling may affect a person's own perception of him-self: he will come to believe that he is what the label says he is — mental and mad. Thus, a 'self-fulfilling prophecy' develops: a person is labelled as mentally ill; he then sees himself as someone who is indeed mentally ill and behaves accord-ingly; this reinforces other people's belief in his condition and their treatment of him. Mental illness is no more — or no less — than the result of these social processes.

The basis for labelling theory

There are *theoretical underpinnings* for labelling theory in the work of inter-actionists. In Chapter 1 we introduced some of the concepts they use, such as self-image, labelling and self-fulfilling prophecy. These concepts are also used, in a somewhat less extreme way, by other workers in the field of mental illness, such as A. Rose whose work we will be considering a little later in this chapter.

There are also some *research findings* which were used by Scheff to support his theory. He studied patterns of admissions and discharges in three hospitals in the

U.S.A. and claimed that psychiatrists tended to give patients very brief, superficial examinations and that they applied diagnostic categories carelessly. Their primary concern seemed to be the attachment of a medical label to people who had been brought to them for 'rule-breaking' by the courts or by their families. This is a serious indictment of psychiatric practice — and its implications are seen by labelling theorists as particularly worrying, since they believe that the application of a label will actually cause people to become what they are labelled.

Criticisms of labelling theory

Scheff's work has not passed unchallenged. One of the most severe critics has been another sociologist, W. Gove, who takes issue with both the assumptions and with the research findings (Gove, 1970). For example, Gove argues that the majority of people who become psychiatric patients suffer from a serious mental disturbance before any 'label' is applied to them. Therefore, their mental problem is *not a result of labelling.* He also criticizes Scheff's claim that once a person is identified as having psychiatric problems, he will be routinely 'processed' and institutionalized; instead, Gove points to the large numbers of patients who are 'screened out'. A similar point is made by the British psychiatrist, J. Wing, who argues that it is difficult to see how social processes would force a person 'to adopt the central schizophrenic syndrome since this would need special coaching from an expert' (Wing, 1973). Scheff has also been criticized for making unwarranted generalizations from limited research: even if the situation was as he described in the three hospitals in the U.S.A. in the early 1960s, this does not mean that all psychiatric practice is in this vein, or that there is no validity in the concept of mental illness.

In summary, it appears that the labelling theorists have drawn attention to some important considerations, such as the effects of stigma on patients. However, at present their case is unproven, and some of them have perhaps been guilty of trying to explain too much with inadequate theory and too little fact.

10.1.4   Critics of the concept of mental illness: conclusions

A. Miles has summarized some of the characteristics of the writers we have mentioned and considered the implications of their work (Miles, 1981). She claims:

'The various critics of the "illness" approach to mental disorder write from different perspectives and pursue different lines of argument, but there is a curiously common theme in their writings: an assumption that people become psychiatric patients through the ill-will and victimisation of others around them. In Laing's writings it appears that the schizophrenic patient is the victim of his family's particular dynamics and scapegoating; and Szasz emphasises that psychiatrists carry out the wishes of a hostile group when they call innocent, but non-conforming persons 'mentally disturbed'. Scheff, without spelling it out, implies that psychiatrists' endorsement of lay labelling means a medical approval of incompetent or malicious lay verdicts . . . . What is not crystallised in the various writings is why society or certain groups within it, should exhibit such hostility towards some, especially as the victims appear to be a diverse set of people. . . . Neither is any evidence given to show that the hostility exists. . . . On the contrary, there is considerable research evidence to show that family members and other lay associates of prospective patients apply the mental illness label with great reluctance and as a last resort.'

There are clearly many strands in the work of those who criticize the concept of mental illness. Their work forms an integral part of the 'anti-psychiatry' lobby.

10.2 The anti-psychiatry approach: contributions and criticisms

Miles provides a useful assessment of the 'anti-psychiatry' approach. She recognizes that it may make a valuable contribution in encouraging lay people to think critically about the quality of care provided for psychiatric patients and to be aware of the controversial nature of many issues concerning mental illness. Also, it highlights the importance of social processes in diagnosis and treatment.

However, there have been a number of unfortunate repercussions of their work:

(1) It tends to discredit psychiatry, particularly with those members of the reading public who are interested in health and social matters; they may consequently become less likely to press for improvements in psychiatric services.
(2) The relatives of psychiatric patients and other potential helpers tend to be confused by the arguments and may withdraw from providing support for patients.
(3) The work of the anti-psychiatry movement casts doubts on the motives, not only of the professionals, but also of the families of disturbed patients. For example, the writings of Laing and his colleagues suggest that it may well be the family which has driven the patient mad. This shifts the blame on to families who may be trying very hard to help a mentally ill relative, often at great cost.
(4) The anti-psychiatry approach seems to be singularly lacking in positive, constructive and well-tried alternatives. As Miles (1981) puts it:

'Meanwhile, what happens to the mentally disturbed, to those who are unable to leave the house because of a phobia, or to carry out simple actions because they feel themselves forbidden to do so . . .; or to those who suffer from many other incapacitating fears, threats, compulsions or distresses? The most serious charge that can be levied against the advocates of anti-psychiatry is that they leave suffering, helpless individuals without assistance and expose them, and their families and associates, to potential harm.'

We have devoted some space to discussing these issues because they are important both theoretically and practically. Since the ideas of the anti-psychiatry approach have affected public attitudes, they need to be discussed and debated by all concerned and nurses need to be as well informed as possible. It would therefore be useful if readers working in the psychiatric field could follow up references at the end of this chapter so that they can make up their own minds on these very controversial matters.

We will now consider some of the other ways in which sociologists have contributed to discussions of mental illness, assuming from now on that there is such a thing as mental illness and that reasonable agreement exists about its nature. First, we will look at ways in which social factors may play a part in its causation.

10.3   Social factors in the causation of mental illness

10.3.1   Mental illness and social class

One of sociology's major contributions to the study of mental illness has been the investigation of its social distribution. Numerous researchers have demonstrated a correlation between social class and psychiatric disorders. Lower socio-economic groups tend to suffer more from mental disorders in general, and from personality disorders and schizophrenia in particular. However, neuroses and manic depressive psychoses tend to be found more frequently among higher income groups (Faris and Dunham, 1939; Hollingshead and Redlich, 1958; Srole et al., 1962).

Three kinds of factors have been put forward to explain this correlation with social class: genetic factors, stress and social selection.

Genetic factors

Recent studies of monozygotic twins and adopted twins have shown that genetic factors alone cannot account for the onset of a psychiatric disorder such as schizophrenia; they may be significant, but sociocultural factors are also important (Dohrenwend, 1975).

Stress

The suggestion is that members of lower social classes are subjected to greater stress as a result of living in a deprived situation and having fewer resources with which to cope with the pressures and demands of life.

Social selection

Social selection, or the 'downward drift' hypothesis, maintains that more people with mental disorder are found in the lower social strata because they are unable to obtain or to hold responsible, well-paid jobs and so they have to resort to unskilled work. As their condition deteriorates, they 'drift' down the occupational scale and may also be forced to move into poor neighbourhoods with cheap housing. In other words, they suffer 'downward social mobility' as a result of their mental illness.

This hypothesis is not a satisfactory account of the cause of mental illness, for it does not explain why a person becomes afflicted in the first place. However, it seems to fit the case histories of many patients, especially schizophrenics. Several research studies have been undertaken to try to test it, but they have come up with differing results. For example, a British study (Goldberg and Morrison, 1963) considered the social background of 509 schizophrenic male patients. The researchers found a disproportionate number in social class V, even though their fathers' occupations were typical of the general population and not concentrated in this class. Therefore, there was a discrepancy between the social class position of fathers and sons, which suggested that the sons had indeed 'drifted' down the social scale. However, American studies such as the famous work by Hollingshead and Redlich (1958) have not found data to support the hypothesis and a lively debate has ensued.

In general, it seems that mental illness is such a complex phenomenon that it may be necessary to consider a variety of contributory causes, and it is probable that several processes may be involved in the relationship between psychiatric disorder and social class.

10.3.2 Mental illness and social stress

Social stress is another social factor which is often claimed to contribute to the development of mental illness. Stress may clearly be related to social class, but there are many stressful situations which occur independently of class position. A study which tried to disentangle some of the many causes of depression was undertaken by Brown and Harris (1978). They worked with two groups of women living in an Inner London borough; one group was a random sample of women aged 18–65; the other group was receiving treatment for depression. The study showed an association between certain 'stressful situations' or 'life events' and depression. These life events included, for example, the loss of a job or the threat of eviction from lodgings for non-payment of rent. Examples of stressful situations included living in a damp flat or the discovery that a son was taking drugs.

The study showed large differences between the social classes, with more depression among working class women than their middle class counterparts. But the pattern was not straightforward. For example, there seemed to be no class difference for women without children; but for women with children at home, there was a much greater likelihood of depression among the working class women — 1 in 5 compared with 1 in 20 for the middle class group.

Brown and Harris suggest four factors which may make women vulnerable to depression:

(1) Lack of social support such as that provided by a close relationship with someone who can act as a confidante.

(2) Loss of mother before the age of 11.
(3) Three or more children under 14 living at home.
(4) Not having any employment outside the home.

Three of these factors were found to be class-related; the fourth was not.

Such studies are useful for nurses because they highlight situations which are likely to predispose people to depression. They can alert us to cues and 'cries for help', and, by increasing our understanding of the factors involved, enable us to respond more appropriately.

√ 10.3.3   The interactionist approach to the development of mental illness

The relationship between social experience and the development of mental illness has been studied by interactionists other than those discussed earlier in the chapter. Two notable examples are included below.

Rose on neurosis

A. Rose has adopted this approach in a theory of the development of neurosis. Rose (1962) begins by emphasizing that many factors, including physiological ones, may be involved in the causation of neurotic disorders. He defines as 'neurotic' a person who holds a negative attitude towards himself, and he attempts to identify some of the *interpersonal* experiences which may be involved in the development of such an attitude. He begins by referring to G.H. Mead's idea of the 'self' — that concept of 'me' which is a reflection of the way a person perceives other people's reactions to him — and to Charles Cooley's closely related idea of the 'looking glass self'. He suggests that if other people react negatively, a person will tend to develop a poor self-image and low self-esteem. This may generate feelings of inadequacy and self-devaluation, and a tendency to behave in ways which are consistent with this low self-esteem, making him become, for example, withdrawn and unsociable. This in turn may engender negative responses from other people, which will confirm and intensify his already negative feelings about himself. The result is a downward spiral:

> 'If the reaction of others is generally negative, and the individual gets a correct perception of this negative reaction, and if he accepts this negative evaluation, our proposition is that the individual becomes neurotic. In other words, an element in the chain of causes leading to neurosis is held to be the social–psychological factor of self-mutilation . . . . A depreciated or "mutilated" self is a major factor in the development of neurosis . . . .'

This approach to the development of mental disorder has clear implications for the way in which we relate to each other. It highlights the importance of making people feel that they are individuals worthy of love, esteem and appreciation, particularly during the formative years of childhood when a young person is establishing his own self-image.

But the implications go far beyond childhood. Rose extends his analysis to the development of neurotic disorders such as involutional melancholia in adults, and suggests that the tendency for this condition to develop between the ages of 45 and 55 for women, and 55 and 70 for men, may be associated with changing social roles. These are the years when, in our society, traumatic changes in life-roles occur: women lose their child-rearing and maternal functions as children grow to independence; and men lose their occupational roles as they reach retirement age. Both men and women may feel useless and that their lives no longer have any purpose or meaning. Rose therefore suggests that the kind of depression which often characterizes men and women in these age groups may have social origins and that the tendency to attribute it to physiological causes such as the glandular changes associated with the menopause or other ageing processes may be an oversimplification.

The therapeutic recommendations following from this analysis include psychotherapy which helps the individual to redefine his self-image in more positive ways which will in turn help him to establish more positive social relationships and a more satisfying way of life:

> 'Our own contribution here limits itself to a psychotherapy of redefining the situation, redefining the self through a redefinition of the situation, and to a broader treatment process which involves changing the objective social situation. The goal is the development of a positive attitude towards the self, and a realistic recognition of the attainable ways in which the changing self can continue to function in a changing social environment.'

Becker on psychosis

E. Becker offers a similar kind of analysis, which considers some of the ways in which unhappy social experiences may lead to difficulties in forming good relationships and to problems of interpersonal communication (Becker, 1962). However, instead of applying his work to the development of neuroses, Becker refers to the psychoses, particularly schizophrenia. In addition, Cox (1973) argues that the 'redefinition of self' is a major component in group psychotherapy, as the title of his article indicates: 'Group psychotherapy as a redefining process'.

10.4   The social experience of being a patient

Sociologists have shown particular interest in the ways in which people who suffer from mental illness are treated, particularly in institutions. One of the most famous of these studies is by E. Goffman who also uses the interactionist approach (Goffman, 1961).

10.4.1   Goffman and the 'total institution'

Goffman's book *Asylums* is not written specifically about institutions for the mentally ill; however, it is sub-titled: 'Essays on the Social Situation of Mental

Patients and Other Inmates'. One of Goffman's key concepts is the 'total institution' — a place where inmates live together, sharing all aspects of life, including working, eating and sleeping, and where their time is organized for them by the officials in charge. Total institutions can be of various kinds: mental hospitals, prisons, monasteries, convents and boarding schools. However, a key factor in evaluating the effects of total institutions is the extent to which an inmate's stay is voluntary or enforced. This is particularly important because Goffman suggests that an important characteristic of total institutions is their tendency to change people. If someone wishes to be changed — as, presumably, a monk might wish to develop his spiritual life — this may be desirable. But if a person is coerced into such an institution, the experience may not be desired and may even be harmful.

Goffman describes some of the routines which are often adopted in total institutions and suggests that they may result in depersonalization and loss of identity. Such routines include the admission procedures, which may involve loss of personal possessions and clothing — a person's own 'identity kit'. Also, in some places, inmates are 'initiated' by being forced to undergo certain humiliating procedures. Then there are various experiences of 'contamination' associated with having to carry out personal and intimate procedures in public, or in close proximity to other people. This is often very traumatic, since it represents a hurtful invasion of privacy and can arouse feelings of repugnance. These unpleasant and humiliating experiences may be exacerbated, Goffman suggests, by the culture of the institution which sets up divisions between staff and inmates. Staff, for example, may assume the right to adopt intimate forms of address, which represent an invasion of privacy and an asymmetrical relationship of staff authority and inmate deference.

In essence, Goffman suggests that total institutions may be psychologically very destructive if they adopt routines which are humiliating and which erode the autonomy and the identity of inmates.

Goffman's book was written over twenty years ago. It attracted considerable attention, and many attempts have since been made to try to reform the ways in which mental hospitals are run. However, it is well worth reading in order to see to what extent you think his account may still be relevant, not only for mental hospitals, but also for other kinds of residential institution such as homes and hospitals for the chronic sick and the elderly.

10.4.2   Towell on psychiatric nursing

The care of patients in hospital has also been studied in detail in D. Towell's work *Understanding Psychiatric Nursing* (Towell, 1975). Towell portrays a psychiatric hospital and describes the work of nurses in admission, therapeutic community and geriatric wards. He found that the nurses' attitudes to the treatment of patients varied on the different types of ward and these differences were related to their relationships with and care of patients. For example, on the admission ward, nursing perspectives were strongly influenced by the 'medical model' of treatment based on medical diagnostic categories, and variations in the extent to which patients were regarded as 'ill' affected the nurses' relationships with them:

'. . . patients not regarded as "ill" (notably those described as "hysterical" or having "personality disorders") thereby lost their claim to receive help, were less likely to be shown acceptance by the nurses, and more likely to be responded to with negative sanctions when engaging in behaviour deviating from ward expectations.'

The orientation of nurses to patients was somewhat different on the other two types of ward: on the therapeutic community ward there was a strong emphasis on patients' personal problems, whereas the geriatric ward was characterized by 'little staff concern for treatment'. There, 'the categories used to describe patients were derived directly from the problems patient behaviours constituted for nurses in carrying out the daily routines which were their dominant concern. In the course of action there was a tendency for patients to become the partially depersonalised objects of these task-centred routines; a tendency encouraged by the use of organicist interpretations of patient behaviours drawn from the wider medical context'.

Towell concludes that these and other findings have far-reaching implications. He suggests that they indicate a need not only for more resources for psychiatric services, but also 'careful consideration of the need for innovations in conceptions of treatment, staff training and hospital organisation'.

10.5 Rehabilitation of ex-psychiatric patients

10.5.1 Post-patient experiences

Many patients who have been in psychiatric hospitals experience problems after they are discharged into the community. There is nothing new in this. Miller (1970) quotes an anonymous Elizabethan poet who described the plight of 'Poor Tom' once he had been released from 'Bedlam' – the colloquial historic name given to Bethlem Hospital, London, an institution for the mentally ill:

In the bonny halls of Bedlam,
Ere I was one-and-twenty,
I had bracelets strong, sweet whips ding-dong,
And prayer and fasting plenty.
Now I do sing, 'Any food, any feeding,
Feeding, drink or clothing?
Come dame, or maid, be not afraid,
Poor Tom will injure nothing'.

Miller goes on to say:

'What happens to patients inside mental hospitals has changed greatly in the four centuries since Poor Tom sang his song. What happens to them outside has changed too, but not nearly so much — the labelling and stigma, the loss of livelihood, the feelings of isolation, worthlessness, bitterness and depression. "Once a patient, always a patient", a released state mental patient told us. She was talking about the feelings of disgrace and hopelessness that follow them, like a long haunting shadow, often for the rest of their lives.'

Stigma and stigma management

Much of the research on the experiences of ex-mental patients has been concerned with the effects of the stigma which arises because of the cultural stereotype of mental illness and the generally negative attitudes of the public to mental patients. For example, a number of studies have shown that many people perceive former psychiatric patients as incompetent, undesirable and unpredictable. It is therefore not surprising that many patients are very apprehensive about facing the world again when they leave hospital.

In a study of discharged patients, Cumming and Cumming (1968) claim: 'We found two basic evidences of stigmatization: the first an outright expression of shame or inferiority because of hospitalization, and the second an expectation of discrimination or inferior treatment from others.'

Goffman also discusses this problem and uses the phrase 'stigma management' to depict ways in which ex-patients cope with the situation. One way is to adopt the strategy of 'passing', whereby a person conceals his identity as an ex-psychiatric patient. This strategy carries with it the cost of perpetual fear of discovery. Consequently, others may choose to speak openly about their experiences and hope to demonstrate that they are now reformed and 'acceptable' persons.

In a study of over 1000 former mental patients in California, Miller (1970) tried to identify factors which would help an ex-mental patient to remain out of hospital. Four factors were highlighted:

(1) Adequate material and professional support.
(2) The availability of someone who cared about the patient and provided close support in his attempts to cope with the outside world.
(3) The opportunity to develop a series of spontaneous positive relationships.
(4) A situation in which the patient could exercise some degree of control.

10.5.2   Home and hospital care

Any account of the conditions necessary for effective rehabilitation of ex-psychiatric patients in the community must consider the relative advantages and disadvantages of home and hospital care. Since the mid-1950s the emphasis has been on community care and there has been a tendency for more rapid discharge from hospital. However, as Mechanic (1969) has pointed out, some patients who have shown signs of remission in hospital suffer a return of symptoms when they go home. This may indicate problems in the home environment which have persisted and which confront the patient on his discharge. Relapses may also be due to the cyclical nature of some psychiatric conditions. Whatever the reason for relapse, the recurrence of problems and the associated need to readmit some patients has resulted in the cynical comment that the policy of the 'open door' has developed into the policy of the 'revolving door'.

This is, of course, no argument against the development of community care; rather, it emphasizes the importance of community psychiatric services and the role of the community psychiatric nurse. And it also indicates that decisions about whether to opt for hospital or community care may depend on the characteristics of each individual case. Merely to conclude that institutional life is dehumanizing and therefore necessarily bad — a reaction of some people to critiques, such as those by Goffman described above — is to overlook situations in which it may be the better alternative.

10.6   Allegations of the over-use and abuse of psychiatry

Before we leave the subject of the care of the mentally ill, we should refer to another area of contemporary controversy which needs to be recognized by anyone interested in this subject: allegations of the 'over-use' and of the 'abuse' of psychiatry.

10.6.1   'Over-use' of psychiatry

There are some workers, such as Freidson (1973), who argue that more and more behaviour is being included under the umbrella of psychiatry. For example, some kinds of problems are now seen as the prerogative of the psychiatrist which in previous eras were seen as requiring the attention of the law or of the church:

> 'The increasing emphasis on the label of illness, then, has been at the expense of the labels of both crime and sin and has been narrowing the limits if not weakening the jurisdiction of the traditional control institutions of religion and law.'

This can have insidious consequences. For example, Kittrie (1971) argues that the labelling of the deviant as 'ill' may lead to greater infringements of his liberty, albeit for humanitarian reasons, than other kinds of social response. For example, a convicted offender who is sent to a special hospital, such as Broadmoor, has no formal 'sentence' and therefore no idea of how long he may be kept there. This may be harder to bear than the fate of an offender who is sent to prison. Even if the prison sentence is long, it does have an end-point and the prisoner can adjust to this. Also, there is a great onus of responsibility on the medical staff who must decide if and when a patient should be discharged. Agonizing decisions may have to be made in the attempts to achieve the right balance between the safety of the public and the desire for freedom of individual patients.

10.6.2 'Abuse' of psychiatry

The concern here is with the use of psychiatry as an explicit agent of social and political control. While it can be argued that this may happen in any society, it is perhaps seen in its most extreme form in some modern totalitarian societies. For example, the use of psychiatry to 'treat' political and religious dissidents in the U.S.S.R. has been well documented and the brutality of some of the treatments has been described in the Amnesty International Report (1975). Lader (1977) also discusses the abuse of psychiatry, particularly in the Soviet Union, and condemns the practice of using it as a means of repression and coercion. So we conclude where we began: with controversy, and an exhortation to read the work of some of these writers and to make up your own minds.

■ Summary

The controversy as to whether mental illness exists is explored. Szasz claims that there is no such thing, but just actual 'illnesses' or 'problems of living', while other writers argue against current ideas of mental illness. The 'labelling theorists', such as Scheff, accept the fact of mental illness, but suggest that labelling people as mentally ill can actually cause such illness. These workers are criticized by more orthodox thinkers, such as Miles, who consider that the case is unproven due to the use of inadequate theory and too little fact. Social factors are believed to contribute to mental illness, and Rose's analysis of neurosis suggests that negative attitudes of other people, especially during an individual's formative years, and the changes in social roles at middle age may be involved in the causation of neurotic disorders.

Of particular interest to sociologists are the effects that institutions and the attitudes of nurses have upon patients, and the works of Goffman and of Towell on these aspects are instructive. Sociologists also recognize the adverse effects that social stigma has on the discharged patient. Finally, the chapter mentions other controversies — the alleged over-use and abuse of psychiatry.

■ Questions

1. Give a brief account of the following:
   (a) the 'myth of mental illness';
   (b) the 'family as a cause of schizophrenia'.
   (c) labelling theory.

2. In what ways have sociologists criticized the 'medical model' of mental illness? Do you agree with them?
3. How may sociology enhance our understanding of some of the processes in the causation, experience and treatment of mental illness?
4. Compare and contrast some of the criticisms of the 'use' and 'abuse' of psychiatry in Britain and the U.S.S.R.

References

Amnesty International Report (1975). *Prisoners of Conscience in the USSR: Their Treatment and Conditions*, London, Amnesty International.

Becker, E. (1962). 'Socialization: command of performance and mental illness', *American Journal of Sociology*, vol. 67; reprinted in *A Sociology of Medical Practice*, Cox, C. and Mead, A. (Eds.), London, Collier Macmillan, 1975.

Brown, G.W. and Harris, T. (1978). *Social Origins of Depression: A Study of Psychiatric Disorder in Women*, London, Tavistock.

Cox, M. (1973). 'Group psychotherapy as a redefining process', *International Journal of Group Psychotherapy*, vol. 23, no. 4, pp. 465–473.

Cumming, J. and Cumming, E. (1968). *On the Stigma of Mental Illness*, in *The Mental Patient*, Spitzer, S.R. and Denzin, N.K. (Eds.), New York, McGraw-Hill.

Dohrenwend, B.P. (1975). 'Sociocultural and social-psychological factors in the genesis of mental disorders', *Journal of Health and Social Behaviour*, vol. 16, pp. 365–392.

Faris, R.E.L. and Dunham, H.W. (1939). *Mental Disorders in Urban Areas*, Chicago, University Press.

Freidson, E. (1973). *Profession of Medicine: A Study of the Sociology of Applied Knowledge*, New York, Dodd & Mead.

Goffman, E. (1961). *Asylums: Essays on the Social Situation of Mental Patients and Other Inmates*, New York, Doubleday.

Goldberg, E.M. and Morrison, S.L. (1963). 'Schizophrenia and social class', *British Journal of Psychiatry*, vol. 109, pp. 785–802.

Gove, W. (1970). 'Societal reaction as an explanation of mental illness: an evaluation', *American Sociological Review*, vol. 35, pp. 873–884.

Hollingshead, A. and Redlich, R.C. (1958). *Social Class and Mental Illness*, New York, John Wiley.

Kittrie, N. (1971). *The Right to be Different: Deviance and Enforced Therapy*, Baltimore and London, The Johns Hopkins Press.

Lader, M. (1977). *Psychiatry on Trial*, Harmondsworth, Penguin.

Laing, R. and Esterson, A. (1964). *Sanity, Madness and the Family*, London, Tavistock.

Mechanic, D. (1969). *Mental Health and Social Policy*, Englewood Cliffs, New Jersey, Prentice-Hall Inc.

Miles, A. (1981). *The Mentally Ill in Contemporary Society*, Oxford, Martin Robertson.

Miller, D.H. (1970). 'Worlds that fail', in *Where Medicine Fails*, Strauss, A. (Ed.), Chicago, Aldine.

Rose, A.M. (1962). 'A socio-psychological theory of neurosis', in *Human Behaviour and Social Processes*, Rose, A. (Ed.), London, Routledge & Kegan Paul; reprinted in *A Sociology of Medical Practice*, Cox, C. and Mead, A. (Eds.), London, Collier Macmillan, 1975.

Roth, M. (1976). 'Schizophrenia and the theories of Thomas Szasz', *British Journal of Psychiatry*, vol. 129, pp. 317–326.

Scheff, T. (1966). *Being Mentally Ill: A Sociological Theory*, Chicago, Aldine.

Srole, L., Langner, T.S., Michael, S.T., Opler, M.K. and Rennie, T.A.C. (1962). *Mental Health in the Metropolis: The Midtown Manhattan Study*, New York, McGraw-Hill.

Szasz, T. (1961). *The Myth of Mental Illness*, New York, Harper.

Towell, D. (1975). *Understanding Psychiatric Nursing: A Sociological Analysis of Modern Psychiatric Nursing Practice*, London, Royal College of Nursing.

Wing, J. (1973). *Schizophrenia: Medical and Social Madness*; quoted in Clare, A., *Psychiatry in Dissent*, London, Tavistock.

Wing, J. (1978). *Reasoning about Madness*, London, Oxford University Press.

Further reading

Altschul, A. (1972). *Patient–Nurse Interaction: A Study of Interaction Patterns in Acute Psychiatric Wards*, Edinburgh, Churchill Livingstone. A book which raises profoundly important questions for nurses concerning the theoretical basis for sound nursing practice; the training in personal relationships given to nurses; communication between members of the psychiatric team; and the criteria for evaluating nursing care.

Lader, M. (1977). *Psychiatry on Trial*, Harmondsworth, Penguin. Written by a psychiatrist who is concerned about the use of psychiatry for political purposes: 'When a branch of medicine deals with intangibles like delusions, when it cannot agree on diagnosis, when treatments are introduced on insufficient evidence, when its relationships with the law are vague and contentious, it is open to manipulation from within and without.' Recent developments in the Soviet Union are discussed — where political and religious dissidents with no hint of emotional instability are diagnosed as 'schizophrenic', committed to prison mental hospitals and subjected to forcible drug treatments.

Miles, A. (1981). *The Mentally Ill in Contemporary Society: A Sociological Introduction*, Oxford, Martin Robertson. A comprehensive account of some of the major contemporary issues in the sociology of mental illness. Delightfully jargon-free. Well referenced. A very useful source book.

Occupational therapy at the Royal Hospital and Home for Incurables (© RHHI; reproduced by permission of the RHHI)

(It is the challenge for those who care for the chronic sick to find sources of fulfilment for their patients . . . — see p. 165)

11 Sociological aspects of the care of the chronic sick

Many writers have suggested that our present health care system is based on a 'medical model' of disease and cure which is particularly appropriate for acute illnesses. However, as we saw in Chapter 2, patterns of morbidity and mortality are changing, and there are now growing numbers of people in our society who suffer from some form of handicap or chronic illness. Tuckett (1976) points to some implications of these changes:

> 'The present pattern of disease means that doctors are now mainly called upon to treat conditions that prevent individuals from performing self-supporting activities or from developing the intellectual and physical potentialities needed to achieve an inner sense of well-being — that is, conditions like chronic rheumatism and arthritis, chronic bronchitis, diabetes, epilepsy, anaemia, multiple sclerosis, and various forms of mental "difficulties". With these kinds of diseases the main danger is not that inadequate practice on the part of the doctor will lead to the patient's death, but that it will lead to unnecessary suffering, discontent, inconvenience, or humiliation. Furthermore, since modern medical techniques often keep alive a patient who in earlier times might have died, the doctor now has to help a patient react to and cope with the handicaps that the onset of a condition may impose.'

For 'doctors' read 'nurses', and for 'treat' read 'care for' and the relevance of this passage for nursing is clear.

11.1 The characteristics of chronic illness

Fabrega and Manning (1972) have classified illnesses according to the following characteristics:

(1) Duration; for example, short and relatively predictable as in measles, or long-term and perhaps ultimately fatal as in multiple sclerosis.
(2) Prognosis, or the possibility of cure and recovery.

(3)   The degree of discomfort and incapacity involved.
(4)   The 'potential for self-degradation', or the degree of stigmatization which patients may incur.

Chronic illnesses differ on all these characteristics from short-term, acute illnesses, since they often (a) are less clearly defined at onset and in duration; (b) are much more uncertain in the course they take; (c) bring the prospect of a future characterized by varying degrees of permanent disability and distress; (d) involve a degree of social stigma.

11.1.1   Chronic illness and social stigma

Fabrega and Manning differentiate 'non-stigmatizing' conditions, such as cardiac disease and those which, in our society, are 'stigmatizing', because they set the individual apart from other people in everyday life in ways which are humiliating. Thus, they bring not only physical suffering and inconvenience, but also psychological distress and feelings of inferiority.
Goffman (1963) describes stigma in this way:

> '...we believe the person with a stigma is not quite human. On this assumption we exercise varieties of discrimination, through which we effectively, if often unthinkingly, reduce his life chances... . We tend to impute a wide range of imperfections on the basis of the original one... . Further, we may perceive his defensive response to his situation as a direct expression of his defect.'

Goffman highlights one of the effects of stigma as 'spoiled identity'. This is most likely to happen with conditions resulting in physical deformity and with some psychiatric conditions (see Chapter 10). Goffman emphasizes that people who are afflicted in such a way suffer from the additional problem that their stigmatized identity overrides their other attributes. Thus, instead of being seen as an 'ordinary' person who happens to have a particular affliction, they are seen instead primarily in terms of that affliction. Their individual characteristics, abilities and aspirations tend to be overlooked. Moreover, they tend to see themselves as others see them.
Davis (1963) describes some of the dilemmas experienced by such people in his account of the poignant experiences of polio victims:

> '...it is more than likely that he will share, initially at least, many of the prejudiced and squeamish attitudes that are commonly shown toward the handicapped. He will tend, openly or secretly, to place a high value on many activities and pursuits that are closed to him because of his impairment. His attempts, if any, to be accepted by "normals" as "normal" are doomed to failure and frustration: not only do most "normals" find it difficult to include the handicapped person fully in their own category of being, but he himself, in that he shares the "normal" standards of personal evaluation, will in a sense support their rejection of him... .'

It is important to remember that physical disability and chronic illness affect not only the individual but also his family. Their range of activities may become severely curtailed and, if the disability is one which carries stigma, they may acquire what Goffman calls a 'courtesy stigma' — one which results from close association with someone who is stigmatized. Therefore, they too may suffer not only worry and inconvenience, but also embarrassments and inhibitions in personal relationships.

11.2 Care of the chronic sick in institutions

The experience of hospitalization for a patient with a clearly defined condition which is susceptible to treatment, even if such treatment is unpleasant and lengthy, is clearly very different from that of a patient in long-term or indefinite care for a chronic condition. For the former, the 'medical model' of treatment and rehabilitation applies and there is an expectation of recovery. His ordeal can be alleviated by hope. But for the latter, his future may lie wholly within the institution, and his only prospect is one of continued infirmity and eventual death.

Another difference lies in the type of institution caring for the chronic sick. A number of sociological studies have compared the attitudes and behaviour of staff caring for the chronic sick with those of staff caring for other kinds of patients.

11.2.1 The findings of Coser

Coser (1963), for example, in a study of a community hospital in the U.S.A., showed how tensions could develop if staff had been trained to think in terms of 'curability' which were inappropriate for the conditions of their patients. When such staff were responsible for the long-term care of patients who could not be cured, they tended to become apathetic and 'alienated'.

In Coser's discussion of 'alienation' she referred to experiences described by sociologists writing about people working in other occupations (Seeman, 1959) and she found that the nurses in her study had similar experiences:

(1) They felt *powerless*, in that they were unable to achieve any goal which they perceived as worthwhile.
(2) Their work felt *meaningless*, because they could see no gratifying results and consequently they could not achieve a satisfying self-image.
(3) They therefore felt '*self-estranged*', because they could not develop satisfactory social and occupational identities.
(4) They were also often *isolated*. This isolation was of two kinds. First, professional isolation, with little contact with other colleagues working in the same field; second, geographical isolation, because the chronic sick were cared for in buildings which were set apart from others.

As a result of this tendency towards alienation, staff were likely to adopt one of two alternative kinds of adjustments:

(a) *Ritualism* — where they concentrated on meticulously following the rules of the institution, without attempting any individual initiatives or imaginative innovations in patient care.

(b) *Retreatism* — where they just escaped as far as possible from any involvement or commitment.

The significance of Coser's findings is highlighted by a comparison she made between the attitudes of these nurses and of other nurses who were working on a rehabilitation ward. She asked both groups of nurses a number of questions: when they thought the ward looked at its best; what were the most important needs of the ward; what they liked most and least about their work; and what they saw as their most important tasks. Analysis of the answers revealed that the nurses on the long-stay ward found their work more mechanical, task specific and concerned with 'housekeeping'; nurses on the rehabilitation ward were more interested in patients' activities and social relationships, and with their own professional achievements.

11.2.2 The findings of Miller and Gwynne

Another small-scale study which compared two different kinds of care of the chronic sick is that of Miller and Gwynne (1974). These authors adopt somewhat provocative labels to designate two models of care in institutions for the young chronic sick: the 'warehousing' and the 'horticultural' models. As the names imply, the former depicts those institutions which are primarily concerned with their patients' physical condition. They may encourage dependence and do little to promote the realization of their patients' potential. The latter are likely to provide more individualized care and to encourage patients to be self-sufficient. However, Miller and Gwynne point out that each model has its problems. The former may inhibit patients from living as full a life as possible; the latter may make too many demands on their patients and cause them distress, especially if they are going through a stage of relapse in which they would welcome more support and care.

Miller and Gwynne therefore suggest that a balance needs to be struck between the assumptions behind these models of care and in the policies which follow from them. They also highlight a very disturbing feature of the institutional care of the young chronic sick — the phenomenon which they describe as 'social death'. (This term appears elsewhere in this book, with a rather different meaning — see Chapter 13, where its use by Sudnow is mentioned, in the distinction he makes between 'biological' and 'social' death.) Here, Miller and Gwynne use the term to describe the unhappy situation in which young people with chronic illness or handicap who are admitted to an institution may become socially isolated: their families and friends may rarely, if ever, visit them and they can become cut off from the wider world.

11.2.3 The findings of Roth

A third example of work which analyses some of the problems in providing institutional care for the chronic sick by Roth (1970). He describes the situation at 'Farewell Hospital' — a 'chronic care institution' — and points out that its purpose was to rehabilitate patients, but that this was a misplaced aim as the life for which they were being rehabilitated was one which most of them would never have the opportunity to lead. He describes the atmosphere and tempo of the hospital:

> 'The chronic custodial institution, in comparison with a short-term treatment institution, seems like a study in slow motion. Even the staff of several years' experience are often misled about the pace at which their programme moves. Their predictions about when a patient will reach a given point in his programme almost always fall short. "Transfer to two weeks" becomes three months.... "Will have information from his consultation next week" means information two months later. It is something the staff becomes accustomed to.... It is something the patients also become accustomed to, but with much more bitterness. Another characteristic common to such institutions is that they foster social and economic dependence....'

In 'Farewell Hospital', many staff only come for short periods to obtain experience. But of those who stay longer, most:

> 'come to more or less accept the limited selection of patients, the delays, the institutional assaults upon the patient's initiative, and the fact that the rehabilitation programme has little relationship to the larger institution where most people end up feeling rejected and abandoned. It is not surprising therefore that most of the most experienced staff members turn their backs on the therapy programme and spend as much of their time as possible building professional enclaves of research, administration and teaching — activities which, in part, serve as an escape from a treatment programme which offers little satisfaction and reward.'

11.2.4 Discussion of the foregoing sociological studies

The studies cited above sound like a formidable indictment of the staff who are trying to care for the chronic sick, often in very difficult circumstances. It is therefore important to point out that writers such as Coser are not seeking to criticize the nurses, but to show how problems and shortcomings in the care provided for patients are rooted in the culture of the organization in which they work. In other words, many of the problems were caused by the inappropriateness of the 'medical model', with its emphasis on cure, which was so inadequate for the care of those for whom there was no cure. For example, staff had been trained or 'socialized' into this medical model, and they consequently sought goals associated with 'cure'; where these were unattainable, they had little else by which to judge their work or to provide a basis for job satisfaction. Similarly, patients were often left without any therapeutic regime or any strategy for making the most of their limited capacities.

It thus appears that there is a need for staff who work in all institutions caring for the chronic sick to set a series of goals, appropriately graded for each patient, which will provide him with the most advantageous blend of opportunity for self-fulfilment to the limit of his capacities, together with the appropriate level of care to help with his disabilities. This would help to individualize care and to improve the quality of life of the patients; it would also help to make the work of staff more meaningful and rewarding. This approach is, of course, already adopted in many places. But the studies described above suggest that there may be others where this is not yet the case; and if the problems they describe still exist, this may be to the detriment of both patients and staff.

11.3   The care of the chronic sick in the community

11.3.1   The investigations of Kratz

Two studies will be used to illustrate problems associated with the care of the chronic sick in their own homes. First, the study by Kratz (1978), which had two objectives: (a) to investigate the problems of patients with long-term illness in the community, observing which factors motivated nurses to give different levels of care to patients with similar disabilities; (b) to provide experience in the application of sociological research methods to nursing problems.

Kratz was interested in the nursing care provided in the community for patients suffering from the effects of a 'stroke'. She found that nurses tended to base their performance on the knowledge and values acquired during their general training in hospital. For example, they knew about, and valued, some kinds of care more than others:

(1) They knew about, and valued, the care of seriously ill patients.
(2) They valued the care of patients waiting to go into hospital, and were reasonably knowledgeable about their care.
(3) They were not very clear about the care they should provide for patients who were getting better, but they quite valued looking after them.
(4) They did not know about caring for patients who were not getting better and they did not value caring for them very highly.

In discussing her findings, Kratz distinguished two components of the nurses' knowledge: knowing why something was done, and knowing how to do it. The former gave a sense of purpose to an action; the latter was associated with the level of skill. Thus, when caring for acutely ill patients, nurses knew both why and how to act; similarly, with patients awaiting admission to hospital, they knew within certain limits what needed to be done and how to do it. However, with patients who were not getting better, they felt uncertain about what they should be doing and consequently received little satisfaction. These findings are summarized in *Figure 11.1.*

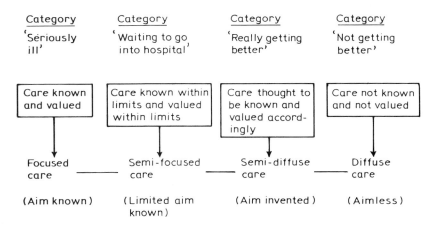

Figure 11.1   The continuum of care (From Kratz, 1978, by courtesy of Churchill Livingstone, publishers, Edinburgh)

In essence, Kratz found that where nurses knew, or thought they knew, what care was needed, they gave it and valued doing so. But where they were uncertain, nurses did not value caring for patients and often failed to meet their needs.

Kratz also found that nurses tended to expect patients to learn to 'manage' and to become independent of their ministrations as soon as possible. Associated with this attitude was a perception of some patients who refused to 'manage' as 'unfair': they took up too much of that scarce commodity — the nurse's time.

11.3.2   McIntosh on communicating with patients in their homes

There are some similarities between Kratz's findings and those of J. McIntosh's study of the care of the chronic sick in the community (McIntosh, 1981). She found that community nurses tended to categorize relatives caring for patients at home in terms of two stereotypes: 'copers' and 'non-copers'. She found that 'non-copers' were identified by nurses in the few cases in which there was evidence of neglect of patients, all of whom were suffering from a stroke. In these instances, relatives seemed unable to confront the painful change which had come into their lives, so they turned away from the situation and neglected the patient.

McIntosh says:

'It is worth considering why nurses describe "neglect" as "not coping". This is an important issue because it shows how in-built attitudes and assumptions can prevent nurses from giving the most practical advice. One starting point is the fact that almost everyone holds values about caring for the sick, and to most people it seems unnatural and inhuman to neglect a patient. "Neglect" is not acceptable to most nurses, and strong professional and societal norms reinforce the desirability of "good nursing care". Since "neglect" is rarely recognised as an adaptation process, it is tempting for the community nurse to stereotype such relatives as "non-copers" and to regard them as "failures".'

She goes on to describe how nurses will consequently confine their contributions to correcting 'failings', and points out that this is likely to generate hostility or apathy, as in the following case:

'One home where the wife was neglecting her husband was visited by a number of nurses, and many of them expressed their disapproval of this state of affairs. Their feelings were understandable since clean clothes were never put out, the house smelt of stale urine, and the husband always looked unkempt with trails of spilt food down his shirt-front. Most of the nurses' remarks to the wife referred explicitly or implicitly to her "failings". However, one day while the nurse was giving a bed bath and chatting to the patient, the observer heard a conversation between the wife and a visitor just outside the bathroom door. The wife tearfully explained how the continual washing was "getting her down", that meal times were a trial because his eating habits nauseated her, and his double incontinence disgusted her.'

McIntosh concludes that this old lady's failure to put out clean linen was actually a 'coping mechanism' for avoiding the burden of washing, and the failure to help with feeding her husband was a response to her problems of coping with the sad consequences of his stroke. The nurses' disapproval of her behaviour had acted as a barrier to fruitful discussion about ways of overcoming her difficulties — such as using a feeding cup.

It is important to realize that this illustration is not intended as an implied criticism of the nurses involved, but to show how community nurses need to be aware of the complex reasons which may lie behind the phenomenon which may be perceived as 'neglect'. As McIntosh points out:

'If nurses were taught to regard an old lady's sad neglect of her husband as one among several alternative coping mechanisms that relatives can adopt, then their communication with both patient and relative might be much more effective.'

11.4 Chronic illness and the quality of life

'Why is a fifty-year-old woman, "a prisoner in my bathroom", compulsively (and unnecessarily) irrigating a colostomy for twelve hours every other day — six years after successful cancer surgery?' 'Why does a thirty-five-year-old mother with three children remain a virtual recluse — five years after the loss of a breast in a successful battle against cancer?' These questions are asked by Bard (1970) who goes on to say:

> 'Tragic stories like these are dramatic evidence of the gap between today's remarkable advances in medical technology and the unpredictable paradoxes of human emotions and behaviour. Such stories of "death expectancy" reveal untold suffering for people whose lives have been saved, and for their families. They suggest a disturbing thought — more lives are being saved, but *for what?* Why should the gift of life be so bitter to the survivors of major illnesses who, only a few years ago, would have invariably died?'

11.4.1   Emotional stresses on cancer patients

In the article 'The price of survival for cancer victims', Bard (1970) looks at some of the problems encountered by people afflicted with this particular form of chronic illness:

> 'Cancer patients must be regarded as people under a special and severe form of stress. Cancer is commonly perceived as an always-fatal and particularly loathsome disease, not "clean" and uncomplicated like, for example, the frequently more fatal heart disease. In addition to the expectation of prolonged and intense pain, it carries the threat of disability and, even more frighteningly, recurrence and the repeated threat of death. Thus cancer becomes an unusually stressful experience which disrupts the most important lifelong patterns of behaviour.'

Bard goes on to describe the 'reality sequence', which is similar to that for other diseases, but carries particularly frightening connotations resulting from the diagnosis of cancer. It consists of four stages: (a) the onset of symptoms; (b) the diagnosis; (c) the hospitalization; (d) the convalescence.

Onset of symptoms and the diagnosis

The patient's initial fears commence with the first two stages in the reality sequence:

> 'When the first symptom is recognized, the patient immediately begins to anticipate what he thinks will happen to him during treatment. This anticipation is based on the generally frightening ideas many people have about cancer . . . . For example, patients may project into the future their concern about recurrence; or anticipate social rejection if mutilating surgery is necessary; or develop feelings of unacceptability.'

Hospitalization

Hospitalization may carry special fears and anxieties for the patient with cancer:

> 'Some patients interviewed on the day of admission to the hospital express feelings of being trapped and helpless . . . . If they are ward patients, they observe the experience of other patients in a highly selective way to corroborate their

fears. The importance of the day of admission cannot be over-emphasized. His very presence in the hospital reinforces for the patient all the fears and anticipations which first occurred at the onset of symptoms and continued throughout the period of diagnosis.'

Bard goes on to describe the psychological states of many patients before and after surgery, pointing out that dejection, acute anxiety and even thoughts of suicide are all likely to be experienced. The importance of recognizing these tendencies and of providing emotional support cannot be over-emphasized:

'It is important to remember that, although they are commonly regarded as regressive reactions, depression and dependence are both appropriate and temporary for most patients. Often they can be regarded as a prelude to the process of emotional repair. To what extent these feelings persist depends a great deal on the amount of help the patient gets in solving his problems. Unless he has adequate help, the patient may not be able to solve them, and chronic depression, restriction of function, and pathological dependence may persist long after hospitalization.'

Convalescence

Bard draws our attention to some of the problems which may await patients returning home after treatment for cancer. They include fears of being unacceptable because of the nature of the disease — especially if it has resulted in mutilating surgery; and fears of being unable to cope with the demands of daily living, on account of physical weakness.

Finally, the importance of communication is stressed:

'In general, then, the problem of emotional adaptation to cancer and its treatment is inseparable from the larger problems of human communication. Anxiety, present in every cancer patient, is a formidable barrier between him and those around him. It causes distortions, shifts in emphasis, indeed, inability to comprehend, to remember, or even to hear. If one wants to be sure communication is successful, efforts must be made to allay disruptive anxiety. More often than not, allaying anxiety rests more on non-verbal than on verbal means: the "how" of communicating is infinitely more important than the "what" communicated . . . . It seems logical to devote as much energy to preserving the psychic integrity as we now devote to preserving physiological integrity. The patient saved from a serious illness should be enabled to live with dignity and self-respect — not merely to exist.'

11.5   Positive goals of care

Many studies relating both to residential and to community care highlight the problem of the perceived absence of positive goals of care. With a prevailing ethos which places a premium on 'cure', it may be hard to provide staff with something towards which they feel they can work. But this is not a counsel of despair, for all kinds of nursing bring their own demands and challenges. It is the challenge for those who care for the chronic sick to find sources of fulfilment for their patients, within their capabilities, and to achieve their own professional satisfaction in providing care where there is no chance of cure.

■ Summary

The characteristics of chronic illness are enumerated and the effects of social stigma on sufferers from chronic sickness are described. It is shown that families of such patients can suffer from a 'courtesy stigma'. There are many difficulties facing those who care for the chronic sick. One such problem is the absence of positive goals of care in situations where cure is impossible.

The author concludes that the challenge for those who care for the chronic sick is to find sources of self-fulfilment for their patients and to provide appropriate care, in order to maximize benefit to the patient and provide professional satisfaction to health care staff.

■ Questions

1. What do you understand by the terms 'horticultural' and 'warehousing' models of care?
2. Why is the term 'social death' sometimes used in connection with the institutional care of the chronic sick? What measures might be taken to try to avoid this?
3. What are some of the major problems and challenges confronting those who care for the chronic sick?

References

Bard, M. (1970). 'The price of survival for cancer victims', in *Where Medicine Fails*, Strauss, A. L. (Ed.), Chicago, Aldine.

Coser, R. (1963). 'Alienation and the social structure: a case analysis of a hospital', in *The Hospital in Modern Society*, Freidson, E. (Ed.), New York, Free Press.

Davis, F. (1963). *Passage Through Crisis: Polio Victims and Their Families*, Indianapolis, Bobbs-Merrill.

166

Fabrega, H. and Manning, P. K. (1972). 'Disease, illness and deviant careers', in *Theoretical Perspectives on Deviance*, Scott, R. A. and Douglas, J. D. (Eds.), New York, Basic Books.

Goffman, E. (1963). *Stigma: Notes on the Management of Spoiled Identity*, Englewood Cliffs, New Jersey, Prentice-Hall.

Kratz, C. (1978). *Care of the Long-Term Sick in the Community*, Edinburgh, Churchill Livingstone.

McIntosh, J. (1981). 'Communicating with patients in their own homes', in *Communication in Nursing Care*, Bridge, W. and Macleod Clark, J. (Eds.), London, H.M. & M.

Miller, E. J. and Gwynne, G. V. (1974). *A Life Apart: A Pilot Study of Residential Institutions for the Physically Handicapped and Young Chronic Sick*, London, Tavistock.

Roth, J. (1970). 'The public hospital: refuge for damaged humans', in Strauss, A. L. (Ed.), Chicago, Aldine.

Seeman, M. (1959). 'On the meaning of alienation', *American Sociological Review*, vol. 24, pp. 783–791, December.

Tuckett, D. (Ed.) (1976). *An Introduction to Medical Sociology*, London, Tavistock.

Further reading

Kratz, C. (1978). *Care of the Long-term Sick in the Community*, Edinburgh, Churchill Livingstone. This book is strongly recommended as an excellent example of the application of sociology to nursing. Chapter 1 explains the type of sociological approach adopted (symbolic interactionism) and the problems encountered in the research, which used participant observation. The findings raise thought-provoking questions about the challenges confronting nurses who are responsible for caring for patients for whom it seems that little can be done by way of cure.

Old THOMAS PARR of
Winnington in Shropshire,
Who lived in the Reign of Ten Kings & Queens.
He died in the Strand, 1634. Aged 152 Years.

Old Thomas Parr (Courtesy BBC Hulton Picture Library)

(. . . as the balance shifts to a higher proportion of the 'elderly elderly', there is likely to be a greater demand for resources to provide for their needs — see p. 170)

12 Sociological aspects of the care of the elderly

12.1 Who are the elderly?

'You're as old as you feel.' This colloquial saying is reflected in a distinction made by some of those who write about old age. They wish to emphasize the fact that 'the elderly' are not a homogeneous group of people who can be satisfactorily considered as a clear-cut statistical category, but they vary greatly in the degree of their physical well-being and personal independence. Also, there is a distinction between the 'young elderly' and the 'elderly elderly'. It is thus important to beware of crude generalizations about old age.

However, for general purposes, the 'elderly' are usually defined in terms of retirement age. We saw in Chapters 2 and 3 that the numbers of people surviving to old age have increased dramatically over recent decades, as a result of general improvements in the standard of living, coupled with advances in medical science and health care.

12.1.1 The increasing proportion of elderly people

Table 12.1 shows how the proportion of the population over retirement age increased from 6 per cent at the turn of the century to 14 per cent in 1951 and almost 18 per cent in 1981; and how the proportion aged 75 years or more has increased fourfold. In the late 1970s, more than one person in twenty — about 3 million people — were in this age group, and their numbers are expected to increase as we move into the twenty-first century.

TABLE 12.1   The elderly as a proportion of the total population

	1901 (%)	1951 (%)	1979 (%)	1981* (%)	2001* (%)
Over retirement age	6.3	13.6	17.4	17.7	16.5
Over 75 years	1.3	3.5	5.5	5.7	6.4

(Source: Adapted from 'Social Trends', Central Statistical Office, HMSO, 1980 and 1981)
*Indicates 1979-based projections.

Looking to the years ahead, the situation is summarized in 'Social Trends' (1981), published by the Central Statistical Office of H.M.S.O.:

'Although the total number of people over retirement age in Great Britain will remain at about 9.5 million up to the end of the century, the balance between the younger and more active element will change considerably. The numbers of those 75 and over, for instance, will increase by 21% between 1979 and the end of the century, while those between retirement age and 75, will decrease by 11% during the same period.'

Clearly, there are implications here for those health and welfare services which care for the frail and infirm: as the balance shifts to a higher proportion of the 'elderly elderly', there is likely to be a greater demand for resources to provide for their needs.

Another point: these figures conceal significant differences between men and women. In 1979, there were 4.4 million men and 6.3 million women over 60, while 68 per cent of people over 75 were women — a proportion which rises to 76 per cent of the 85-year-olds. So, when we look more closely at the 'elderly elderly' we find they are predominantly women, who are very likely to be either widowed or single.

12.2 Where do the elderly live?

We saw in Chapter 4 that the nuclear family is the most common type of family in a modern industrial society such as Britain. We also noted that nuclear families tend to be geographically mobile and to become separated from the older generation. Moreover, the type of housing which is characteristic of our cities and suburbs is not suitable for accommodating extended families. Neither are many village dwellings. Thus it is not surprising that many elderly people live alone. In 1978, one-quarter of those aged 65–69 were living alone — a figure which rises to 40 per cent of those aged over 70.

12.2.1 Family support

However, living alone and loneliness are not the same thing, although obviously they may be closely connected. Married couples, as their children grow up and leave home, often become extremely dependent on each other; but, as the years progress, one of them is likely to die and to leave the other not only alone, but also lonely. One approach to the measurement of loneliness is to try to measure 'social isolation' by assessing the frequency of social contacts. Townsend (1963) studied elderly people living in Bethnal Green, London, and discovered that they were not so isolated as the general stereotype of the 'lonely old person' might have led us to expect. For example, among the 203 elderly people in his study, nearly one-half actually lived with relatives other than a spouse, and only 4 per cent did not see at least one of their children every week. Overall, two-thirds of them could count on relatives to help in times of illness or other crisis. However, the remaining one-third — who were mainly single, or widowed, or had sons but no daughters — did tend to have no one nearby to whom they could turn for help.

These findings are for an area of London which other research (Young and Willmott, 1957) showed was strong in community ties. It is therefore interesting to compare them with another study, which looked at the situation of the elderly in three different countries: the U.S.A., Britain and Denmark (Shanas *et al.*, 1968). They found that between one-quarter and one-third of all the elderly people in their study had been ill during the year prior to interview, and that for those who had no spouse, children were the most important source of help with practical tasks such as shopping, cooking and cleaning the home. For example, for the elderly in the British sample, 77 per cent had received help from their family with housework; 80 per cent and 82 per cent with meals and personal toilet.

Therefore, in general, the picture is not one of old people being neglected by the younger generation. However, there were significant differences between the care available for those elderly people who had children and those without, as well as between those who had daughters, compared with those who only had sons. Those without daughters were very much more vulnerable to social isolation and to neglect in times of illness. Others who were particularly vulnerable were those who had recently been widowed. The title of a study by Parkes, Benjamin and Fitzgerald (1969) — 'Broken heart: a statistical study of increased mortality among widowers' — tells its own story.

12.2.2 Stress on relatives

However, the availability of help and support for the elderly from their families may bring its own problems. Some of these are indicated in a study undertaken in Glasgow by Isaacs (1971), who analysed the reasons for admission of 280 patients from their own homes into a geriatric unit. Isaacs found that two-thirds were coming into hospital because of a lack of basic care at home or because of excess strain on relatives. Of all admissions, 32 per cent were due to strain on relatives. This was defined in terms of a burden of care arising from the patient's illness which threatened the physical or mental well-being of relatives. Excess strain usually occurred when the patient lived in the same house as the relatives and was exacerbated by incontinence, immobility and mental problems such as confusion.

Isaacs' study highlights some of the dilemmas confronting those who are responsible for providing care for the elderly who are ill or infirm. The problems of institutionalization, repeatedly emphasized by sociologists in their critiques of institutional care (Goffman, 1961; Townsend, 1962), have been influential in shifting policy towards community care. But, as Pinker (1978) points out, this may bring its own problems: isolation and loneliness for vulnerable individuals, and a burden of responsibility for relatives and neighbours. Many are able to accept this responsibility, and do so willingly. Indeed they would not wish anything different. Yet for others it may cause very real problems — both personal and financial. Pinker suggests that it is women who are most likely to suffer, as it is they who are generally expected to provide care. Therefore we should be careful to avoid creating a new form of 'sexual exploitation', in which the hidden expenses of community care are carried by female relatives, sometimes at great personal cost.

12.3   Theories of ageing

Several theories have been put forward to explain ways in which people adjust to the experience of growing old. We shall consider three of these — the disengagement, activity and continuity theories.

12.3.1   Disengagement theory

This theory stems from the structural functionalist approach in sociology (see Chapter 1) and suggests that people adapt to old age in ways which are 'functional' both for society and for themselves. Two of its main proponents, E. Cumming and W. Henry put forward three basic propositions (Cumming and Henry, 1961):

(1)   Old age is characterized by a process of mutual withdrawal of ageing individuals and society.
(2)   This process of withdrawal is inevitable.
(3)   The withdrawal is necessary for 'successful' ageing.

Withdrawal is seen as being functional for society because it enables the gradual phasing out of individuals, so that their eventual deaths cause minimum disruption to the smooth running of the social order. For example, formal retirement from work can be anticipated; it enables the organization to offer responsibility and leadership opportunities to younger people and to prepare new individuals for the posts being vacated. It also allows the outgoing individual to prepare for his new life-style. The process of phasing out individuals from the mainstream of social life is often institutionalized in the form of 'rites de passage' — such as retirement ceremonies — in which the social group can express its appreciation of the retiring person's contribution.

The theory also suggests that the process of disengagement is beneficial for the elderly people themselves: it allows them to become less active and more preoccupied with their personal interests.

This theory has not passed unchallenged. For example, it has been argued that many elderly people may not wish to become 'disengaged' and that individual disengagement, if it does occur, is probably a much more complex phenomenon than the theory allows. Therefore, the theory should not be accepted uncritically. However, it does highlight some of the social processes involved when the needs of society — for example, for older people to make way for younger people in certain occupations — intersect with the individual's life-cycle.

Cockerham (1978) summarizes its significance:

'By setting a specific age, usually sixty-five, as the time of retirement, disengagement becomes institutionalized and orderly and inevitable, just as ageing itself is inevitable. Some degree of disengagement appears to be inherent in the ageing process for many people and disengagement theory helps to explain what happens in certain specific situations.'

12.3.2 Activity theory

Activity theory rests on fundamentally different assumptions from disengagement theory. Havighurst (1963) gives three basic premises:

(1) The majority of normally ageing people will maintain fairly constant levels of activity.
(2) The extent of disengagement, or continuing engagement, is not inherent in the process of ageing, but will be influenced by other factors such as previous life-style.
(3) It is essential to maintain a considerable degree of social, physical and mental activity if the process of ageing is to be 'successful'.

The definition of 'successful' ageing, according to Havighurst, is the degree to which an older person can maintain a level of activity comparable to that of middle-aged persons. Research by Palmore (1968) has given some support to this approach: a longitudinal study covering a 10-year period found that older men maintained levels of activity and satisfaction with life, but that older women tended to experience some loss of both. Palmore also found that, in general, the more active a person was, the happier he or she was likely to be, and he concluded that continued engagement, rather than disengagement, was characteristic of a healthy, happy old age.

However, it should be noted that this theory rests on the assumption that older people judge their quality of life by reference to middle age. This may not always be appropriate: they may not wish to do so, or they may be unable to sustain a middle-aged life-style for physical or financial reasons.

Therefore activity theory, like the disengagement theory, may shed light on the experience of ageing for some people but not for all.

12.3.3 Continuity theory

This approach, found in the work of writers such as Atchley (1972), emphasizes an essential continuity throughout the different phases of a person's life-cycle. It suggests that individuals develop fairly stable habits, attitudes and values, which become part of their personalities. These are likely to be retained as people become older, and will influence their reactions to the process of ageing. However, the very process of growing older may bring changes which require modification of previous behaviour, and this is recognized by the continuity theorists. Their approach therefore includes a wide range of responses to ageing and is thus perhaps more flexible and comprehensive than either the disengagement or activity theories. However its very flexibility makes it difficult to test by research.

Whatever theories exist about people's responses to ageing, there comes a time for many of them when illness or frailty result in their admission into an institution.

12.4   Institutional care of the elderly

One early sociological study of residential care of the elderly was P. Townsend's *The Last Refuge* (Townsend, 1962). The inside cover of the book sets the tone:

> "'Grim and sombre". This was the first impression Peter Townsend had of the Victorian workhouse which had become an institution for old people . . . frightful overcrowding in sparsely furnished dormitories. Day rooms bleak and uninviting in which sat watery-eyed and feeble men, their spirit and pride drained away by the hopelessness of the surroundings: the shocking lack of privacy . . . .'

Subsequent improvements in the provision of care for the elderly should not diminish our concern over the continued existence of some of the problems highlighted by Townsend in this study. Moreover, some of the problems which, as we have seen, are encountered in the institutional care of the mentally ill or the chronic sick (for example, Coser, 1963; Goffman, 1961) also arise with long-term patients in a geriatric ward or hospital. And these problems may be compounded by others — such as difficulties in communication.

12.4.1   Communicating with geriatric patients

Fielding (1981) points to the significance of degenerative diseases in the elderly and stresses the importance of communication between nurses and patients. She reminds us that geriatric patients are often depressed or inarticulate; therefore, it is particularly important to look for non-verbal cues in their facial expressions and gestures, which can communicate anxiety or depression more eloquently than any words. Fielding gives a useful account of a number of studies of verbal and non-verbal communication. One such study by Wells (1980) is sobering. It consisted of 'live' tape recordings of conversations between nurses and elderly patients and showed that personal communication was infrequent and usually brief — the average length was 90 seconds. As Fielding points out: 'The brevity of the conversation indicates that the nurses did not give high priority to this aspect of a patient's care.'

12.5   Types of institutional care

We have seen that the number of old, and especially very old, people is growing and that many will survive to a stage of life where they suffer from some kind of infirmity and so will need some form of care. A great deal of care can be offered in the community, with support from health and welfare services, such as home helps, chiropodists, meals on wheels and community nurses. However, there may come a time for many elderly people when they cannot cope and admission to hospital is necessary. Apart from private nursing homes — which are prohibitively expensive for all but a small minority — there are five main types of residential care: local authority sheltered housing or Part III accommodation; geriatric hospitals; geriatric wards in general hospitals; and residential homes run by voluntary associations. In many parts of the country, there are long waiting lists, especially for admission to local authority accommodation and to the homes run by voluntary organizations. So, general practitioners and relatives often have to seek admission for the elderly to beds for acute cases, and this may be far from satisfactory.

12.5.1   Wade's analysis of care provision for the elderly

The shortage of appropriate accommodation reflects the low priority given to provision for the elderly and may result in considerable distress. Attempts to obtain more and better facilities should therefore be made and should take into account the preferences of the elderly themselves. In this context, research such as that undertaken by B. Wade is very relevant (Wade, 1983). Following a review of the literature (Wade and Sawyer, 1981), she argues that 'a "positive" environment for the elderly would: (a) be more domestic or homely; (b) foster social interaction; (c) provide opportunities for choice; (d) give recognition to the adult status of the elderly; (e) provide opportunities for the elderly to undertake activities which are salient to their lives; (f) feature participation and consultation in the care regime by the elderly themselves.'

Wade and colleagues describe some of the findings in the study 'Different Care Provisions for the Elderly' (Wade, Sawyer and Bell, 1982). This study was funded by the Department of Health and Social Security with the aim of identifying a potential clientele for a state system of nursing homes. The researchers observed the facilities and care provided for elderly people in hospital wards, Part III homes and private nursing homes. They found differences within and between these settings. For example, there were variations not only in physical facilities, but also in the extent to which staff were encouraged to sit down and talk to patients, and in the attitudes of staff to visitors. Each kind of setting showed a continuum of attitudes and behaviour, from very 'routinized' and 'task-oriented' to more individualized forms of care.

This study also considered the attitudes of the elderly themselves, concerning such matters as the extent to which they were consulted before being admitted to an institution, whether they felt lonely and whether they felt happy living in their current situation. In response to the question on loneliness, there was little difference in the proportions who said 'Never' among the elderly living in the community (55.6 per cent), in hospital (54.5 per cent) and in local authority Part III accommodation (52.8 per cent); but the proportion in private nursing homes (63.3 per cent) was somewhat higher. Differences were more marked in the replies given to the question which asked the elderly people to say whether they were happy living in their current situation: the proportions answering 'Yes' ranged from 75.9 per cent of those living in the community and 75 per cent of those in private nursing homes, to 46.2 per cent of those in hospital and 44.1 per cent of those in Part III accommodation.

Wade quotes some of the remarks made by the elderly which ranged from contentment to acceptance and despair. For example:

'I'm very happy here, they're all very kind and very loving, it is homely.'

'Not happy but try to make myself contented.'

'I'm fed up with sitting in this chair day after day. I've been sitting in this blooming chair since last September. I never go anywhere, but sit here all day long. Nobody to talk to. I wish I could go home.'

Comments similar to this last one were made by one-third of all the patients with whom interviews were attempted in hospital and in Part III homes, but were less frequently heard from those in private nursing homes.

Finally, Wade offers four different models of care: supportive, protective, controlled and restrained. Their characteristics are summarized in *Figure 12.1*. She advocates the 'supportive' model and recommends that developments in the provision of care for the elderly should allow for adequate levels of staffing by '*nurses who have been trained in the giving of total patient care*'.

The poet Robert Browning wrote very cheerfully about old age:

Grow old along with me,
The best is yet to be,
The last of life, for which the first was made . . . .

(Rabbi Ben Ezra)

It may be that this happy vision of the latter part of life becomes a reality for many elderly people. For many others, however, old age is fraught with problems and saddened by loneliness. And sometimes, elderly people are made to feel demoralized, demeaned and diminished by the attitudes of those who care for them, especially in institutions where staff can appear brusque or patronizing. The poem reproduced on page 178, which was found in the bedside locker of an elderly lady who had died, is a salutary reminder to us all:

Person Centred

Supportive model	Protective model
Consultation	Consultation
Patient/resident committee	Limited choice
Choice	Little or no involvement of visitors/volunteers
Salience	No outings
Involvement of visitors/ volunteers	Provision of diversional activities
Outings/activities suggested by the elderly themselves	Therapeutic input
Therapeutic input	
Unrestricted visiting	

Open - - - - - - - - - - - - - - - + - - - - - - - - - - - - - - **Closed**

Controlled model	Restrained model
Emphasis on routine	Emphasis on routine
Lack of choice	Lack of choice
Activities/outings organized by staff/ volunteers	Restricted visiting
Unrestricted visiting	Non-involvement of relatives/visitors in the care regime
Little therapeutic input	No outings
	Little therapeutic input

Task Centred

Figure 12.1 Different models of care for the elderly (From Wade, 1983, by courtesy of B. Wade and the Editor of *Nursing Times*)

POETIC THOUGHTS OF AN OLD WOMAN

What do you see nurses, what do you see?
Are you thinking when you are looking at me
A crabbit old woman, not very wise
Uncertain of habit, with far away eyes
Who dribbles her food and makes no reply,
When you say in a loud voice 'I do wish you'd try'.
Who seems not to notice the things that you do
And forever is losing a stocking or shoe
Who unresisting or not, lets you do as you will,
With the bathing and feeding, the long day to fill?
Is that what you're thinking, is that what you see?
Then open your eyes nurse you're not looking at me.

I'll tell you who I am as I sit here so still;
As I move at your bidding, as I eat at your will —
I'm a small child of ten with a father and mother
Brothers and sisters who love one another;
A girl of sixteen with wings on her feet;
Dreaming that soon now a lover she'd meet;
A bride soon at twenty my heart gives a leap,
Rememb'ring the vows that I promised to keep;
At twenty-five now I have young of my own
Who need me to build a secure happy home;
A woman of thirty my young grow so fast
Bound to each other with ties that should last;
At forty my young sons now grown and will be gone
But my man stays behind to see I don't mourn;
At fifty once more babies play round my knee
Again we know children my loved one and me.
Dark days are upon me, my husband is dead
I look to the future, I shudder with dread,
For my young ones are all busy rearing young of their own
And I think of the years and the love that I've known.
I'm an old woman now and nature is cruel
'Tis her jest to make old age look like a fool.
The body it crumbles, grace and vigour depart
There is now a stone where I once had a heart.
But inside this old carcass a young girl still dwells
And now and again my battered heart swells.
I remember the joys, I remember the pain
And I'm loving and living life over again.
I think of the years all too few gone too fast
And accept the stark fear that nothing can last.
So open your eyes nurses, open and see
Not a crabbit old woman, look close — see me.

■ Summary

Statistical evidence shows that the population trend is towards a higher proportion of the 'elderly elderly'; this has clear implications for the health and welfare services and the allocation of resources. Perhaps unexpectedly, it is seen that old people are not neglected by the younger generation, although those elderly people without children, especially daughters, are more vulnerable to social isolation and neglect in times of illness. Three sociological theories of the way people adjust to growing old are considered — the disengagement, activity and continuity theories. Although institutional care has been vastly improved since the days of the 'grim and sombre' Victorian workhouse, the author feels we should still be concerned about the continued existence of other problems. Alternatives in care, utilizing the range of health and welfare services, are seen to be important, as is a 'positive' environment for those patients in residential care.

The chapter concludes with a moving poem, found in the bedside locker of an elderly lady after her death, from which there are many lessons to be learned.

■ Questions

1. Why has the number of elderly people increased so greatly in recent decades? What are the implications for the health and welfare services?
2. Briefly outline two theories of ageing. Indicate which you hope will describe your own experience — and why!
3. Give an account of B. Wade's model of care provision for the elderly. Discuss ways in which it applies to the most recent situation in which you have cared for elderly people.

References

Atchley, R. C. (1972). *The Social Forces in Later Life*, Belmont, California, Wadsworth.
Cockerham, W. C. (1978). *Medical Sociology*, Englewood Cliffs, New Jersey, Prentice-Hall.
Coser, R. A. (1963). 'Alienation and the social structure: a case analysis of a hospital', in *The Hospital in Modern Society*, Freidson, E. (Ed.), New York, Free Press.
Cumming, E. and Henry, W. E. (1961). *Growing Old: The Process of Disengagement*, New York, Basic Books.
Fielding, P. (1981). 'Communicating with geriatric patients, in *Communication in Nursing Care*, Bridge, W. and Macleod Clark, J. (Eds.), London, H.M. & M. Publishers.

180

Goffman, E. (1961). *Asylums*, Harmondsworth, Penguin.
Havighurst, R. (1963). 'Successful aging', in *Processes of Aging*, Williams, R., Tibitts, C. and Donahue, W. (Eds.), New York, Atherton.
Isaacs, B. (1971). 'Geriatric patients: do their families care?', *British Medical Journal*, vol. 4, p. 282.
Palmore, E. (1968). 'The effects of ageing on activities and attitudes', *Gerontologist*, vol. 8 (winter), pp. 259–263.
Parkes, C. M., Benjamin, B. and Fitzgerald, R. G. (1969). 'Broken heart: a statistical study of increased mortality among widowers', *British Medical Journal*, vol. 1, pp. 740–743.
Pinker, R. (1978). 'A nurse for all seasons', *Nursing Mirror*, vol. 146, no. 21, pp. 31–34.
Shanas, E., Townsend, P., Wedderburn, D., Friis, M., Millhoj, P. and Stenouwer, J. (1968). *Old People in Three Industrial Societies*, London, Routledge & Kegan Paul.
Townsend, P. (1962). *The Last Refuge*, London, Routledge & Kegan Paul.
Townsend, P. (1963). *The Family Life of Old People*, Harmondsworth, Penguin.
Wade, B. (1983). 'Different models of care for the elderly', paper presented to the Royal College of Nursing Research Society Annual Conference, Durham; *Nursing Times* Occasional Paper, vol. 79, no. 12, pp. 33–36.
Wade, B. and Sawyer, L. (1981). 'Different Care Provisions for the Elderly: Review of the Literature', unpublished Report to D.H.S.S., September, Department of Social Administration, The London School of Economics.
Wade, B., Sawyer, L. and Bell, J. (1982). 'Different Care Provisions for the Elderly', Final Report to D.H.S.S., Department of Social Administration, The London School of Economics.
Wells, T. J. (1980). *Problems in Geriatric Nursing Care*, Edinburgh, Churchill Livingstone.
Young, M. and Willmott, P. (1957). *Family and Kinship in East London*, Harmondsworth, Penguin.

Further reading

Brown, P. (1982). *The Other Side of Growing Older*, London, Macmillan.
Evers, H. (1981). 'Tender loving care? Patients and nurses in geriatric wards', in *Care of the Aging*, Copp, L. A. (Ed.), Edinburgh, Churchill Livingstone.
Redfern, S. (1981). 'Evaluating care of the elderly — a British perspective', in *Care of the Aging*, Copp, L. A. (Ed.), Edinburgh, Churchill Livingstone.
Wade, B. (1983). 'Different models of care for the elderly', *Nursing Times* Occasional Paper, vol. 79, no. 12, pp. 33–36.

Father Time (Courtesy BBC Hulton Picture Library)

(... death was much more commonplace — stalking society, ever ready to strike people of all age groups ... — see p. 183)

13 Sociological aspects of the care of the dying

'Timor mortis conturbat me'.

William Dunbar (1465–1530)

13.1 Death in modern society

In Britain today, as in most industrial societies, many people become adult without ever seeing a dead person. Death therefore tends to have an aura of mystery. This is in striking contrast to earlier times when, as we saw in Chapters 2 and 3, death was much more commonplace — stalking society, ever ready to strike people of all age groups through killer diseases, especially in epidemics which could suddenly ravage entire communities. Infant deaths were a common experience and most families expected to lose some of their children. And as most deaths occurred at home, the process of dying and the presence of a corpse in the house were not unfamiliar events.

Nowadays, our expectations of life are so high that we do not expect to die before our 'three score years and ten'. Nor do we expect those whom we love to do so. Most people, in times of peace, do not think about death very much. Although death and violence may figure prominently in films and novels, 'real' death — involving ourselves or those whom we know — does not often feature in our thinking. Consequently, it is likely to be all the more shocking when it does occur. We may be unprepared to cope with it as individuals; and for society, death tends to be a taboo subject.

Writers such as Ariès (1974) or Gorer (1965) argue that it is more difficult nowadays to talk openly about death than in earlier times. For example, Gorer in his interesting book *Death, Grief and Mourning in Contemporary Britain*, argues that there is a major difference between pre-industrial and industrialized societies in the way in which the bereaved are allowed to behave. In many pre-industrial societies, people who have lost someone whom they love are often encouraged to express their grief openly. But in industrial societies, like our own, people are expected to hide their grief and to control their feelings in public. Gorer suggests that this is not psychologically sound and may lead to greater emotional distress and additional suffering.

This tendency to keep death, bereavement and grief out of the public view is reinforced by the increase in the number of deaths 'hidden' in institutions. A hundred years ago, less than one-third of the population died in hospitals, asylums or workhouses, whereas nowadays more than one-half of all deaths occur in hospital.

Along with this increase in the institutionalization of dying is an increase in our ability to 'manage' death. This may of course be beneficial. Control of pain and discomfort are obviously welcome, and some prolongation of life may help the terminally ill to prepare for death. But the ability to 'manage' death brings responsibilities and raises many issues. Among these are decisions about how best to manage the 'awareness' of impending death for the terminally ill person and for his relatives. Such decisions will be influenced by variations in the type of death and its duration — or what sociologists call the 'dying trajectory'.

13.2   Patterns of death

13.2.1   Dying trajectories

The concepts of 'trajectories of dying' and of 'contexts of awareness' have been described by two sociologists, A. Strauss and B. Glaser. They depict the idea of a dying trajectory in this way (Strauss and Glaser, 1968):

> 'The course of dying — or "dying trajectory" — of each patient has at least two outstanding properties. First, it takes place over time: it has duration. Second, a trajectory has shape: it can be graphed. It plunges straight down; it moves slowly but steadily downwards; it vacillates slowly, moving slowly up and down before diving downwards radically; it moves slowly down at first, then hits a long plateau, then plunges to death.'

Dying trajectories are important because they affect everyone concerned with an impending death. Expectations may build up concerning the time-scale, and psychological adjustments may be based on them which can be shattered if the trajectory takes an unexpected turn. For example, Strauss and Glaser suggest:

> 'In an intensive care unit where cardiac patients die frequently, the mood is relatively unaffected by one more speedy death; but if a hopeless patient lingers on and on, or if his wife, perhaps, refuses to accept his dying and causes "scenes", then both mood and work itself are profoundly affected.'

Normally, certain events or stages of dying occur, which are described by Strauss and Glaser as 'critical junctures':

(1)   The patient is defined as dying.
(2)   Staff and family prepare for his death; the patient also may do so, if he is aware of his condition.
(3)   The stage when it is felt that there is 'nothing more to do' to prevent death.
(4)   The final descent — which may vary in length from weeks to hours.
(5)   The 'last hours'.
(6)   The death watch.
(7)   The death itself.

Strauss and Glaser discuss the implications of different kinds of trajectories. Slow trajectories in particular bring with them both hazard and opportunity. They can be 'too long', with sustained tension and prolonged suffering; but they can also provide a chance for the dying person to come to terms with his impending death and to terminate his life in dignity with those he loves.

13.2.2 Context of awareness

A slow trajectory brings a particular responsibility for those concerned with the management of the death to arrange the 'context of awareness', so that the patient, the relatives and the staff can communicate as effectively and helpfully as possible. Strauss and Glaser define the 'awareness context' as 'what each interacting person knows of the patient's defined status, along with his recognition of others' awareness of his own definition'. They then describe four kinds of awareness context:

(1) Closed awareness — where the patient does not recognize that he is dying, although everyone else around him does.
(2) Suspected awareness — when the patient suspects that he may be dying and tries to find out what his prognosis is.
(3) Mutual pretence awareness — where everyone knows the patient is dying, but all pretend that they do not.
(4) Open awareness — where the patient, his relatives and the staff all admit that death is inevitable and speak and act accordingly.

The desirability of the different awareness contexts may vary from one situation to another and they may also vary over time for a particular patient and his family. For example, the appropriateness of an awareness context may be affected by the stages through which dying patients may pass, especially those who experience a slow trajectory and who may have to live for quite a long time with the knowledge that they have a fatal illness. Thus it is important to 'match' the awareness context with the level of awareness of the patient — allowing, for example, an 'open awareness' context to develop when the patient has reached the stage where he is willing and ready to acknowledge that he has a fatal condition.

13.3   Kübler-Ross: the stages of dying

Kübler-Ross (1969) has described in detail the various stages through which many dying people may pass. Not all dying people go through these experiences, nor do they do so in the order described below. But these are some of the phases typically encountered by those who know that they have a terminal disease. An understanding of these stages may help us to respond more sensitively and helpfully when caring for patients who are experiencing them.

13.3.1 Denial and isolation: 'No, not me, it cannot be true'

This stage may last for a few seconds or for months, and is often accompanied by feelings of intense isolation. However, denial and disbelief can serve as a 'buffer system' that allows the patient time to collect his thoughts, to muster his energies and to develop his coping mechanisms. Some patients may also regress to this state of denial from time to time as a reprieve from the nightmare of impending death.

13.3.2 Anger: 'Why me?'

Very few patients maintain a state of denial. When this gives way to a realization that death is inevitable, they often experience feelings of rage, resentment and bitterness. This can be a very trying time for relatives and for staff. Nurses are often a target for their anger and some understanding of why the patients are so aggressive may help them to respond more sympathetically. This can be a particularly traumatic time for relatives, who have to encounter their loved one's negative feelings and bitterness at a time when they too are feeling sad and vulnerable. As Kübler-Ross (1969) says: 'They then either respond with grief and tears, guilt or shame, or avoid future visits, which only increases the patient's discomfort and anger.'

If the nursing staff perceive what is happening, it can be very helpful if they explain, so that the family can understand and feel a little less hurt.

13.3.3 Bargaining: 'Yes, me ... but ...'

'Just a bit longer.' 'Let me live long enough to see my son married.' These are the sorts of reactions encountered at this stage. Underlying them is a plea for extension of time, often couched in terms of some kind of bargain. Patients may ask God, or hospital staff, for a few more months. But once the time is up, they may still be reluctant to accept that death is inevitable. Kübler-Ross suggests that 'psychologically, promises may be associated with quiet guilt, and it would therefore be helpful if such remarks by patients were not just brushed aside by the staff'. Patients may indeed need time, and the opportunity to talk to relatives or staff in order to cope with this stage. Kübler-Ross suggests that the chaplain, in particular, may often be able to help with any deep-seated problems of guilt and fear.

13.3.4 Depression: 'Yes, me'

This is the stage when the terminally ill patient can no longer deny the full impact of his illness — when he cannot 'smile it off'any more. Kübler-Ross distinguishes two kinds of depression which may be experienced now; she argues that as they are different, they should be dealt with differently.

First, there is a 'reactive' depression, resulting from anxiety, fear and grief over loss. Such loss may be a direct result of the illness — as with the loss of a breast for a mastectomy patient, and the effects on self-esteem resulting from a mutilated body-image. Or there may be other kinds of loss, such as the loss of a job and the financial anxieties associated with this.

The second type of depression is more concerned with impending losses and can be seen as a kind of preparatory grief — an anticipation of the grief of leaving loved ones.

In giving advice on how to help patients who are suffering from such depression, Kübler-Ross urges:

> 'The patient should not be encouraged to look at the sunny side of things, as this would mean he should not contemplate his impending death. It would be contraindicated to tell him not to be sad, since all of us are tremendously sad when we lose one beloved person. The patient is in the process of losing everything and everybody he loves. If he is allowed to express his sorrow he will find a final acceptance much easier, and he will be grateful to those who can sit with him during this stage of depression without constantly telling him not to be sad.'

13.3.5 Acceptance: 'Yes, me . . . and I'm as ready as I ever will be'

'My time is close now, and it's all right.' This typifies the final stage reached by many patients, when they experience peace and tranquillity. Very often they are physically quite weak and may spend much of the time sleeping. There are similarities between the state of infancy described by Bettelheim (1967) and this stage of dying described by Kübler-Ross: 'Indeed it was an age when nothing was asked of us and all we wanted was given.'

This is a time when perhaps the relatives need even more support and comfort than the patient. As Parkes (1972) reminds us:

> 'For the family and patient, the period of terminal care can be a time of growth and shared preparation, as it can be a time of defeat and mutual destruction. It can be a fulfilment and completion of marriage. It can mar the memory of good relationships and undermine the health of the survivor for years.'

This account of the stages of dying may alert us to the experiences of terminally ill patients and help us to understand their reactions to impending death. However, it is important to repeat that not all patients pass through all these stages, and that they may experience them in a different order. Kübler-Ross's work should therefore be seen as a sensitizing account, to be interpreted appropriately for each patient.

13.4   Communication with the dying patient and his family

An underlying theme in the work of Strauss and Glaser and of Kübler-Ross is the importance of appropriate communication with the dying person and his relatives. Other writers, such as Saunders (1976) and Raven (1975) also emphasize this. However, some research studies of the ways in which medical and nursing staff actually look after the dying have shown that they may adopt various *strategies of avoidance* — sometimes as a matter of policy, and sometimes perhaps more by default. Four studies illustrate the diversity of ways in which professionals may communicate with the dying.

First, Bond (1978) studied the interaction between nurses and patients in a radiotherapy department and found that the nurses often avoided discussion of important issues. Most interactions with patients were short and related to physical care; nurses 'managed' conversations to avoid 'difficult' topics and adopted 'escape' tactics often used by medical staff or more senior nurses. However, there were some nurses who were perceptive and sensitive to patients' distress and who indicated that they would have liked to do more to help — if they only knew how and if only they had the time.

Second, McIntosh (1977), in a study of doctors and cancer patients, found that doctors frequently avoided telling patients the nature of their diagnosis unless patients were insistent in their demands to be told 'the truth'. Generally, 'the cornerstone of the doctors' philosophy on telling was the belief that the great majority of patients should not be told'. In terms used by Strauss and Glaser, these doctors believed in the benefits of maintaining a state of 'closed awareness'.

Thirdly, Hinton (1980) talked to 80 terminally ill cancer patients in an attempt to shed light on the difficult question of whether or not 'to tell'. Two-thirds of the patients were aware of the likelihood of their impending death. In general, however, they tended to talk about their death with their family or the interviewer rather than with staff. Hinton stresses the importance of staff making themselves available. Many patients are prepared to talk if only people are prepared to listen to them.

Fourthly, the work of Qvarnstrom (1978) highlights the kinds of fear which many dying people experience, including:

(1)   Fear of the pain and suffering that their illness may entail.
(2)   Fear of loneliness, and of dying alone.
(3)   Fear for their relatives and for how they will cope with the situation.
(4)   Fear of what will happen after death.

It is clear that some at least of these fears could be alleviated if nursing staff were willing and available to listen and to discuss. For example, the patient could be reassured that someone will be with him when he dies.

One of the principles of care in hospices for the terminally ill is that patients should not suffer pain and loneliness during the process of dying, and every effort is made to try to ensure that the experience of death is shared by the family, who will be supported and helped to adjust.

13.5   The place of death

The mention of hospices introduces the topic of the place of death. As we saw earlier, more and more people are dying in hospitals; however, many do still die at home, and some die in places established specifically to care for the terminally ill — such as the hospices.

13.5.1   Dying in hospital

There have been various studies of the experiences of dying in different settings. One of the most disturbing studies of dying in hospital was undertaken by an American, D. Sudnow, who made a distinction between 'biological' death and 'social' death and suggested that the two are not always simultaneous (Sudnow, 1967). While 'biological' death is defined by medical criteria such as 'brain' death, this may not occur at the same time as a patient is perceived as being 'as good as dead' by the staff, and treated accordingly. In some cases, patients for whom the staff saw no hope of recovery were treated more as corpses than as living human beings — and were, in effect, relegated to the category of deceased.

Sudnow gives some examples of ways in which patients while still alive may be treated as though already dead — as when, after admission, they were kept on stretchers in corridors rather than being transferred to a proper bed, or when a nurse repeatedly attempted to begin some of the procedures usually undertaken as part of last offices, such as closing a patient's eyes, while he was still alive.

Obviously, these examples of treating patients as dead before they have died physically are not meant to suggest that this represents the typical care of patients who die in hospital. However, there may be real difficulties in caring for the dying in the setting of a general hospital. Some of these may be practical; others may be a matter of attitudes.

Location of the dying patient's bed

Among the practical problems are the choice of location of the dying patient's bed. Clearly, the lack of privacy of a bed in the middle of a busy ward is not ideal for either the patient or his relatives. But the gradual progression of a patient with a slow dying trajectory from the middle of the ward to a bed nearer the nurses' desk and then to a side ward, indicates his deterioration more eloquently than any words. If he and/or his relatives have not been told that he is dying or have not accepted the implications of death — that is, if there is a situation of 'closed awareness' or 'mutual pretence awareness' — his transfer can cause acute anxiety. Moreover, relegation to a side ward can often bring isolation and loneliness, particularly if the medical and nursing staff are adopting avoidance strategies which are themselves often associated with closed awareness contexts. In the words of Strauss and Glaser (1968):

'A staff's failure in understanding a patient's attempts at achieving psychological closure on his life contributes to another process: the patient's increasing isolation . . . . In all the countries we have observed, we found strong tendencies to isolate a dying patient during his last days in the hospital. Isolation techniques — perhaps "insulation" is a better term — have their source in various structural conditions . . . . At the last, the staff tends to put him either into a single room or with a comatose patient. Of course, when patients are moved to an intensive care ward, they are quite isolated from people other than staff, including their families . . . . On the whole, then, under these kinds of structural conditions, it is much easier for patients to gain relative privacy from staff intrusions than to get attention. To the extent that patients fail in either aim, they lose the contest over the shaping of their own passing.'

Conversely, of course, the privacy of a side ward may be desirable for the patient himself, for his relatives and for the other patients on the ward. The important consideration is the need to ensure that, wherever the patient is placed, he is not left to face death alone and without the opportunity to share his fears and anxieties at the time and stage when he feels ready to do so.

Attitudes of staff to the dying patient

Perhaps the most fundamental problem concerns attitudes rather than practicalities. It has been suggested by many writers that one of the reasons why staff find it difficult to discuss death with patients is rooted in our contemporary culture. We noted at the beginning of this chapter that death nowadays does not feature as a part of everyday life. It is often 'hidden' and people feel awkward when talking about it. It has become such a taboo subject (Bond, 1980) that our culture has even been described as a 'death-denying' culture. One of the repercussions of this situation may be a great emphasis on keeping people alive at almost any cost, and a tendency in medical care to regard death as a 'failure'.

The results of such attitudes may be twofold. First, there may be heroic attempts to maintain some kind of life — a situation which has led Cecily Saunders to call for the need to recognize 'a difference between prolonging living and what can really only be called prolonging dying'. The other result may be a tendency to define the dying patient's situation as one in which 'there is nothing more to do' and to relegate him to a minimum level of care and attention. As Qvarnstrom (1978) points out: 'His need for psychological support will be relegated to the background whenever the personnel's care perspective is dominated by hopes that the patient will recover.'

13.5.2 Dying at home

Although a majority of people now die in hospital, there is still a substantial minority, about one-third, who die in their own homes. In their study *Life Before Death*, Cartwright, Hockey and Anderson (1973) found that patients who die at home, and their relatives, often require a great deal of support. For example, 84 per cent of those dying at home suffered from problems such as incontinence or senility which demand a great deal from those who care for them. These writers also found that the family structure was closely associated with decisions as to where a patient spends his last months or weeks. If there are female relatives available to care for him, he is more likely to be able to die at home: 60 per cent of those patients with unmarried daughters were cared for at home, compared with 34 per cent who only had unmarried sons. However it was clear that once relatives began to take responsibility for the care of the dying patient, they often did not receive much relief or help from other sources.

It is therefore important to try to ensure that adequate support is provided for the patient who chooses to die at home, and for his relatives who accept the responsibility of caring for him. McNulty (1978) has indicated a number of 'essentials' for the care of the dying at home. They include:

(1) Adequate numbers of trained staff who are familiar with the needs of the terminally ill.
(2) A fully available 24-hour cover of both medical and nursing care, with staff who have sufficient time to allow patients and families to discuss their anxieties, fears and problems.
(3) Good communication between all members of the health care team and between hospital and community services.
(4) Availability of adequate drugs.
(5) Out-patient and day centre facilities, with appropriate transport arrangements.
(6) Quick access to hospital beds should admission become necessary.
(7) A follow-up service for the bereaved.

13.5.3   Dying in a hospice

The word 'hospice' means 'travellers' house of rest' and symbolizes the philosophy which has inspired their development. Although a few hospices had been in existence for many years, developments in the care of the terminally ill — such as the pioneering work of Cecily Saunders — led to the creation of many new units specifically intended to provide appropriate care for the dying person and support for his relatives. They were designed as separate institutions because of the difficulties of integrating the needs of the dying patient with the busy routines and regimes of general hospitals. In hospices there is a commitment to the total care of each patient, and help is available from a multidisciplinary team to assist him with physical, psychological, spiritual and social problems. The family is also helped and supported as they share the patients' last months, weeks or days. Many hospices also have a home-care programme which, in co-operation with local community services, enables patients to die at home, if appropriate, with continuing support for them and for their families.

13.6   Care of the bereaved

Clearly, any nurse involved with dying patients will encounter those whom the patients love and who love them. Appropriate communication will depend on an understanding of their predicament. It is important to remember that the stages of awareness may differ between the patient and his family. And the family may also be undergoing processes of adjustment, perhaps similar to those experienced by the dying: denial; anger; depression and anticipatory grief. But whereas the dying person may reach the stage of acceptance and some degree of tranquillity, those who love him have to face the prospect of life after his death — and of adjustment to bereavement.

When a love tie is severed, emotional and behavioural reactions are set in train which Parkes (1972) calls 'the cost of commitment'. The intensity of grief will be influenced by many factors, such as the depth of attachment to the departed person and previous experience in coping with crises and hardships. The need for help for the bereaved in their suffering and in their attempts to readjust their lives has been receiving growing recognition. There are now a number of organizations such as the Cruse Club, established in 1959, to help widows; or the Society of Compassionate Friends, which is a self-help group run by parents who have lost a child or who have a child who is dying. Much of the help and support provided by these organizations comes from people who have themselves been through the grief and tragedy of this particular form of bereavement and who can therefore offer sympathy and practical advice on the basis of their own experience. The fact that they have learnt the hard way — by knowing at first hand what it is like — gives them something to offer which is real and relevant.

However, one of the problems frequently mentioned by writers concerned with the care of the dying and the bereaved is that many doctors and nurses lack any training and preparation which enables them to offer appropriate help or to cope with their own fears and anxieties.

13.7   Education for the care of the dying

Birch (1979) studied anxiety experienced by student nurses and found that the care of the terminally ill, the dying and the bereaved ranked among the top 7 out of 56 most anxiety-provoking situations. He also found that students thought that they had been given less preparation for these tasks than their tutors believed they had provided. This finding is similar to a conclusion in a study by Whitfield (1979), where student nurses alleged a lack of discussion, help and support from tutors and school staff on matters of psychological support for patients, which contrasted with adequate discussion and support on matters relating to patients' physical needs.

Other writers have also emphasized a general inadequacy in the provision of education and help for students in the health care professions concerning the care of the dying and the bereaved. Therefore, these recommendations of Strauss and Glaser (1968) are particularly relevant:

(1)   Training for terminal care should be amplified and deepened in schools of medicine and nursing.
(2)   The psychological, social and organizational aspects of terminal care should be reviewed and explicitly planned.

(3) There should be explicit planning for the phases of the dying trajectory that occur before and after residence at the hospital.

(4) Medical and nursing personnel should encourage public discussion of issues that transcend professional responsibilities for terminal care.

The last recommendation raises a wider issue — the profound ethical problems encountered by those who care for the dying. Their actions and decisions will be shaped by their consciences in the light of their personal beliefs, but these beliefs do not develop or operate in isolation from the rest of society. Fundamental decisions about the prolongation or termination of life for particular patients may have to be made by physicians and nurses. But they cannot claim a professional prerogative on decisions of general principle and policy. In a democratic society, these must be discussed, debated and decided by a wider public — with due recognition of the views of professionals who have a particular contribution to offer which is based on experience and knowledge.

Nurses therefore have an obligation to ensure that the contribution made by the health care professions both directly — in the actual care given to the dying and their relatives — and indirectly — in influencing decision-making and policy formation — is founded on as sound a knowledge base as possible. The implications for nursing education and practice are clear.

■ Summary

In earlier times most people died at home and death was a familiar event. Now, death has an aura of mystery and has become a taboo subject. More than half of all deaths occur in hospitals, where there is an increase in our ability to 'manage' death, but a tendency to regard death as a 'failure'. Two sociological concepts — trajectories of dying and contexts of awareness — are discussed, and the description of the stages of dying by Kübler-Ross are outlined. Many writers underline the importance of appropriate communication with the dying person and his family and also with bereaved relatives, and studies illustrating the way that professionals deal with this subject are reviewed. The place of death and the problems of coping with the dying in hospitals, in the home and in hospices are discussed.

Education of health care professionals about care of the dying is believed by many to be inadequate, and recommendations for improvement are given. Ethical questions concerning issues such as the prolongation and termination of life are seen to require greater debate between professionals and a wider public.

■ Questions

1. What do you understand by the following:
    (a) trajectories of dying;
    (b) contexts of awareness?

How may these concepts help you to understand some of the social aspects of the care of the dying?
2. Give an account of Kübler-Ross's 'stages of dying'. What are some of the social implications of these stages?
3. What are the considerations you would bear in mind when arranging for a patient to receive terminal care at home?

References

Ariès, P. (1974). *Western Attitudes Towards Death: From the Middle Ages to the Present*, Baltimore, Maryland, Johns Hopkins University Press.

Bettelheim, B. (1967). *The Empty Fortress*, New York, Free Press.

Birch, J. (1979). 'The anxious learners', *Nursing Mirror*, 8 Feb.

Bond, S. (1978). 'Process of communication about cancer in a radiotherapy department', unpublished *Ph.D. thesis*, University of Edinburgh.

Bond, S. (1980). 'A taboo of our times', *Nursing Mirror*, 13 March.

Cartwright, A., Hockey, L. and Anderson, J. (1973). *Life Before Death*, London, Routledge & Kegan Paul.

Gorer, G. (1965). *Death, Grief and Mourning in Contemporary Britain*, London, Cresset Press.

Hinton, J. (1980). 'Whom do dying patients tell?', *British Medical Journal*, vol. 281, 15 Nov., pp. 1328–1330.

Kübler-Ross, E. (1969). *On Death and Dying*, New York, MacMillan.

McIntosh, J. (1977). *Communication and Awareness in a Cancer Ward*, London, Croom Helm.

McNulty, B. (1978). 'Out-patient and domiciliary management from a hospice', in *The Management of Terminal Disease*, Saunders, C. M. (Ed.), London, Arnold.

Parkes, C. M. (1972). *Bereavement — Studies of Grief in Adult Life*, London, Tavistock.

Qvarnstrom, U. (1978). 'Patients' reactions to impending death', *Ph.D. thesis*, University of Stockholm.

Raven, R. W. (1975). *The Dying Patient*, London, Pitman Medical.

Saunders, C. M. (1976). *Care of the Dying*, London, Macmillan.

Strauss, A. L. and Glaser, B. G. (1968). 'Patterns of dying', reprinted in *A Sociology of Medical Practice*, Cox, C. and Mead, A. (Eds.), London, Collier Macmillan.

Sudnow, D. (1967). *Passing On: The Social Organisation of Dying*, Englewood Cliffs, New Jersey, Prentice-Hall.

Whitfield, S. (1979). 'A descriptive study of student nurses' ward experiences with dying patients and their attitudes towards them', *M.Sc. thesis*, University of Manchester.

Further reading

Doyle, D. (Ed.) (1979). *Terminal Care*, Edinburgh, Churchill Livingstone. A collection of papers from a multidisciplinary conference. They cover topics such as the provision of a home care service; the role of the primary care team; grief; the meaning of death and ministry to the dying. Particularly relevant is L. Hockey's contribution on 'The role of the nurse'.

Saunders, C. M. (Ed.) (1978). *The Management of Terminal Disease*, London, Arnold. A wide-ranging collection of essays covering philosophical and practical aspects of the care of the dying and their families.

Part V

Conclusion

Hippocrates of Cos, the Father of Medicine, 460–375 B.C., from a woodcut in the 'surgery' of Ambroise Paré, sixteenth century (Courtesy BBC Hulton Picture Library)

(. . . many subjects have contributed to the body of medical [and nursing] knowledge and practice — see p. 203)

14 Nursing and sociology: the need for critical collaboration

This final chapter draws together many of the threads of the preceding chapters. It reviews some of the implications of sociology for nursing practice, management and education; it discusses some of sociology's dilemmas and problems; and it concludes by recommending the development of a creative partnership between sociology and nursing.

14.1   The sociological contribution: a review

This book has attempted to show that sociology is relevant to nurses. First, we looked at ways in which it can help us to understand the society in which we all — health care professionals, patients, clients — live and work. Sociological studies of family life, of education or of social class may all shed light on the social processes which shape our lives and influence our relationships with one another. Therefore, some understanding of the ways in which sociologists have described and analysed such social processes may provide us with a pair of sociological 'spectacles' — enabling us to view these processes from a sociological perspective.

Secondly, we considered studies which show the importance of social factors in the delivery and uptake of health care and we discussed work which focuses on a number of situations of particular relevance to nursing — the care of the mentally ill, the chronic sick, the elderly and the dying.

So, hopefully, the case has been made that sociology can provide insights and information which are relevant to nursing practice and to the organization of nursing care. In addition, sociology may be especially relevant in the implementation of the nursing process, when the assessment, planning and evaluation of patient care requires social and cultural factors to be taken into account.

We can therefore argue that sociology should be taught to all student nurses, midwives and health visitors. Although it already features on the syllabuses of many basic and post-basic courses, more systematic coverage might be developed. If this is to be the case, it might be helpful to those who have the responsibility for organizing curricula if we conclude with a brief account of some of the issues confronting contemporary sociology. In this context, two problems will be mentioned: the commitment of some sociologists to a 'critical' stance; and sociology's own internal conflicts. These topics have been chosen, because they are the ones which most often cause consternation and confusion for non-sociologists.

14.2 Current issues and problems in sociology

14.2.1 Sociology as a 'critical' discipline.

Sociology has an honourable reputation as a 'critical' discipline and many contemporary sociologists are deeply committed to a critical stance. This is justifiable in at least two ways. First, as we saw in Chapter 1, a critical attitude towards knowledge lies at the heart of the scientific enterprise. The principle of 'falsifiability', emphasized by Popper (1963), embodies the idea that the scientific community never 'rests on its laurels'. Knowledge is always seen as tentative and theories are always 'up for testing'. It is only by trying to be critical — by always being prepared to have our ideas, assumptions and practices challenged — that we can ever gain any measure of confidence in the validity of our knowledge and practice. Therefore, scientifically, a critical stance is appropriate for any academic discipline.

The second strand in sociology's commitment to a critical stance lies in its reformist role. Many sociologists have been concerned about the social problems around them and have sought to document and publicize them, with a view to bringing about social change.

So far, so good. There is much sociology which is both critical of certain social arrangements and highly respected academically. However, there is another aspect to this commitment to a critical stance which has been felt by many to be less desirable; that is, the tendency in the work of some sociologists to be so 'critical' that they overstate their case — making gross generalizations or offering too simplistic an account of a reality which is very complex. After all, sociologists, like everyone else, are inevitably limited in the grasp they can obtain of everything which is going on. There may therefore be times when their analysis does not ring true and does not accurately represent the authentic experience of those whom they are studying. For example, a nurse who had attended a medical sociology seminar was furious because a sociologist had said that when nurses spoke about being anxious while working on the wards, they were just putting forward 'red herrings' and avoiding 'real issues'. As a nurse who had at times felt acute anxiety while working on the wards (who has not?), she felt that this sociologist's account was inaccurate and arrogant.

It is this kind of attitude in the work of some sociologists which has prompted another sociologist, B. Heraud, to take his colleagues to task. In his book *Sociology in the Professions* (Heraud, 1979) he observes that some sociologists:

'reflect an attitude of arrogance and disdain for the day-to-day work of professionals and for the decisions which have to be made by them . . . decisions by
which such professionals have to stand or fall, while the sociologist may remain
safely on the sidelines.'

Heraud also regrets the tendency of some contemporary sociologists to adopt
such a critical stance that they see nothing good or positive in what they observe.
They thus appear cynical and carping:

'The weakness shows itself particularly in the contemporary analysis of the professions, where the sociologist takes a very serious view of his role as everlast-
ing social critic by ignoring or distrusting any of the positive, pragmatic or
optimistic forces of opinion in such institutions or in the wider society . . . .'

Responding to 'critical' sociology

These tendencies in the work of some contemporary sociologists have been
mentioned here, in case readers encounter them in other contexts — for example,
on courses in colleges of further and higher education. They can understandably
lead to feelings of discomfort or anger. However, the appropriate response is for
those professionals whose work or attitudes are being criticized to be prepared to
consider whether there is validity in the criticism. If there is, it may be a salutary
experience and lead to some improvements in professional practice. If, however,
the criticism is ill-founded, it should be challenged.

Nurses have tended to be too deferential, too ready to accept the judgements of
others and too unwilling to enter into dialogue. It may not be easy to argue with
academics from other subjects. However, they need critical feedback to improve
their own work; and nurses have a wealth of professional experience which has its
own validity and can form a sound basis for counter-arguments. Only by engaging
in such dialogue can we develop a situation in which sociologists can be helped to
make as effective a contribution as possible to nursing.

14.2.2   Conflicts within sociology

As we have seen, sociology consists of a number of 'schools' based on different
approaches. This is inevitable, given the complexity of social reality and the limits
of our knowledge. No one school has attained a position where it can explain all the
multifaceted aspects of human experience and behaviour. Most sociologists
recognize this, and adopt a position of 'pluralism' — respecting the contributions
and recognizing the limitations of the different schools. However, some indulge in
such acrimonious argument with their fellow sociologists that the situation has
been described by a professor of sociology, J. Rex, as resembling 'wars of religion'
(Rex, 1978a).

In considering such conflicts, it is necessary to distinguish between academic
criticism (valid and necessary) and emotional, ideological conflict (to be expected
on political platforms, but not in the classroom or the academic textbook). Some
conflict may be understandable because of the controversial nature of much of the
subject matter of sociology. But if sociology is presented in a curriculum as an

academic subject, it should not violate the generally accepted standards of academic practice. Herein lies one of modern sociology's most thorny problems.

At the heart of this problem lie deep conflicts among sociologists themselves concerning the criteria to be used to assess the validity of sociological knowledge and practice. Two examples will be mentioned here to give some idea of the kinds of issues involved; we have already touched on them briefly, in Chapter 1. They are: first, the extent to which sociologists try to take account of all available relevant evidence in testing their theories; secondly, the extent to which their work is, or can be, value-free or unbiased.

14.2.3 Use of all available relevant evidence

One of the most important criteria of established scientific practice is the use of all available relevant evidence to test theories. In other words, a scientist, whether a natural scientist or a social scientist, must not select just those facts which suit his own theory. This means that sociologists should, where appropriate, adopt a comparative approach to discover whether the situations they describe are unique; or whether they are only found in particular types of social setting or society; or whether they are universal human phenomena. This is important, because unless we can make these distinctions we cannot begin to try to look for causes.

Marxist writers and their critics

There is a tendency in some sociological studies to concentrate exclusively on problems in one kind of society and to ignore the fact that they occur elsewhere. For example, writers of a Marxist persuasion often focus exclusively on the problems of capitalist societies in their critiques of health, welfare and education. There is an abundance of books of this type, such as the influential book on education by Bowles and Gintis (1976) entitled *Schooling in Capitalist America*. Such books often assert that educational and welfare institutions in capitalist societies are repressive, that they are tools of the state and that they serve to legitimize the *status quo*. They may do so, and this may be a matter for genuine concern and form the basis for proposals for reform, especially if some people suffer as a result. But books such as these are open to criticism for their lack of comparative analysis, for the authors refrain from pointing out that similar social problems are found in other societies — sometimes in an even more acute form.

Another sociologist, the late Professor P. Halmos, made this point when reviewing a book on social welfare written in this vein (Halmos, 1976):

> '. . . there is a complete silence on the failures of the so-called socialist welfare states in the areas so often featuring in the critique of capitalist welfare states: suicide, drug addiction, alcoholism, crime, mental illness and so on; the catalogue of "social problems" recognised by the fifteen or so contemporary socialist states are just as frequent in these states as they are in capitalist ones. A book devoted to highlighting the failures of the British Welfare State since 1955 and prescribing a socialist revolutionary answer for this failure has no business to be silent about the record of the socialist precedents in this area of human experience . . . .'

Unscientific approach

It is important to emphasize that the issues at stake here are not merely political, but scientific. For if writers focus all their attention on the problems of one kind of society — in this case, capitalist society — then the impression is created that it is this kind of society which 'causes' the problems. Unless or until a comparative study considers the extent to which similar problems occur in other types of society, it is unscientific to imply a causal relationship or to recommend solutions based on such assumed causes.

The work of some Marxist sociologists has been used as the example for criticism here, because such work has been prolific in recent years. However, similar criticism should be applied to any sociology which does not take comparative data into account in attempts to test theories. This does not mean that there is no place for descriptive and analytical studies — indeed, we saw their usefulness in Chapter 8. They can provide 'illuminative' data which tell their own story, like a good novel. However, any attempts to develop and to test general theories about society or social institutions must use experimental or comparative methods. And because, for obvious ethical and practical reasons, sociologists can only very rarely establish rigorous experimental situations, they must rely on comparative studies. However, without a commitment to seeing whether theories 'hold' in different situations, and to using available relevant evidence to discover which factors are associated with the phenomena under study, sociology cannot be deemed a 'science' in the generally accepted meaning of that term. It is partly because of the complexity of issues such as these that some sociologists argue that sociology cannot and should not try to be a 'science'. The debate continues.

14.2.4   Problem of bias

Rex (1978b) has highlighted an additional problem which is clearly related to the points just made concerning the selective use of facts to support theories. He is concerned about the extent to which some sociologists' passionate convictions lead them to operate in ways which are ideological and political rather than academic. While they are naturally entitled, as we all are, to engage in political activity as private citizens, it is not generally regarded, in western societies, as valid academic practice to use the school, the college or the academic textbook for partisan political purposes.

Pluralism

We noted in Chapter 6 that one of the generally accepted objectives of education in democratic societies is to encourage students to think for themselves, to consider critically the available relevant evidence and to make up their own minds. Hence, there is a traditional commitment to the principle of 'pluralism'. This means teaching in ways which introduce students to different approaches, encouraging them to assess the alternative theories, and to draw their own conclusions. But Rex (1978b) has soberly pointed out that sociology:

'. . . is dangerous because it enters into a field which is partly claimed by ideology and the political ideologist may all too easily seek to pass off his product as sociology, seeking to use the university as a means of establishing his political as well as intellectual hegemony.'

Solemn warnings

In practical terms, this means that sociology can sometimes degenerate to an ideologically motivated civil war — as Rex has noted:

'It is not for nothing that we live in an age of academic revolution. The events of 1968 have left us with dogmas and cults, even with intellectual wars of religion. Of course, the versions of the new paradigms which are disseminated to the mass of sociology students . . . are not the sophisticated political doctrines of Frankfurt or Paris or Berkeley. They are taken to mean too often that truth and falsity themselves are bourgeois notions, that right and wrong are only labels used by the oppressors to hold young people in bondage. At the end of this road we find the Baader-Meinhoff gang and the Symbionese Liberation Army.'

These solemn warnings from senior representatives of sociology have been quoted in order to help newcomers to the subject to understand some of the conflicts and tensions in the discipline. The purpose of quoting them is not to be destructive, but to be helpful. If you come into contact with sociology in places where such conflicts are occurring — and they are not found everywhere — or where sociology is being presented in a biased and politically partisan way, it may be less disconcerting to have some understanding of what is happening. To be forewarned is to be forearmed.

14.3   A forward look

14.3.1   Interdisciplinary collaboration in teaching and research

Awareness of sociology's internal conflicts and problems may be especially relevant now, when nursing is developing links with sociologists for service teaching and multidisciplinary research. For example, sociology now features on the syllabuses of many courses in nursing, midwifery and health visiting, and there is an increasing likelihood that sociologists will be invited to help with teaching. This can be excellent, because multidisciplinary collaboration may be mutually enriching.

14.3.2 Contributions from other disciplines to nursing

I have argued elsewhere (Cox, 1982) that nursing research needs contributions from other disciplines in the development of the body of nursing knowledge — in the same way that disciplines such as law and medicine have drawn on work from other fields. In Chapter 2, for example, we saw that many subjects have contributed to the body of medical knowledge and practice.

However, it is important to ensure that colleagues from other disciplines contribute to nursing in ways which are constructive. This does not mean that we should be averse to criticism — this point has been made already. But it does mean that such colleagues should accept the responsibilities of 'service' teaching — note that word 'service' — and of 'collaborative' research. They should therefore adapt their academic expertise and knowledge so that their contributions in teaching and research are primarily guided by a genuine wish to help nurses to provide better nursing care.

14.3.3 Contribution of nursing to sociology

Nurses sometimes say that they are not in a position to judge or to criticize the contributions from other people because they have no criteria by which to judge them. This is not so. One criterion which we should use is the extent to which at least one of the goals of teaching or research is the enhancement of the quality of nursing practice. This is something which nurses are uniquely qualified to judge.

Sociology has much to offer nursing: at the level of clinical practice; in the implementation of the nursing process; in the organization and management of nursing care; and in the education of students. Nursing and nurses also have much to offer to sociology. There is thus great potential for fruitful collaboration, like that advocated by Wing (1980), between sociology and psychiatry. In his words, we need: '. . . creative partnerships . . . based on a realistic appraisal of each other's talents and limitations. This is the way forward now.'

■ Summary

This chapter is split into three main parts. First, a review is given of the aims of the book, detailing the coverage which the various chapters have given to the study of society, to the importance of social factors in health care and to demonstrating the relevance of sociology for student nurses, midwives and health visitors. Secondly, there is a discussion of the current issues and problems in sociology, emphasizing that sociologists often take a 'critical' stance and play a reformist role, but should avoid unwarranted generalizations and especially the pitfall of selecting evidence to support theories. In this respect, it is regretted that some sociologists operate in ways which are so politically biased that education may become indoctrination. Lastly, the chapter looks into the future and to the likelihood that sociologists will be invited to help with teaching nurses, midwives and health visitors. This is seen to be desirable, provided that these contributions are guided by the wish to help health care professionals give better care.

Due to their professional experience and expertise, health care professionals have much to offer sociology in return, and thus the author sees great potential for fruitful collaboration between the disciplines.

■ Questions

1. In what ways may sociology contribute to our understanding and implementation of the concept of 'total patient care'?
2. 'No man is an *Island*, entire of it self' (J. Donne). How does sociology help us to understand man as a social being and to care for him accordingly?
3. Give a brief account of those aspects of sociology which have:
   (a) most interested you;
   (b) most irritated you;
   (c) most bored you;
   (d) most helped you in your nursing, midwifery or health visiting.
   Give reasons for your choice.

References

Bowles, S. and Gintis, H. (1976). *Schooling in Capitalist America*, London, Routledge & Kegan Paul.

Cox, C. (1982). 'Frontiers of nursing in the twenty-first century: implications for nursing education', *International Journal of Nursing Studies*, vol. 19, no. 1, pp. 1–9.

Halmos, P. (1976). Review of *Ideology and Social Welfare* by George, V and Wilding P., 1976 (Routledge & Kegan Paul), published in *The Times Higher Educational Supplement*, 18 June.

Heraud, B. (1979). *Sociology in the Professions*, London, Open Books.

Popper, K. (1963). *Conjectures and Refutations: The Growth of Scientific Knowledge*, London, Routledge & Kegan Paul.

Rex, J. (1978a). 'British sociology's wars of religion', *New Society*, vol. 44, no. 814, pp. 295–297.

Rex, J. (1978b). 'The pressures on sociology teaching', *New Society*, vol. 44, no. 816, pp. 414–416.

Wing, J. K. (1980). 'Sociology and psychiatry', paper presented to the Annual Conference of the British Sociological Association, Lancaster.

Further reading

Cox, C. (1979). 'Who cares? Nursing and sociology: the development of a symbiotic relationship', *Journal of Advanced Nursing*, vol. 4, pp. 237–252.

Marks, J. (1983). *Science and the Making of the Modern World*, London, Heinemann. A fascinating, very readable account of the historical development of science and of the ways in which it has influenced different societies; also, a clear statement of the philosophy of science and of open, liberal societies.

Popper, K. (1976). *Unended Quest — An Intellectual Autobiography*, London, Fontana. An account of the development of Karl Popper's political and philosophical ideas. This is particularly relevant for an understanding of the concept of pluralism, which is discussed in this chapter and which underpins this entire book.

Index

References in *italics* are to illustrations.